Twelfth Edition

The State
of
Church Giving
through 2000

John L. Ronsvalle

Sylvia Ronsvalle

empty tomb,®*inc.*
Champaign, Illinois

The State of Church Giving through 2000
by John and Sylvia Ronsvalle
published by empty tomb, inc.
First printing, October 2002

empty tomb, inc.
301 N. Fourth Street
P.O. Box 2404
Champaign, IL 61825-2404
Phone: (217) 356-9519
Fax: (217) 356-2344
www.emptytomb.org

ISBN 0-9679633-2-X
ISSN 1097-3192

The Library of Congress has catalogued this publication
as follows:
The state of church giving through …—19uu- Champaign, Ill. :
Empty Tomb, Inc.,
v. : ill. ; 28 cm. Annual.
1. Christian giving Periodicals.
2. Christian giving Statistics Periodicals.
3. Church finance—United States Periodicals.
4. Church finance—United States Statistics Periodicals.
   BV772 .S32 98-640917

CONTENTS

TABLES AND FIGURES

PREFACE _____

Located in the Midwest, one is surrounded by great rivers: the Mississippi, the Missouri, the Ohio and the Illinois, for example. There is an awareness of how these waterways build and gain momentum as they move from a source to a destination.

History is like these rivers. Through the faithful work of church officials beginning in 1916, the flow of information has continued and grown. The *Yearbook of American and Canadian Churches* (*YACC*) series, and its predecessor publications, have collected this information and made it available for church leaders, researchers and others.

All who care about the church owe a debt of gratitude to those denominational officials who collect, process and share these numbers, so that the data stream continues.

The National Council of the Churches of Christ in the U.S.A. (NCC) has carried on the publication that began with the *Federal Council Year Book* in 1916. By continuing this rich tradition, Robert W. Edgar, NCC General Secretary, has displayed true church statesmanship.

Eileen Lindner, *YACC* editor, and her assistants, Marcel Welty and Nathan Hanson, have been a joy to work with, and their leadership of the *Yearbook* is greatly appreciated. Their efforts to survey the denominations and publish the data extends the base of knowledge for the benefit of present and future church leaders, researchers, and members in general.

As anyone who works on a publication knows, many people play a part. The staff members of empty tomb remain courageous in their pursuit of faithful servant leadership, and supportive of the vision of a more faithful church. In particular, Peter Helfrich, Administrative Assistant, has shared directly in the production of this volume. Financial supporters and volunteers are another key component of the works through empty tomb. We want to express appreciation for volunteers Don Thompson and Chuck Gray who helped in the production stage, and John K. Jones for his helpful input.

The analyses that follow are, on one level, numbers on a page. On another level, the numbers provide a thermometer of church member commitment. On a third level, these numbers represent the potential for increased faithfulness among church members in the United States. We offer them with the hope that they will be one means to "spur one another on toward love and good deeds" (Hebrews 10:24, NIV).

John L. Ronsvalle, Ph.D.
Sylvia Ronsvalle

Champaign, Illinois
October 2002

SUMMARY_____

The State of Church Giving through 2000 is the most recent report in an annual series that began with *The State of Church Giving through 1989*. These analyses consider denominational giving data for a set of denominations first analyzed in a study published in 1988. The present report reviews data for a composite set of denominations from 1968 to 2000 that includes 30 million full or confirmed members, and just over 100,000 of the estimated 350,000 religious congregations in the U.S.

The findings of the present church member giving analysis include the following.

- Per member giving to Total Contributions and Congregational Finances increased as a portion of income between 1968 and 2000, with giving to Congregational Finances recovering to mid-1970 levels. In 2000, per member giving as a portion of income to Benevolences reached its lowest point in the 1968-2000 period.

- The composite set was expanded to include 44 Protestant communions, and data was compared for 1999-2000. As a portion of income, giving to Total Contributions and Congregational Finances increased while the Benevolences level declined.

- An analysis of data for a subset of mainline Protestant denominations and a subset of evangelical Protestant denominations found giving higher in the evangelical Protestant denominations, but a steeper decline in giving patterns among the evangelicals over the 1968-2000 period. Evangelical denominations were increasing in membership during these years, but their members were giving a smaller contribution as a portion of income. In the mainline denominations, giving as a portion of income to Congregational Finances was higher in 2000 than in 1968; however, Benevolences continued to decline.

- A review of giving and membership patterns in 11 Protestant denominations from 1921 to 2000 found that per member giving as a portion of income began to decline in 1961, and membership began to decline as a percent of U.S. population in 1962. Giving as a percentage of income was lower in 2000 than in either 1921 or 1933.

- Data was analyzed using both linear and exponential regression.

  - The increase in giving as a portion of income to Congregational Finances apparent in recent years produced levels that were higher than either regression series for 1968-2000 suggested. Benevolences continued to decline but the actual numbers have evidenced a plateau since 1993, yet reached a low point in 2000.

- Membership analyses of various groupings of communions suggested that there was a decline in church membership as a portion of U.S. population in the 1968-2000 period.

- If church members were to reach a congregationwide average of 10% giving, an additional $139 billion dollars would be available to assist both local and global neighbors in need.

- The second annual Report Card on Philanthropy Measurement evaluated the contributions of twelve entities to public knowledge about charitable giving in the United States. The overall quality of philanthropy measurement merited a C-.

- The last chapter presents proposals to encourage church members to fulfill more of their potential in the area of financial discipleship, including giving to the church. The proposals include: (1) Church leadership making a decision to mobilize all members in behalf of a positive agenda for affluence; and (2) Church structures developing a Web-based feedback system to increase the practical partnership between congregations and denominational mission efforts.

INTRODUCTION_____

An historical series of financial and membership data in the United States extends back to 1916. Church statesmen took a broad overview of organized religion as a major social institution. They collected and preserved the data through publications and archives.

This information tradition continues through the present. Individual congregations initially provide the data to the regional or national denominational office with which the congregation is affiliated. The denominational offices then compile the data. The *Yearbook of American and Canadian Churches* (*YACC*), of the National Council of the Churches of Christ in the U.S.A., requests the data from the national denominational offices, publishing it in annual *YACC* editions.

The data published by the *YACC*, in some cases combined with data obtained directly from a denominational source (as noted in the series of tables in Appendix B), serves as the basis for the present report. The numbers on the following pages are not survey reports. Rather, they represent the actual dollar records included in reports submitted by pastors and lay congregational leaders to their own denominational offices.

By following the same data set of denominations over a period of years, trends can be seen among a broad group of church members. In addition, since the data set includes communions from across the theological spectrum, subsets of denominations within the larger grouping provide a basis for comparing patterns between communions with different perspectives.

In an ongoing fashion, efforts are made to use the latest information available. As a result, *The State of Church Giving through 2000* provides information available to date.

Definition of Terms. The analyses in this report use certain terms that are defined as follows.

Full or Confirmed Members are used in the present analysis because it is a relatively consistent category among the reporting denominations. Certain denominations also report a larger figure for Inclusive Membership, which may include, for example, children who have been baptized but are not yet eligible for confirmation in that denomination. In this report, when the term "per member" is used, it refers to Full or Confirmed Members, unless otherwise noted.

The terms "denomination" and "communion" are used interchangeably. Both refer to a group of church people who share a common identity defined by traditions and stated beliefs.

The phrase "historically Christian church" refers to that combination of believers with a historically acknowledged confession of the faith. The broad spectrum of communions represented in the National Church Leaders Response Form list indicates the breadth of this definition.

Total Contributions Per Member refers to the average contribution in either dollars or as a percentage of income which is donated to the denominations' affiliated congregations by Full or Confirmed Members in a given year.

Total Contributions combines the two subcategories of Congregational Finances and Benevolences. The definitions used in this report for these two subcategories are consistent with the standardized *YACC* data request questionnaire.

The first subcategory of Congregational Finances includes contributions directed to the internal operations of the individual congregation, including such items as the utility bills and salaries for the pastor and office staff, as well as Sunday school materials and capital programs.

The second subcategory is Benevolences. This category includes contributions for the congregation's external expenditures, beyond its own operations, for what might be termed the larger mission of the church. Benevolences includes international missions as well as national and local charities, through denominational channels as well as programs of nondenominational organizations to which the congregation contributes directly. Benevolences also includes support of denominational administration at all levels, as well as donations to denominational seminaries and schools.

As those familiar with congregational dynamics know, an individual generally donates an amount to the congregation which underwrites both Congregational Finances and Benevolences. During the budget preparation process, congregational leadership considers allocations to these categories. The budget may or may not be reviewed by all the congregation's members, depending on the communion's polity. However, the sum of the congregation's activities serves as a basis for members' decisions about whether to increase or decrease giving from one year to the next. Also, many congregations provide opportunities to designate directly to either Congregational Finances or Benevolences, through fund-raising drives, capital campaigns, and special offerings. Therefore, the allocations between Congregational Finances and Benevolences can be seen to fairly represent the priorities of church members.

When the terms "income," "per capita income," and "giving as a percentage of income" are used, they refer to the U.S. Per Capita Disposable (after-tax) Personal Income series from the U.S. Department of Commerce Bureau of Economic Analysis (BEA), unless otherwise noted.

The Implicit Price Deflator for Gross National Product was used to convert current dollars to 1996 dollars, thus factoring out inflation, unless otherwise specified.

Appendix C includes both U.S. Per Capita Disposable Personal Income figures and the Implicit Price Deflator for Gross National Product figures used in this study.

Analysis Factors. *Chained Dollars.* The analyses in *The State of Church Giving through 2000* are keyed to the U.S. BEA series of "chained (1996) dollars."

Income Series. The U.S. Department of Commerce Bureau of Economic Analysis has published the 11th comprehensive revision of the national income and product accounts, with the benchmark year being 1996. The U.S. Per Capita Disposable Personal Income series used in the present *The State of Church Giving through 2000* is drawn from this national accounts data.

Rate of Change Calculations, 1985-2000. The following methodology is used to calculate the rate of change between 1985 and the most recent calendar year for which data is available, in the present case, 2000.

The rate of change between 1968 and 1985 was calculated by subtracting the 1968 giving as a percentage of income figure from the 1985 figure and then dividing the result by the 1968 figure.

The rate of change between 1985 and 2000 was calculated as follows. The 1968 giving as a percentage of income figure was subtracted from the 2000 figure and divided by the 1968 figure, producing a 1968-2000 rate of change. Then, the 1968-1985 rate of change was subtracted from the 1968-2000 figure. The result is the 1985-2000 rate of change, which may then be compared to the 1968-1985 figure.

Rounding Calculations. In most cases, Total Contributions, Total Congregational Finances, and Total Benevolences for the denominations being considered were divided by Full or Confirmed Membership in order to obtain per capita, or per member, data for that set of denominations. This procedure occasionally led to a small rounding discrepancy in one of the three related figures. That is, by a small margin, rounded per capita Total Contributions did not equal per capita Congregational Finances plus per capita Benevolences. Similarly, rounding data to the nearest dollar for use in tables and graphics led on occasion to a small rounding error in the data presented in tabular or graphic form.

Giving in Dollars. Per member giving to churches can be measured in dollars. The dollar measure indicates, among other information, how much money religious institutions have to spend.

Current dollars indicate the value of the dollar in the year it was donated. However, since inflation changes the amount of goods or services that can be purchased with that dollar, data provided in current dollars has limited information value over a time span. If someone donated $5 in 1968 and $5 in 2000, on one level that person is donating the same amount of money. On another level, however, the buying power of that $5 has changed a great deal. Since less can be bought with the $5 donated in 2000 because of inflation in the economy, on a practical level the value of the donation has shrunk.

To account for the changes caused by inflation in the value of the dollar, a deflator can be applied. The result is inflation-adjusted 1996 dollars. Dollars adjusted to their chain-type, annual-weighted measure through the use of a deflator can be compared in terms of real growth over a time span since inflation has been factored out.

The deflator most commonly applied in this analysis designated the base period as 1996, with levels in 1996 set equal to 100. Thus, when adjusted by the deflator, the 1968 gift of $5 was worth $19.02 in inflation-adjusted 1996 dollars, and the 2000 gift of $5 was worth $4.68 in inflation-adjusted 1996 dollars.

Giving as a Percentage of Income. There is another way to look at church member giving. This category is giving as a percentage of income. Considering what percentage or portion of income is donated to the religious congregation provides a different perspective. Rather than indicating how much money the congregation has to spend, as when one considers dollars donated, giving as a percentage of income indicates how the congregation rates in light of church members' total available incomes. Has the church sustained the same level of support from its members in comparison to previous years, as measured by what portion of income is being donated by members from the total resources available to them?

Percentage of income is a valuable measure because incomes change. Just as inflation changes the value of the dollar so $5 in 1968 is not the same as $5 in 2000, incomes, influenced by inflation and real growth, also change. For example, per capita income in 1968 was $3,119 in current dollars; if a church member gave $312 that year, that member would have been tithing, or giving the standard of ten percent. In contrast, 2000 per capita income had increased to $25,205 in current dollars; and if that church member still gave $312, the member would have been giving only a little more than 1% of income. The church would have commanded a smaller portion of the member's overall resources.

Thus, while dollars donated provide a limited picture of how much the church has to spend, giving as a percentage of income provides some measure of the church member's level of commitment to the church in comparison to other spending priorities. One might say that giving as a percentage of income is an indication of the church's "market share" of church members' lives.

In most cases, to obtain giving as a percentage of income, total income to a set of denominations was divided by the number of Full or Confirmed Members in the set. This yielded the per member giving amount in dollars. This per member giving amount was divided by per capita disposable personal income.

Data Appendix and Revisions. Appendix B includes the aggregate denominational data used in the analyses in this study. In general, the data for the denominations included in these analyses appears as it was reported in editions of the *YACC*. In some cases, data for one or more years for a specific denomination was obtained directly from the denominational office or another denominational source. Also, the denominational giving data set has been refined and revised as additional information has become available. Where relevant, this information is noted in the appendix.

chapter 1

Church Member Giving, 1968-2000

HIGHLIGHTS

Data for a composite set of denominations, including approximately 100,000 of the estimated 350,000 religious congregations in the U.S., yielded the following information about giving patterns from 1968-2000.

- Per member giving to churches increased in both current and inflation-adjusted 1996 dollars between 1968 and 2000. Because dollars did not keep pace with increases in income, giving as a percentage of income declined, from 3.10% in 1968 to 2.64% in 2000, a decline of 15% in the portion of income donated to the church from the 1968 base.

- Congregational Finances, funding local operations, increased in inflation-adjusted dollars from 1968 to 2000. Giving as a portion of income to this category declined from 2.45% in 1968 to 2.24% in 2000, a decline of 9%. Although sporadic from year to year, a general increase in giving to Congregational Finances began in 1993. By 2000, giving as a portion of income to this category had recovered to mid-1970 levels.

- Benevolences, funding the larger mission of the church, increased in inflation-adjusted dollars from 1968 to 2000. As a portion of income, Benevolences declined 39% from 0.66% in 1968 to 0.40% in 2000. In unrounded numbers, the 2000 level of giving to Benevolences as a percent of income was the lowest in the 1968-2000 period.

- In 1968, 21¢ of every dollar donated funded Benevolences. By 2000, 15¢ of every dollar went to Benevolences. Of each additional inflation-adjusted dollar donated to the church between 1968 and 2000, 93¢ went to Congregational Finances.

- If the portion of income donated to the church had not declined between 1968 and 2000, congregations and denominations would have had, in aggregate dollars, 9% more for Congregational Finances and 62% more for Benevolences in 2000.

NARRATIVE

The Composite Denominations The first study that provided a basis for the present series was published in 1988. The *Yearbook of American and Canadian Churches* (*YACC*) series publishes church member giving data. Data for the years 1968 and 1985 could be confirmed for 31 denominations.[1] The data year 1968 was selected because, beginning that year, a consistent distinction was made between Full or Confirmed Membership and Inclusive Membership in the *YACC* series. The denominations that published data for both 1968 and 1985 included 29,477,705 Full or Confirmed Members in 1985. They comprise approximately 100,000 of the estimated 350,000 religious congregations in the U.S.

The present church member giving report series extended the analysis for the original set of denominations beyond 1985. The current report analyzes the data set through 2000, the most recent year for which data was available at the time the report was written.[2] Also, data for the intervening years of 1969 through 1984, and 1986 through 1998, was included in the composite data set, as available.[3]

Giving Categories. When a dollar is given to the church, it is allocated into one of two major subcategories, as defined by the annual reporting form of the *YACC*. Congregational Finances refers to those expenditures that support the operations of the local congregation, such as utilities, pastor and staff salaries, insurance and Sunday school materials. Benevolences refers to expenditures for what might be termed the broader mission of the church, beyond the local membership. Benevolences includes everything from regional and national denominational offices to the local soup kitchen, from seminaries to international ministries. Total Contributions is the sum of Congregational Finances and Benevolences.

---

[1]John Ronsvalle and Sylvia Ronsvalle, *A Comparison of the Growth in Church Contributions with United States Per Capita Income* (Champaign, IL: empty tomb, inc., 1988).

[2]Two of the original 31 denominations merged in 1987, bringing the total number of denominations in the original data set to 30. As of 1991, one denomination reported that it no longer had the staff to collect national financial data, resulting in a maximum of 29 denominations from the original set which could provide data for 1991 through 2000. Of these 29 denominations, one reported data for 1968 through 1997, but did not have financial data for 1998 through 2000 available in time for this report; this communion indicated its intention to supply the missing years' data in late 2002. A second denomination merged with another communion not included in the original composite set but since added; having merged, this new denomination did not plan to collect financial data for 2000-2002 from its congregations, although conversations continue about the preservation of the historical data stream that extends back to at least 1968. Therefore, the composite data for 2000 includes information from 27 communions in the data set. Throughout this report, what was an original set of 31 denominations in 1985 will be referred to as the composite denominations. Data for 31 denominations will be included for 1968 and 1985, as well as for intervening years, as available.

[3]For 1986 through 2000, annual denominational data has been obtained which represented for any given year at least 98.92% (the 2000 percentage) of the 1985 Full or Confirmed Membership of the denominations included in the 1968-1985 study. For 1986 through 2000, the number of denominations for which data was available varied from a low of 27 denominations of a possible 30 in 2000 to a high of 29 in 1987 through 1997. For the years 1969 through 1984, the number of denominations varied from a low of 28 denominations of a possible 31 in 1970-1972 and 1974-1975 to 31 in 1983, representing at least 99.74% of the membership in the data set. The denominational giving data considered in this analysis was obtained either from the *Yearbook of American and Canadian Churches* series, or directly in correspondence with a denominational office. For a full listing of the data used in this analysis, including the sources, see Appendix B-1.

Financial Categories. Calculating contributions on a per member basis accounts for any changes in membership, either through growth or decline, that might have taken place during the period under review. The dollars given can be considered from two points of view. The *number of dollars given* by members indicates how much money the church has to spend. On the other hand, *giving as a percentage of income* places donations in the larger context of income available to church members.

Within the category of dollars given, there are two approaches as well: (1) current dollars; and (2) inflation-adjusted dollars.

Current dollars refers to the value that the dollar had in the year it was donated. However, inflation affects the value of dollars. A dollar in 2000 bought fewer goods or services than it did in 1968, an issue that members understand at the grocery store but seem to have greater difficulty understanding at church. In order to account for this factor, giving in inflation-adjusted dollars factors out the economic impact of inflation.

The second general category is giving as a percentage of income. This category considers not only the dollars given, but what portion those dollars represent of the resources available to the donor. One might say that looking at the amount of dollars donated indicates how much churches had to spend, while considering giving as a percentage of income reflects how the donation rated in the donor's overall lifestyle choices.

Giving in Dollars. Table 1 presents per member contributions in both current and inflation-adjusted dollars for the composite denominations data set.

Each data series is considered in the three categories of Total Contributions Per Member and the two subcategories of Congregational Finances and Benevolences.

Current Dollars, 1968-2000. As can be seen in Table 1, the per member amount given to Total Contributions, Congregational Finances, and Benevolences increased in current dollars each year during the 1968-2000 period.

Overall, from 1968 to 2000, Total Contributions to the church in current dollars increased $567.48 on a per member basis. Of this amount, $487.20 was directed to increase the per member Congregational Finances expenditures, for the benefit of members within the congregation. Benevolences, or outreach activities of the congregation, increased by $80.28.

One effect of this allocation distribution was that Benevolences shrank as a portion of Total Contributions. In 1968, 21¢ of each dollar went to Benevolences. By 2000, the amount had decreased to 15¢.

Inflation-adjusted Dollars, 1968-2000: The U.S. Bureau of Economic Analysis (U.S. BEA) publishes the deflator series that are used to factor out inflation. These deflators allow dollar figures to be compared more precisely across years. The current year of base comparison in the U.S. BEA series is 1996. By applying the Implicit Price Deflator for Gross National Product to the current-dollar church member giving data, the data can be reviewed across years with inflation factored out. The result of this process is also listed in Table 1. The arrows next to the three inflation-adjusted columns are included to provide a quick reference as to whether giving increased or decreased from one year to the next.

When the effects of inflation were removed, one may note that per member giving decreased in more years than in the current dollar columns. For example, although per member contributions to Total Contributions increased in the majority of years, the six years of 1969, 1970, 1971, 1975, 1991 and 1995 posted declines.

Congregational Finances also generally increased in inflation-adjusted 1996 dollars. Declines appear in 6 years: 1969, 1970, 1974, 1975, 1991 and 1995.

Benevolences also increased in the majority of years. Decreases occurred in 8 years in the 1968-2000 period, in the years 1970, 1971, 1977, 1982, 1987, 1990, 1991 and 1993.

Table 1: Per Member Giving to Total Contributions, Congregational Finances and Benevolences, Current and Inflation-Adjusted 1996 Dollars, 1968-2000

| | Per Full or Confirmed Member Giving to Congregations, in Dollars | | | | | | | | |
| | *Current Dollars* | | | Inflation-Adjusted 1996 Dollars | | | | | |
Year	*Total*	*Cong. Finances*	*Benevol.*	Total	↑↓	Cong. Finances	↑↓	Benevol.	↑↓
1968	$96.79	$76.35	$20.44	$368.16		$290.42		$77.73	
1969	$100.82	$79.34	$21.47	$365.41	↓	$287.58	↓	$77.83	↑
1970	$104.36	$82.87	$21.49	$359.25	↓	$285.27	↓	$73.98	↓
1971	$109.55	$87.07	$22.48	$358.95	↓	$285.30	↑	$73.65	↓
1972	$116.97	$93.16	$23.81	$367.61	↑	$292.78	↑	$74.83	↑
1973	$127.37	$102.01	$25.36	$379.06	↑	$303.59	↑	$75.47	↑
1974	$138.87	$110.79	$28.08	$379.21	↑	$302.54	↓	$76.68	↑
1975	$150.19	$118.45	$31.73	$375.18	↓	$295.91	↓	$79.28	↑
1976	$162.87	$129.15	$33.72	$384.95	↑	$305.24	↑	$79.71	↑
1977	$175.82	$140.23	$35.60	$390.46	↑	$311.40	↑	$79.05	↓
1978	$193.05	$154.74	$38.31	$400.19	↑	$320.78	↑	$79.41	↑
1979	$212.42	$170.17	$42.25	$406.47	↑	$325.62	↑	$80.85	↑
1980	$233.57	$186.90	$46.67	$409.41	↑	$327.61	↑	$81.80	↑
1981	$256.60	$205.15	$51.44	$411.34	↑	$328.88	↑	$82.46	↑
1982	$276.72	$223.93	$52.79	$417.63	↑	$337.96	↑	$79.66	↓
1983	$293.52	$237.69	$55.83	$426.07	↑	$345.02	↑	$81.05	↑
1984	$316.25	$257.63	$58.62	$442.62	↑	$360.57	↑	$82.05	↑
1985	$335.44	$272.95	$62.48	$455.14	↑	$370.35	↑	$84.78	↑
1986	$354.20	$288.74	$65.47	$470.26	↑	$383.34	↑	$86.92	↑
1987	$367.87	$301.73	$66.14	$474.19	↑	$388.93	↑	$85.25	↓
1988	$382.55	$313.15	$69.40	$476.87	↑	$390.36	↑	$86.51	↑
1989	$403.23	$331.07	$72.16	$484.19	↑	$397.54	↑	$86.65	↑
1990	$419.65	$346.48	$73.17	$484.98	↑	$400.42	↑	$84.56	↓
1991	$433.58	$358.68	$74.90	$483.53	↓	$400.00	↓	$83.53	↓
1992	$445.01	$368.29	$76.73	$484.55	↑	$401.01	↑	$83.54	↑
1993	$457.49	$380.55	$76.94	$486.38	↑	$404.58	↑	$81.80	↓
1994	$488.84	$409.36	$79.48	$509.10	↑	$426.32	↑	$82.78	↑
1995	$497.71	$416.01	$81.71	$507.30	↓	$424.02	↓	$83.28	↑
1996	$538.39	$453.34	$85.05	$538.39	↑	$453.34	↑	$85.05	↑
1997	$554.60	$466.07	$88.52	$544.09	↑	$457.25	↑	$86.84	↑
1998	$587.91	$495.57	$92.34	$569.84	↑	$480.34	↑	$89.50	↑
1999	$624.87	$528.04	$96.83	$597.10	↑	$504.58	↑	$92.53	↑
2000	$664.27	$563.55	$100.72	$621.63	↑	$527.38	↑	$94.25	↑

Details in the above table may not compute to the numbers shown due to rounding

Figure 1 presents the changes in inflation-adjusted dollar contributions to the three categories of Total Contributions, Congregational Finances and Benevolences.

Over the 1968-2000 period, per member donations to Total Contributions in inflation-adjusted dollars increased from $368.16 to $621.63, an increase of $253.47, or 69%.

Of the total increase, $236.95 was directed to Congregational Finances. This subcategory increased 82% between 1968 and 2000, from $290.42 to $527.38.

Figure 1: Changes in Per Member Giving in Inflation-Adjusted 1996 Dollars, Total Contributions, Congregational Finances, and Benevolences, 1968-2000

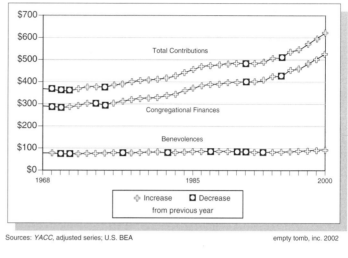

Sources: *YACC*, adjusted series; U.S. BEA   empty tomb, inc. 2002

In contrast, Benevolences increased 21%, from $77.73 in 1968 to $94.25 in 2000, a difference of $16.52.

Of the total inflation-adjusted dollar increase between 1968 and 2000, 93% was directed to Congregational Finances. Stated another way, of each additional inflation-adjusted dollar donated in 2000 compared to 1968, 93¢ was directed to Congregational Finances. This emphasis on the internal operations of the congregation helps explain the finding that Benevolences represented 21% of all church activity in 1968, and 15% in 2000.

Figure 2 provides a comparison of per member giving to the categories of Congregational Finances and Benevolences with changes in U.S. per capita disposable personal income in inflation-adjusted 1996 dollars.

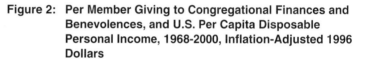

Figure 2: Per Member Giving to Congregational Finances and Benevolences, and U.S. Per Capita Disposable Personal Income, 1968-2000, Inflation-Adjusted 1996 Dollars

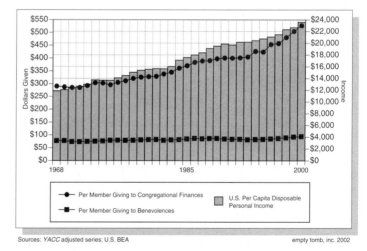

Sources: *YACC* adjusted series; U.S. BEA   empty tomb, inc. 2002

Giving as a Percentage of Income, 1968-2000. The second approach to considering giving is as a portion of income. Unlike dollars, there is no distinction between current or inflation-adjusted dollars when one is considering giving as a percentage of income. So long as one compares current dollar giving to current dollar income when calculating the percentage of income—or inflation-adjusted giving with inflation-adjusted income—the percentage will be the same.

In Table 2, giving as a percentage of income is presented for per member Total Contributions, and the related subcategories of Congregational Finances and Benevolences. As in Table 1 the arrows indicate whether the percentage of income in that category increased or decreased from the previous year. Inasmuch as the percent figures are rounded to the second decimal place, the arrows indicate the direction of a slight increase or decrease for those situations in which the percentage provided appears to be the same numerical figure as the previous year.

Table 2: Per Member Giving as a Percentage of Income, 1968-2000

Per Full or Confirmed Member Giving to Congregations as a Percentage of Income					
Year	Total Contributions Per Member	↑↓	Congregational Finances	↑↓	Benevolences	↑↓
1968	3.10%		2.45%		0.66%	
1969	3.03%	↓	2.38%	↓	0.65%	↓
1970	2.91%	↓	2.31%	↓	0.60%	↓
1971	2.84%	↓	2.26%	↓	0.58%	↓
1972	2.83%	↓	2.25%	↓	0.58%	↓
1973	2.76%	↓	2.21%	↓	0.55%	↓
1974	2.77%	↑	2.21%	↑	0.56%	↑
1975	2.75%	↓	2.17%	↓	0.58%	↑
1976	2.73%	↓	2.17%	↑	0.57%	↓
1977	2.70%	↓	2.15%	↓	0.55%	↓
1978	2.66%	↓	2.13%	↓	0.53%	↓
1979	2.64%	↓	2.12%	↓	0.53%	↓
1980	2.63%	↓	2.11%	↓	0.53%	↑
1981	2.63%	↓	2.10%	↓	0.53%	↑
1982	2.67%	↑	2.16%	↑	0.51%	↓
1983	2.66%	↓	2.15%	↓	0.51%	↓
1984	2.59%	↓	2.11%	↓	0.48%	↓
1985	2.59%	↑	2.11%	↑	0.48%	↑
1986	2.61%	↑	2.13%	↑	0.48%	↑
1987	2.58%	↓	2.12%	↓	0.46%	↓
1988	2.50%	↓	2.05%	↓	0.45%	↓
1989	2.48%	↓	2.04%	↓	0.44%	↓
1990	2.44%	↓	2.02%	↓	0.43%	↓
1991	2.45%	↑	2.03%	↑	0.42%	↓
1992	2.40%	↓	1.99%	↓	0.41%	↓
1993	2.41%	↑	2.01%	↑	0.41%	↓
1994	2.49%	↑	2.09%	↑	0.41%	↓
1995	2.44%	↓	2.04%	↓	0.40%	↓
1996	2.56%	↑	2.15%	↑	0.40%	↑
1997	2.53%	↓	2.13%	↓	0.40%	↑
1998	2.55%	↑	2.15%	↑	0.40%	↓
1999	2.63%	↑	2.22%	↑	0.41%	↑
2000	2.64%	↑	2.24%	↑	0.40%	↓

Details in the above table may not compute to the numbers shown due to rounding

A review of Table 2 yields the following information.

Overall, per member giving as a percentage of income to Total Contributions decreased from 3.10% 2.64%, a decline of 15% in the portion of income donated to the church. Giving as a percentage of income to Total Contributions decreased 21 times out of a possible 32 times, or 66% of the time.

The decline in giving as a percentage of income to Total Contributions is in contrast to the increase to Total Contributions in both current and inflation-adjusted dollars. Giving as a percentage of income takes into account changes in the resources available to the donor. U.S. per capita disposable (after-tax) personal income serves as an average income figure for the broad spectrum of church members included in the composite denominations data set.

U.S. per capita disposable personal income was $3,119 in current dollars in 1968. When that figure is calculated in inflation-adjusted 1996 dollars, U.S. per capita disposable personal income in 1968 was $11,864.

The current-dollar income figure for 2000 was $25,205. When inflation was factored out, 2000 U.S. per capita disposable personal income was $23,587.

Thus, after-tax per capita income in inflation-adjusted dollars increased by $11,723, an increase of 99% from 1968 to 2000. Even though per member Total Contributions increased 69% in inflation-adjusted dollars from 1968 to 2000, the income increase of 99% during the same period explains how church member contributions could be increasing in inflation-adjusted dollars in most of the years from 1968 to 2000, and yet decreasing as a percentage of income in most of the years from 1968 to 2000.

Congregational Finances decreased 20 times during the 32 two-year sets in the 1968-2000 period, or 62% of the time. Congregational Finances declined from 2.45% in 1968 to 2.24% in 2000, a percent change of 9% from the 1968 base in giving as a percentage of income.

Benevolences declined from 0.66% of income in 1968 to 0.40% in 2000, a decline of 39% as a portion of income. In unrounded figures, the 0.40% level of per member giving as a portion of income in the year 2000 was the lowest level in the 1968-2000 period. Out of the 32 two-year sets in the 1968-2000 interval, the portion of income that went to Benevolences declined 23 times, or 72% of the time.

Figure 3 presents per member giving as a percentage of income to Total Contributions, Congregational Finances and Benevolences.

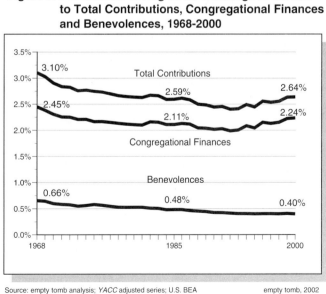

Figure 3: Per Member Giving as a Percentage of Income to Total Contributions, Congregational Finances and Benevolences, 1968-2000

Source: empty tomb analysis; *YACC* adjusted series; U.S. BEA   empty tomb, 2002

Giving in Inflation-adjusted Dollars, 1968, 1985 and 2000. The first report, that served as the basis for the present series on church member giving, considered data for the denominations in the composite for the years 1968 and 1985. With the data now available through 2000, a broader trend can be reviewed for the period under discussion, the 33-year range from 1968 to 2000.

The per member amount donated to Total Contributions in inflation-adjusted 1996 dollars was $86.98 greater in 1985 than it was in 1968 for the denominations in the composite data set. This amount represented an average increase of $5.12 a year in per member contributions. There was an overall increase during the 1985-2000 fifteen-year period as well. In 2000, the per member contribution to the composite denominations, which represented 98.9% of the total 1985 membership of the denominations originally studied, was $166.49 more per member in inflation-adjusted dollars than in 1985. The average annual increase was $11.10 between 1985 and 2000.

Gifts to Congregational Finances also increased between 1968 and 1985, as well as from 1985 to 2000. As in the case of Total Contributions, the annual rate of increase accelerated. Per member contributions to Congregational Finances were $290.42 in 1968, in inflation-adjusted 1996 dollars, and increased to $370.35 in 1985, a total increase of $79.93, with an average annual rate of change of $4.70. From 1985 to 2000, the average annual rate of change more than doubled to $10.47, with per member gifts growing from $370.35 in 1985 to $527.38 in 2000, an increase of $157.02.

In inflation-adjusted 1996 dollars, gifts to Benevolences were $77.73 in 1968 and grew to $84.78 in 1985, an increase of $7.05, with an annual average rate of change of $0.41. Between 1985 and 2000, per member gifts to Benevolences increased to $94.25, an increase of $9.47, with an annual average rate of change of $0.63 for the 1985-2000 period. The rate of change increased from 1985 to 2000, compared to the 1968 to 1985 period.

Table 3 presents per member gifts to Total Contributions, Congregational Finances and Benevolences in inflation-adjusted 1996 dollars for the years 1968, 1985 and 2000.

Table 3: Total Contributions, Congregational Finances and Benevolences, Per Member Giving in Inflation-Adjusted 1996 Dollars, 1968, 1985 and 2000

Year	Giving Per Member in Inflation-Adjusted 1996 Dollars								
	Total Contributions			Congregational Finances			Benevolences		
	Per Member Giving	Diff. from Previous $ Base	Average Annual Diff. in $s Given	Per Member Giving	Diff. from Previous $ Base	Average Annual Diff. in $s Given	Per Member Giving	Diff. from Previous $ Base	Average Annual Diff. in $s Given
1968	$368.16			$290.42			$77.73		
1985	$455.14	$86.98	$5.12	$370.35	$79.93	$4.70	$84.78	$7.05	$0.41
2000	$621.63	$166.49	$11.10	$527.38	$157.02	$10.47	$94.25	$9.47	$0.63

Details in the above table may not compute to the numbers shown due to rounding

Giving as a Percentage of Income, 1968, 1985 and 2000. Between 1968 and 1985, Total Contributions declined from 3.10% to 2.59% as a portion of income. The percentage change in giving as a percentage of income from the 1968 base was -16% in the 17 years from 1968 to 1985.

From 1985 to 2000, giving as a percentage of income to Total Contributions changed from 2.59% in 1985 to 2.64% in 2000. The percentage change in giving as a percentage of income was 1.4% in this fifteen-year interval of 1985-2000. Therefore, the annual percent change in the portion of per capita income donated to Total Contributions measured 0.09% in the 1985-2000 period, compared to the rate of -0.97% in the 1968-1985 period. This data suggests that the rate of annual decline in giving as a percentage of income decreased in the last fourteen years of the 1968 to 2000 period.

Table 4 presents data for Total Contributions per member as a percentage of income in summary fashion for the years 1968, 1985 and 2000.

Table 4: Per Member Giving as a Percentage of Income to Total Contributions, 1968, 1985 and 2000[4]

Year	Total Contributions Per Member as a Percentage of Income	Total Contributions Per Member as a Percentage of Income	Total Contributions Per Member as a Percentage of Income	Total Contributions Per Member as a Percentage of Income
	Total Contributions Per Member as a Percentage of Income	Difference in Total Contributions Per Member as a Percent of Income from Previous Base	Percent Change in Total Contributions Per Member as a Percent of Income Calculated from Previous Base	Annual Average Percent Change in Total Contributions Per Member as a Percent of Income
1968	3.10%			
1985	2.59%	-0.51%	-16.47% from 1968	-0.97%
2000	2.64%	0.04%	1.40% from 1985	0.09%

Details in the above table may not compute to the numbers shown due to rounding

Per member gifts to Congregational Finances measured 2.45% of income in 1968, 2.11% in 1985 and 2.24% in 2000. The annual average percent change in giving as a percentage of income changed direction from -0.81% a year between 1968 and 1985, from the 1968 base, to an increase of 0.35% a year between 1985 and 2000, from the 1985 base. Table 5 presents these numbers. A sporadic trend of increased giving to Congregational Finances began in 1993, and by 2000, the level of giving as a percentage of income had recovered to mid-1970 levels.

---

[4]An explanation as to how the 1968-1985 and 1985-2000 rates of change were calculated may be found in the Introduction.

Table 5: Per Member Giving as a Percentage of Income to Congregational Finances, 1968, 1985 and 2000

Year	Congregational Finances Per Member as a Percentage of Income			
	Congregational Finances Per Member as a Percentage of Income	Difference in Congregational Finances Per Member as a Percent of Income from Previous Base	Percent Change in Congregational Finances Per Member as a Percent of Income Calculated from Previous Base	Annual Average Percent Change in Congregational Finances Per Member as a Percent of Income
1968	2.45%			
1985	2.11%	-0.34%	-13.84% from 1968	-0.81%
2000	2.24%	0.13%	5.18% from 1985	0.35%

Details in the above table may not compute to the numbers shown due to rounding

Between 1985 and 2000, the annual average percent decline in giving as a percentage of income to Benevolences was smaller than that during the 1968-1985 period. From 1968 to 1985, the portion of member income directed to Benevolences decreased from 0.66% to 0.48%. This figure translated to a percent change in giving as a percentage of income of 26% from the 1968 base, with an annual average percent change of -1.55%. In the fifteen-year period from 1985 to 2000, giving as a percentage of income directed to Benevolences declined from 0.48% to 0.40%. The 1985-2000 percent change in giving as a percentage of income of –12.70% produced an annual average percent change of –0.85%, a slowing in the rate of decline compared to the 1968-1985 rate. Table 6 presents Benevolences as a percentage of income in 1968, 1985 and 2000.

Table 6: Per Member Giving as a Percentage of Income to Benevolences, 1968, 1985 and 2000

Year	Benevolences Per Member as a Percentage of Income			
	Benevolences Per Member as a Percentage of Income	Difference in Benevolences Per Member as a Percent of Income from Previous Base	Percent Change in Benevolences Per Member as a Percent of Income Calculated from Previous Base	Annual Average Percent Change in Benevolences Per Member as a Percent of Income
1968	0.66%			
1985	0.48%	-0.17%	-26.31% from 1968	-1.55%
2000	0.40%	-0.08%	-12.70% from 1985	-0.85%

Details in the above table may not compute to the numbers shown due to rounding

Giving in 1999 Compared to 2000. Per member giving as a percentage of income to Total Contributions in 1999 measured 2.63%. In 2000, the figure increased to 2.64%.

Congregational Finances increased from 2.22% in 1999 to 2.24% in 2000, continuing a recent trend of increase in this category that varies from an earlier overall pattern of decline.

In 1999, per member giving to Benevolences as a portion of income was 0.41%. Giving to Benevolences decreased in 2000, rounding to 0.40%.

The implications of these changes, slight though they seem, can be understood when translated to dollars. The unrounded difference between 1999 and 2000 Benevolences as a portion of income was –0.004689% of per capita income. When multiplied by the U.S. per capita income figure of $25,205 in 2000, that figure translated into a decline of only $1.18 less donated per member. However, this group of denominations had 28,681,455 members in 2000. As a result of this slight decline in per member giving as a portion of income to Benevolences, these 27 communions had $33,894,715 less to spend in 2000 on the larger mission of the church than if giving had stayed at the 1999 level.

Potential Giving. What would have been the situation in 2000 if giving had at least maintained the 1968 percentages of income donated?[5]

The implications of the difference become clearer when the aggregate totals are calculated by multiplying the theoretical per member giving at 1968 levels by the number of members reported by these denominations in 2000. Aggregate Total Contributions would then have been $22.3 billion rather than $19.1 billion, a difference of $3.2 billion, or an increase of 17%.

Aggregate Congregational Finances would have been $17.6 billion rather than $16.2 billion, a difference of $1.4 billion, or an increase of 9%.

There would have been a 62% increase in the total amount received for Benevolences. Instead of receiving $2.9 billion in 2000, as these church structures did, they would have received $4.7 billion, a difference of $1.8 billion for the larger mission of the church.

---

[5]For this comparison, only 27 denominations that provided data for both 1968 and 2000 were included.

chapter 2

Church Member Giving for 44 Denominations, 1999 to 2000

HIGHLIGHTS

- The composite denominations data set was expanded to include seventeen additional denominations that reported 1999 and 2000 data to the *YACC*.

- In both the composite set and the expanded set, from 1999 to 2000 per member contributions in current and inflation-adjusted dollars increased to Total Contributions and the two subcategories of Congregational Finances and Benevolences.

- In both the composite set and the expanded set, from 1999 to 2000 per member giving as a percentage of income increased to Total Contributions and Congregational Finances, and decreased to Benevolences.

- The rate of decrease in giving as a percentage of income to Benevolences from 1999 to 2000 was slightly lower in the expanded set of communions than in the composite set.

NARRATIVE

The 1968-2000 analysis in chapter one considers data for a group of denominations that published their membership and financial information for 1968 and 1985 in the *Yearbook of American and Canadian Churches* (*YACC*) series. That initial set of communions, considered in the first report on which the present series on church giving is based, has served as a denominational composite set analyzed for subsequent data years. Twenty-seven of the communions in the 1968-2000 data set provided information for both 1999 and 2000.

Data for both 1999 and 2000 for an additional seventeen denominations was either published in the relevant editions of the *YACC* series, or obtained directly from denominational offices. By adding the data for these 17 denominations to that of the composite group for these two years, giving patterns in an expanded set of communions can be considered.

In this enlarged comparison, the 2000 member sample increased from 28.7 million to 40,768,872 Full or Confirmed Members, and the number of denominations increased from 27 to 44. The larger group of denominations included both The United Methodist Church and The Episcopal Church, which were not included in the original 1968-1985 analysis because of the unavailability of confirmed 1968 data at the time of that study. A list of the denominations included in the present analysis is contained in Appendix A.

Per Member Giving in Inflation-Adjusted 1996 Dollars. As noted in the first chapter of this report, per member giving to Total Contributions increased from 1999 to 2000 for the composite denominations data set in inflation-adjusted 1996 dollars. Specifically, Total Contributions Per Member increased by $24.53 in inflation-adjusted 1996 dollars, from $597.10 in 1999 to $621.63 in 2000. When the group was expanded to 44 denominations, Total Per Member giving increased by $24.72, from $610.85 in 1999 to $635.58 in 2000. The rate of change in giving in inflation-adjusted dollars was similar in the expanded set and in the composite group, although the levels of giving were higher in the expanded set.

The composite denominations increased per member giving in inflation-adjusted dollars to Congregational Finances by $22.80, from $504.58 in 1999 to $527.38 in 2000. The expanded group increased by virtually the same amount at $22.81, from $515.11 in 1999 to $537.92 in 2000.

In the composite communions, per member contributions to Benevolences increased from $92.53 to $94.25 an increase of $1.73. The expanded group of 44 denominations increased by $1.91, from $95.74 to $97.65.

Table 7 presents per member giving data for 1999 and 2000 for the expanded group of 44 denominations, both in inflation-adjusted 1996 dollars, and also as a percentage of income. In addition, the change from 1999 to 2000 in per member contributions in inflation-adjusted 1996 dollars, in giving as a percentage of income, and in the percent change in giving as a percentage of income from the 1999 base are also included.

Table 7: Per Member Giving in 44 Denominations, 1999 and 2000, in Inflation-Adjusted 1996 Dollars and as a Percentage of Income

Year	Total Contributions Per Member		Congregational Finances		Benevolences	
	$s Given in Inflation Adj. '96 $	Giving as % of Income	$s Given in Inflation Adj. '96 $	Giving as % of Income	$s Given in Inflation Adj. '96 $	Giving as % of Income
1999	$610.85	2.69%	$515.11	2.27%	$95.74	0.42%
2000	$635.58	2.69%	$537.92	2.28%	$97.65	0.41%
Difference from the 1999 Base	$24.72	0.00%	$22.81	0.01%	$1.91	-0.01%
% Change in Giving as % of Income from the 1999 Base		0.08%		0.44%		-1.89%

Details in the above table may not compute to the numbers shown due to rounding.

Per Member Giving as a Percentage of Income. In the composite denominations set, from 1999 to 2000, giving as a percentage of income increased to Total Contributions and Congregational Finances, and decreased to Benevolences. The percent given to Total Contributions increased from 2.63% in 1999 to 2.64% in 2000. Congregational Finances increased from 2.22% in 1999 to 2.24% in 2000. Benevolences measured 0.41% in 1999, and 0.40% in 2000.

In the expanded group of 44 denominations, giving as a percentage of income also increased to Total Contributions and Congregational Finances and decreased to Benevolences. In this expanded set, the percent of income given on a per member basis to Total Contributions measured 2.69% in both 1999 and 2000. However, the unrounded numbers posted a small increase. Congregational Finances was 2.27% in 1999 and increased to 2.28% in 2000. Benevolences measured 0.42% in 1999 and 0.41% in 2000.

A comparison of the rate of percent change in giving as a percentage of income from the 1999 base resulted in the following. For Total Contributions, the composite denominations posted a 0.14% change from the 1999 base, compared to 0.08% for the expanded group of 44 denominations. For Congregational Finances, the composite denominations had a rate of 0.53% percent increase, compared to 0.44% for the expanded group of 44 denominations. Benevolences for the composite denominations posted a –2.02% percent decrease, compared to a rate of –1.89% when the group was expanded to include 44 denominations.

chapter 3

Church Member Giving in Denominations Defined by Organizational Affiliation, 1968, 1985, and 2000

HIGHLIGHTS

- During the 1968-2000 period, members of evangelical Protestant denominations gave larger dollar amounts and larger portions of income to their churches than did members of mainline Protestant denominations.

- In 2000, mainline Protestant church members were giving a higher portion of income to the category of Congregational Finances than they did in 1968. All other categories for both groups declined as a portion of income from 1968 to 2000.

- The 1968-2000 rate of decline in giving as a portion of income to Total Contributions was greater among the members of the evangelical denominations than it was among the members of the mainline denominations. While giving as a portion of income to Congregational Finances declined among the NAE-affiliated denominations, it reversed in the NCC-affiliated denominations. The rate of decline in per member giving as a portion of income to Benevolences was similar between the evangelical and the mainline members.

- Membership in the evangelical denominations grew between 1968 and 2000, in contrast to the mainline denominations, which decreased in membership. Therefore, although evangelicals were receiving a smaller portion of income per member, aggregate donations were higher in 2000 than in 1968 for this group.

- Among the mainline denominations, the increase in giving was directed to Congregational Finances. This fact, combined with the loss in membership, may account for the finding that aggregate Benevolences donations in inflation-adjusted dollars were 14 percent smaller in 2000 than in 1968 for these communions.

NARRATIVE_____

The communions included in the composite denominations data set considered in chapter 1 of this volume span the theological spectrum. Reviewing data for defined subsets within the composite group allows for additional analysis.

For example, the theory that evangelical Protestants donate more money to their churches than do members of mainline Protestant denominations can be tested by comparing giving patterns in two subgroups of communions within the composite denominations data set.

In the composite group, membership and financial data is available for 1968, 1985 and 2000 for eight communions affiliated with the National Association of Evangelicals (NAE).

Eight communions affiliated with the National Council of the Churches of Christ in the U.S.A. (NCC) also had membership and financial data available for 1968, 1985 and 2000.

Of course, there is diversity of opinion within any denomination, as well as in multi-communion groupings such as the NAE or the NCC. For purposes of the present analysis, however, these two groups may serve as general standards for comparison, since they have been characterized as representing certain types of denominations. For example, the National Association of Evangelicals has, by choice of its title, defined its denominational constituency. And traditionally, the National Council of the Churches of Christ in the U.S.A. has counted mainline denominations among its members.

Recognizing that there are limitations in defining a denomination's theological perspectives merely by membership in one of these two organizations, a review of giving patterns of the two subsets of denominations may nevertheless provide some insight into how widely spread current giving patterns may be. Therefore, an analysis of 1968-2000 giving patterns was completed for the two subsets of those denominations which were affiliated with one of these two interdenominational organizations.

Using 1985 data, the eight denominations affiliated with the NAE as of 2000 represented 18% of the total number of NAE-member denominations as listed in the *Yearbook of American and Canadian Churches (YACC)* series; 21% of the total number of NAE-member denominations with membership data listed in the *YACC*; and approximately 21% of the total membership of the NAE-member denominations with membership data listed in the *YACC*.[1]

Data for 2000 was also available for eight NCC-member denominations. In 1985, these eight denominations represented 27% of the total number of NCC constituent bodies as listed in the *YACC*; 30% of the NCC constituent bodies with membership data

_____

[1]The 1985 total church membership estimate of 3,388,414 represented by NAE denominations includes *YACC* 1985 membership data for each denomination where available or, if 1985 membership data was not available, membership data for the most recent year prior to 1985. Full or Confirmed membership data was used except in those instances where this figure was not available, in which case Inclusive Membership was used.

listed in the *YACC*; and approximately 29% of the total membership of the NCC constituent bodies with membership data listed in the *YACC*.[2]

Per Member Giving to Total Contributions, 1968, 1985 and 2000. As noted in Table 8, per member giving as a percentage of income to Total Contributions for a composite of those eight NAE-member denominations was 6.15% in 1968. That year, per member giving as a percentage of income to Total Contributions was 3.30% for a composite of these eight NCC denominations.

Table 8: Per Member Giving as a Percentage of Income to Total Contributions, Eight NAE and Eight NCC Denominations, 1968, 1985 and 2000

Year	Total Contributions									
	NAE Denominations					NCC Denominations				
	Number of Denom. Analyzed	Total Contrib. Per Member as % of Income	Diff. in Total Contrib. as % of Income from Previous Base	Percent Change in Total Contrib. as % of Income Figured from Previous Base	Avg. Annual Percent Change in Total Contrib. as % of Income	Number of Denom. Analyzed	Total Contrib. Per Member as % of Income	Diff. in Total Contrib. as % of Income from Previous Base	Percent Change in Total Contrib. as % of Income Figured from Previous Base	Avg. Annual Percent Change in Total Contrib. as % of Income
1968	8	6.15%				8	3.30%			
1985	8	4.74%	-1.41%	-22.94% from '68	-1.35%	8	2.85%	-0.45%	-13.73% from '68	-0.81%
2000	8	4.13%	-0.61%	-9.94% from '85	-0.66%	8	3.17%	0.32%	9.60% from '85	0.64%

Details in the above table may not compute to the numbers shown due to rounding.

In 1985, the NAE denominations' per member giving as a percentage of income level was 4.74%, while the NCC level was 2.85%.

The data shows the NAE-member denominations received a larger portion of their members' incomes than did NCC-affiliated denominations in both 1968 and 1985. This information supports the assumption that denominations identifying with an evangelical perspective received a higher level of support than denominations that may be termed mainline.

The analysis also indicates that the decline in levels of giving observed in the larger composite of 29 denominations was evident among both the NAE-member denominations and the NCC-member denominations as well. While giving levels decreased for both sets of denominations between 1968 and 1985, the decrease in Total Contributions was more pronounced in the NAE-affiliated communions. The percent change in the percentage of income donated in the NAE-member denominations, in comparison to the 1968 base, was -

---

[2]The 1985 total church membership estimate of 39,621,950 represented by NCC denominations includes *YACC* 1985 membership data for each denomination where available or, if 1985 membership data was not available, membership data for the most recent year prior to 1985. Full or Confirmed membership data was used except in those instances where this figure was not available, in which case Inclusive Membership was used.

23% between 1968 and 1985, while the percent change in percentage of income given to the NCC-member denominations was -14%.

A decline in giving as a percentage of income continued among the eight NAE-member denominations during the 1985-2000 period. By 2000, per member giving as a percentage of income to Total Contributions had declined from the 1985 level of 4.74% to 4.13%, a percentage change of -10% in the portion of members' incomes donated over that fifteen-year period.

In contrast, the eight NCC-affiliated denominations increased in giving as a percentage of income to Total Contributions during 1985-2000, from the 1985 level of 2.85% to 3.17% in 2000, a percentage increase of 10% in the portion of income given to these churches.

Because of the decline in the portion of income given in the NAE-affiliated denominations and increase among the NCC-affiliated denominations, in 2000 the difference in per member giving as a percentage of income between the NAE-affiliated denominations and the NCC-affiliated denominations was not as large as it had been in 1968. Comparing the two rates in giving as a percentage of income to Total Contributions between the NAE-member denominations and the NCC-member denominations in this analysis, the NCC-affiliated denominations received 54% as much of per member income as the NAE-member denominations did in 1968, 60% as much in 1985, and 77% in 2000.

For the NAE-affiliated denominations, during the 1985 to 2000 period, the rate of decrease in the average annual percent change in per member giving as a percentage of income to Total Contributions slowed in comparison to the 1968-1985 annual percent change from the 1968 base. The 1968-1985 average annual percent change was -1.35%. The figure for 1985-2000 was -0.66%.

In the NCC-member denominations, the trend reversed. While the average annual percent change from the 1968 base in giving as a percentage of income was -0.81% between 1968 and 1985, the average annual change from 1985 was an increase of 0.64% between 1985 and 2000.

Per Member Giving to Congregational Finances and Benevolences, 1968, 1985 and 2000. Were there any markedly different patterns between the two subsets of denominations defined by affiliation with the NAE and the NCC in regards to the distribution of Total Contributions between the subcategories of Congregational Finances and Benevolences?

In the subcategory of Congregational Finances, a difference was observable. The NCC-related denominations posted an increase from 1968 levels in the portion of income directed to this category. In the NAE-related denominations, the portion of income declined. Table 9 presents the Congregational Finances giving data for the NAE and NCC denominations in 1968, 1985 and 2000.

In the subcategory of Benevolences, both groups posted declines in the portion of income directed to that category. Table 10 presents the Benevolences giving data for the NAE and NCC denominations in 1968, 1985 and 2000.

In 1968, the NAE-affiliated members were giving 6.15% of their incomes to their churches. Of that, 5.01% went to Congregational Finances, while 1.14% went to Benevolences. In 1985, of the 4.74% of income donated to Total Contributions, 3.82%

Table 9: Per Member Giving as a Percentage of Income to Congregational Finances, Eight NAE and Eight NCC Denominations, 1968, 1985 and 2000

	Congregational Finances									
	NAE Denominations					NCC Denominations				
Year	Number of Denom. Analyzed	Cong. Finances Per Member as % of Income	Diff. in Cong. Finances as % of Income from Previous Base	Percent Change in Cong. Finances as % of Income Figured from Previous Base	Avg. Annual Percent Change in Cong. Finances as % of Income	Number of Denom. Analyzed	Cong. Finances Per Member as % of Income	Diff. in Cong. Finances as % of Income from Previous Base	Percent Change in Cong. Finances as % of Income Figured from Previous Base	Avg. Annual Percent Change in Cong. Finances as % of Income
1968	8	5.01%				8	2.67%			
1985	8	3.82%	-1.19%	-23.71% from '68	-1.39%	8	2.40%	-0.27%	-10.06% from '68	-0.59%
2000	8	3.41%	-0.42%	-8.29% from '85	-0.55%	8	2.78%	0.38%	14.15% from '85	0.94%

Details in the above table may not compute to the numbers shown due to rounding.

Table 10: Per Member Giving as a Percentage of Income to Benevolences, Eight NAE and Eight NCC Denominations, 1968, 1985 and 2000

	Benevolences									
	NAE Denominations					NCC Denominations				
Year	Number of Denom. Analyzed	Benevol. Per Member as % of Income	Diff. in Benevol. as % of Income from Previous Base	Percent Change in Benevol. as % of Income Figured from Previous Base	Avg. Annual Percent Change in Benevol. as % of Income	Number of Denom. Analyzed	Benevol. Per Member as % of Income	Diff. in Benevol. as % of Income from Previous Base	Percent Change in Benevol. as % of Income Figured from Previous Base	Avg. Annual Percent Change in Benevol. as % of Income
1968	8	1.14%				8	0.63%			
1985	8	0.92%	-0.22%	-19.51% from '68	-1.15%	8	0.44%	-0.18%	-29.36% from '68	-1.73%
2000	8	0.72%	-0.20%	-17.21% from '85	-1.15%	8	0.38%	-0.06%	-9.76% from '85	-0.65%

Details in the above table may not compute to the numbers shown due to rounding.

was directed to Congregational Finances. This represented a percent change in the portion of income going to Congregational Finances of -24% from the 1968 base. Per member contributions to Benevolences among these NAE-member denominations declined from 1.14% in 1968 to 0.92% in 1985, representing a percent change of -20% from the 1968 base in the portion of income donated to Benevolences.

In 2000, the 4.13% of income donated by the NAE-member denominations to their churches was divided between Congregational Finances and Benevolences at the 3.41% and 0.72% levels, respectively. The percent change between 1985 and 2000 in contributions to Congregational Finances as a percent of income was a decline of -8%. In contrast, the percent change in contributions to Benevolences as a percent of income was a decline of -17% in the same fifteen-year period. The annual rate in the percent change in giving as a percentage of income to Benevolences remained constant at -1.15%. from 1968 to 1985 and from 1985 to 2000.

In 1968, the NCC-member denominations were giving 3.30% of their incomes to their churches. Of that, 2.67% went to Congregational Finances. In 1985, of the 2.85% of income donated to these communions, 2.40% went to Congregational Finances. This represented a percent change from the 1968 base in the portion of income going to Congregational Finances of -10%. In contrast, per member contributions as a percent of income to Benevolences among these same NCC-affiliated denominations had declined from 0.63% in 1968 to 0.44% in 1985, representing a percent change of -29% from the 1968 base in the portion of income donated to Benevolences.

In 2000, the 3.17% of income donated by the NCC-affiliated members to their churches was divided between Congregational Finances and Benevolences at the 2.78% and 0.38% levels, respectively. The increase in per member Total Contributions as a percent of income was directed to Congregational Finances, which increased from 2.40% in 1985 to 2.78% in 2000. The 2000 percent change in contributions to Congregational Finances as a percent of income from 1985 was an increase of 14%. The 2000 level of giving to this category was higher than that posted by these communions in 1968.

The portion of income directed to Benevolences by these NCC-member denominations declined from 1968 to 1985, and continued to decline from 1985 to 2000. The percent change in contributions to Benevolences as a percent of income declined from 0.44% in 1985 to the 2000 level of 0.38%, a decline of 10% in this fifteen-year period. The annual percent change from 1985 in giving as a percentage of income to Benevolences indicated a lower rate of decline at −0.65% between 1985 and 2000, compared to the 1968 1985 annual rate of −1.73%.

Figure 4 presents data for giving as a percentage of income to Total Contributions, Congregational Finances and Benevolences for both the NAE and NCC denominations in graphic form for the years 1968, 1985 and 2000.

Figure 4: Per Member Giving as a Percent of Income to Total Contributions, Congregational Finances and Benevolences, Eight NAE and Eight NCC Denominations, 1968, 1985 and 2000

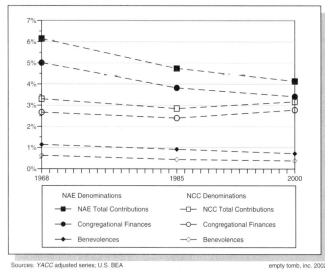

Sources: *YACC* adjusted series; U.S. BEA   empty tomb, inc. 2002

Changes in Per Member Giving, 1968 to 2000. For the NAE-affiliated denominations, per member giving as a percentage of income to Congregational Finances declined from 5.01% in 1968 to 3.41% in 2000, a change of -32% from the 1968 base. In Benevolences, the -37% change reflected a decline from 1.14% in 1968 to 0.72% in 2000.

For the NCC-affiliated denominations, between 1968 and 2000 in the subcategory of Congregational Finances, per member giving as a percentage of income increased from

2.67% to 2.78%, a change of 4% from the 1968 base. That compared to the 39% decline in the subcategory of Benevolences that changed from 0.63% in 1968 to 0.38% in 2000.

Table 11 presents the 1968-2000 percent change in per member giving as a percentage of income to Total Contributions, Congregational Finances and Benevolences in both the NAE- and NCC-affiliated communions.

Table 11: Percent Change in Per Member Giving as a Percentage of Income, Eight NAE and Eight NCC Denominations, 1968 to 2000

Year	NAE Denominations				NCC Denominations			
	Number of Denom. Analyzed	Total Contrib.	Cong. Finances	Benevol.	Number of Denom. Analyzed	Total Contrib.	Cong. Finances	Benevol.
1968	8	6.15%	5.01%	1.14%	8	3.30%	2.67%	0.63%
2000	8	4.13%	3.41%	0.72%	8	3.17%	2.78%	0.38%
% Chg. 1968-'00	8	-33%	-32%	-37%	8	-4%	4%	-39%

Details in the above table may not compute to the numbers shown due to rounding.

Per Member Giving in Inflation-Adjusted 1996 Dollars. The NAE-affiliated group's level of per member support to Total Contributions in inflation-adjusted 1996 dollars was $730.03 in 1968. This increased to $832.67 in 1985, and by 2000 increased to $974.23.

For the NAE-affiliated denominations, per member contributions in inflation-adjusted 1996 dollars to the subcategory of Congregational Finances increased from 1968 to 1985, and again from 1985 to 2000. Per member contributions in inflation-adjusted 1996 dollars to Benevolences increased between 1968 and 1985, and, at a slower rate, between 1985 and 2000. Of the increased per member giving in inflation-adjusted dollars between 1968 and 2000, 86% went to Congregational Finances.

The NCC-affiliated group also experienced an increase in inflation-adjusted per member Total Contributions between 1968 and 2000. The 1968 NCC level of per member support in inflation-adjusted 1996 dollars was $391.71. In 1985, this had increased to $500.13, and in 2000 the figure was $746.57.

The NCC-member denominations experienced an increase in inflation-adjusted per member donations to Congregational Finances in both 1985 and 2000 as well. Although 96% of the increase between 1968 and 2000 was directed to Congregational Finances, gifts to Benevolences increased in inflation-adjusted 1996 dollars between 1968 and 1985, and again between 1985 and 2000.

As a portion of Total Contributions, the NAE-member denominations directed 19% of their per member gifts to Benevolences in 1968, 19% in 1985, and 17% in 2000. The NCC-member denominations directed 19% of their per member gifts to Benevolences in 1968, 16% in 1985, and 12% in 2000.

Table 12 presents the levels of per member giving to Total Contributions, Congregational Finances and Benevolences, in inflation-adjusted 1996 dollars, and the percentage of Total Contributions which went to Benevolences in 1968, 1985 and 2000, for both sets of

Table 12: Per Member Giving, Eight NAE and Eight NCC Denominations, 1968, 1985 and 2000, Inflation-Adjusted 1996 Dollars

Year	NAE Denominations					NCC Denominations				
	Number of Denom. Analyzed	Total Contrib.	Cong. Finances	Benevol.	Benevol. as % of Total Contrib.	Number of Denom. Analyzed	Total Contrib.	Cong. Finances	Benevol.	Benevol. as % of Total Contrib.
1968	8	$730.03	$594.59	$135.44	19%	8	$391.71	$317.19	$74.51	19%
1985	8	$832.67	$671.33	$161.34	19%	8	$500.13	$422.23	$77.90	16%
2000	8	$974.23	$803.83	$170.39	17%	8	$746.57	$656.38	$90.19	12%
$ Diff. '68-'00		$244.20	$209.24	$34.96			$354.87	$339.19	$15.68	
% Chg. '68-'00		33%	35%	26%			91%	107%	21%	

Details in the above table may not compute to the numbers shown due to rounding.

Figure 5: Per Member Giving to Total Contributions, Congregational Finances and Benevolences, Eight NAE and Eight NCC Denominations, 1968, 1985 and 2000, Inflation-Adjusted 1996 $

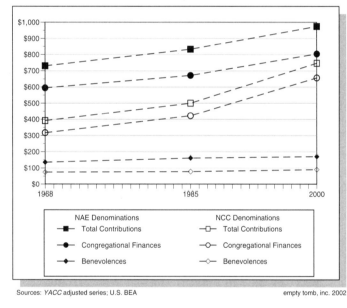

Sources: *YACC* adjusted series; U.S. BEA   empty tomb, inc. 2002

denominations. In addition, the percent change from 1968 to 2000, from the 1968 base, in per member inflation-adjusted 1996 dollar contributions is noted.

Figure 5 presents the data for per member contributions in inflation-adjusted 1996 dollars in graphic form for the years 1968, 1985 and 2000.

Aggregate Dollar Donations, 1968 and 2000. The NCC-member denom-inations and the NAE-member denominations differed in terms of changes of mem-bership. The impact of this difference was evident at the aggregate dollar level.

Table 13 considers aggregate giving data for the eight NAE-member denominations included in this analysis. Membership in these eight NAE-member denominations increased 59% from 1968-2000.

As measured in current aggregate dollars, giving in each of the three categories of Total Contributions, Congregational Finances and Benevolences was greater in 2000 than in 1968 for the NAE-member denominations. This was true even though per member giving as a portion of income declined to all three categories during this period.

The same can be said for the three aggregate categories when inflation was factored out by converting the current dollars to inflation-adjusted 1996 dollars. These denominations

Table 13: Aggregate Giving, Eight NAE Denominations, 1968 and 2000,
Current and Inflation-Adjusted 1996 Dollars

Year	Number of Den. Analyzed	Member-ship	Current Dollars			Inflation-Adjusted 1996 Dollars		
			Total Contributions	Cong. Finances	Benevol.	Total Contributions	Cong. Finances	Benevol.
1968	8	535,865	$102,845,802	$83,765,677	$19,080,125	$391,197,421	$318,621,822	$72,575,599
2000	8	852,206	$887,195,634	$732,025,084	$155,170,550	$830,241,095	$685,031,896	$145,209,199
% Chg.		59%	763%	774%	713%	112%	115%	100%

Details in the above table may not compute to the numbers shown due to rounding.

have been compensated for a decline in giving as a percentage of income to all three categories by the increase in total membership. As long as these denominations continue to grow in membership, their national and regional programs may not be affected in the immediate future by the decline in the portion of income donated.

Table 14 below considers aggregate data for the eight NCC-member denominations. The NCC-related denominations experienced a membership decline of 28% between 1968 and 2000. The increase in current dollar donations was sufficient to result in an increase in aggregate current dollars in each of the three categories of Total Contributions, Congregational Finances and Benevolences.

However, the inflation-adjusted 1996 dollar figures account for the acknowledged financial difficulties in many of these communions, particularly in the category of Benevolences. The impact of the decline in membership was evident at the aggregate dollar level. The increase in giving to Congregational Finances as a portion of income noted above was tempered by a loss of members. Between 1968 and 2000, while the NCC-related communions experienced an increase of 91% in per member giving to Total Contributions in inflation-adjusted 1996 dollars—from $391.77 in 1968 to $746.57 in 2000—aggregate Total Contributions in 2000 to these eight denominations measured only 36% larger in inflation-adjusted 1996 dollars in 2000 than in 1968.

Further, Congregational Finances absorbed all of the increased giving at the aggregate level. The 14% decline in aggregated Benevolences receipts in inflation-adjusted 1996 dollars between 1968 and 2000 provides insight into the basis for any cutbacks at the denominational level.

Table 14: Aggregate Giving, Eight NCC Denominations, 1968 and 2000,
Current and Inflation-Adjusted 1996 Dollars

Year	Number of Den. Analyzed	Member-ship	Current Dollars			Inflation-Adjusted 1996 Dollars		
			Total Contributions	Cong. Finances	Benevol.	Total Contributions	Cong. Finances	Benevol.
1968	8	12,688,864	$1,326,045,714	$1,073,798,710	$252,247,004	$5,043,916,752	$4,084,437,847	$959,478,905
2000	8	9,167,451	$7,313,694,354	$6,430,161,769	$883,532,585	$6,844,183,375	$6,017,370,175	$826,813,200
% Chg.		-28%	452%	499%	250%	36%	47%	-14%

Details in the above table may not compute to the numbers shown due to rounding.

chapter 4

Church Member Giving in Eleven Denominations, 1921-2000

HIGHLIGHTS

Eleven denominations reported data on a fairly consistent basis from 1921 through 2000.

- Per member giving as a portion of income was above three percent from 1922-1933 and again from 1958-1962. However, unlike after 1933, when the country was experiencing the Great Depression followed by World War II, no major national catastrophes explain the downturn in giving that began after 1962.

- Per member giving as a percent of income began to decline in 1961, and membership as a percent of U.S. population began to decline in 1962. While giving as a portion of income showed a slight upward trend beginning in 1993, the decline in membership as a percent of U.S. population continued uninterrupted through the year 2000.

- Considered in five-year segments, between 1950 and 2000, the highest average annual rate of growth in per member giving in inflation-adjusted dollars was from 1995-2000. However, when the increase in dollars given was considered as a portion of average annual income increase, the highest rate was 1950-1955, followed by 1955-1960.

- Giving as a percentage of income was lower in 2000 than in 1921 or in 1933, the depth of the Great Depression.

NARRATIVE

A continuing feature in this ongoing series reviewing church member giving is an analysis of available giving data throughout this century. Because of the fixed nature of the data source, the analysis remains fairly static. However, the data can now be updated to include information through 2000. This data also makes use of the revised U.S. BEA income series, with the benchmark year now being 1996.

For the period 1921 through 2000, the preferable approach would be to analyze the entire composite denominations data set considered in chapter one of this volume. Unfortunately, comparable data since 1921 is not readily available for these communions. However, data over an extended period of time is available in the *Yearbook of American and Canadian Churches* series for a group of 11 Protestant communions, or their historical antecedents. This set includes ten mainline Protestant communions and the Southern Baptist Convention.

The available data has been reported fairly consistently over the time span of 1921 to 2000.[1] The value of the multiyear comparison is that it provides a historical time line over which to observe giving patterns.

Giving as a Percentage of Income. The period under consideration in this section of the report began in 1921. At that point, per member giving as a percentage of income was 2.9%. In current dollars, U.S. per capita disposable (after-tax) personal income was $555, and per member giving was $16.10. When inflation was factored out by converting both income and giving to 1996 dollars, per capita income in 1921 measured $4,705 and per member giving was $136.58.

From 1922 through 1933, giving as a percent of income stayed above the 3% level. The high was 3.7% in 1924, followed closely by the amount in 1932, when per member giving measured 3.6% of per capita income. This trend is of particular interest inasmuch as per capita income was increasing steadily between 1921 and 1927, with the exception of a decline in 1925. Even as people were increasing in personal affluence, they also continued to maintain a giving level of more than 3% to their churches. Even after income began to decline because of the economic reverses in the Great Depression, giving measured above 3% from 1929 through 1933.

The year 1933 was the depth of the Great Depression. Per capita income was at the lowest point it would reach between 1921 and 2000, whether measured in current or inflation-adjusted dollars. Yet per member giving as a percentage of income was 3.3%. Income had decreased by 17% between 1921 and 1933 in inflation-adjusted 1996 dollars, from $4,705 to $3,904. Meanwhile, per member giving had decreased 6%, from $136.58 in 1921 to $127.81 in 1933, in inflation-adjusted dollars. Therefore, giving as a percentage of income actually increased from 2.9% in 1921 to 3.3% in 1933, an increase of 13% in the portion of income contributed to the church.

Giving in inflation-adjusted 1996 dollars declined from 1933 to 1934, although income began to recover in 1934. Giving then began to increase again in 1935. In inflation-adjusted dollars, giving did not surpass the 1927 level of $209.62 until 1953, when giving grew from $201.58 in 1952 to $221.68 in 1953.

During World War II, incomes improved rapidly. Meanwhile, church member giving increased only modestly in current dollars. When inflation was factored out, per member

---

[1]Data for the period 1965-1967 was not available in a form that could be readily analyzed for the present purposes, and therefore data for these three years was estimated by dividing the change in per member current dollar contributions from 1964 to 1968 by four, the number of years in this interval, and cumulatively adding the result to the base year of 1964 data and subsequently to the calculated data for the succeeding years of 1965 and 1966 in order to obtain estimates for the years 1965-1967.

giving was at $132.12 in 1941, the year the United States entered the war. It declined to $128.01 in 1942, increased in 1943 to $129.71 and then to $142.86 in 1944. However, income in inflation-adjusted dollars grew from $6,379 in 1941 to $7,401 in 1942, $7,907 in 1943, and reached a high for this period of $8,368 in 1944, a level that would not be surpassed again until 1953. Thus, giving as a percentage of income reached a low point during the three full calendar years of formal U.S. involvement in World War II, at levels of 1.73% in 1942, 1.64% in 1943, and 1.71% in 1944.

In 1945, the last year of the war, U.S. per capita income was $8,260 in inflation-adjusted dollars. Giving in inflation-adjusted dollars increased from 1944 to 1945, to $161.78, the highest amount it had been since 1930. Although per member giving increased 27% between 1933 and 1945, per capita income had increased 112%. Giving as a percentage of income therefore declined from the 3.3% level in 1933, to 2.0% in 1945.

The unusually high level of per capita income slumped after the war but had recovered to war levels by the early 1950s. By 1960, U.S. per capita income was 11% higher in inflation-adjusted 1996 dollars than it had been in 1945, increasing from $8,260 in 1945 to $9,134 in 1960. Meanwhile, per member giving in inflation-adjusted dollars had increased 77%, from $161.78 in 1945 to $285.64 in 1960. Giving recovered the level it had been from 1922 through 1933, and stayed above 3% from 1958 through 1962. Giving as a percentage of income reached a postwar high of 3.13% in 1960, and then began to decline.

For the second time in the century, giving levels were growing to, or maintaining a level above, three percent of income even while incomes were also expanding. From 1921-1928, incomes expanded 24%. During this time giving grew to above 3% and stayed there. From 1950-1962, incomes grew 20%. Again, giving grew to above 3% in 1958 and stayed there through 1962. In both cases, church members increased or maintained their giving levels even as their incomes increased.

In the 1920s, the economic expansion was interrupted by the Great Depression, followed by World War II.

In contrast to the economic upheaval earlier in the century, however, the economy continued to expand through the 1960s. Yet the portion of income given was not sustained above 3%. By 1968, giving as a percentage of income had declined to 2.6% for this group of 11 communions. U.S. per capita income increased 30% in inflation-adjusted 1996 dollars between 1960 and 1968, from $9,134 in 1960 to $11,864 in 1968. In comparison, per member giving increased 10% in inflation-adjusted dollars, from the 1960 level of $285.64 to the 1968 level of $314.08.

By 1985, per member giving had increased 33% in inflation-adjusted 1996 dollars, from $314.08 in 1968 to $419.30 in 1985. U.S. per capita income measured $17,559, an increase of 48% over the 1968 level of $11,864. Giving as a percentage of income, therefore, measured 2.4% in 1985, representing a 10% decline from the 1968 level of 2.6%.

The year 2000 was the latest year for which data was available for the eleven denominations considered in this section. In that year, per member giving as a percentage of income was 2.6%, a 7% increase from the 1985 level. Per member giving increased 44% in inflation-adjusted 1996 dollars, from $419.30 in 1985 to $603.31 in 2000. U.S. per capita income increased 34% during this period, from the 1985 level of $17,559 to the 2000 level of $23,587. Thus, the percentage of income given increased.

Figure 6 contrasts per member giving as a percentage of income for a composite of eleven Protestant denominations, with U.S. disposable personal income in inflation-adjusted 1996 dollars, for the period 1921 through 2000.

Figure 15: **Per Member Giving as a Percent of Income in 11 Denominations, and U.S. Per Capita Income, 1921-2000**

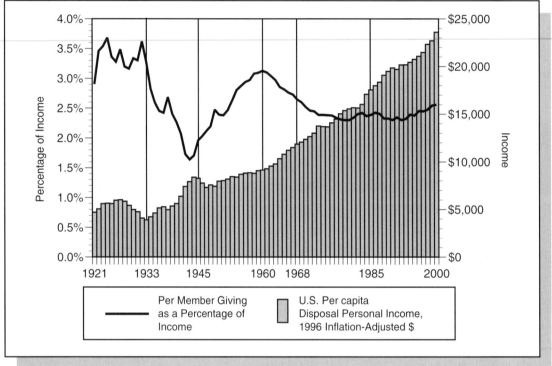

Source: empty tomb analysis; *YACC* adjusted series; U.S. BEA   empty tomb, inc. 2002

Membership and Giving, 1921-2000. Membership was changing for this group of 11 denominations during the 1921-2000 period as well.

Between 1921 and 1961, the portion of U.S. population that this group of 11 denominations represented grew from 16.1% of the U.S. population to 20%, or one-fifth of the United States.

In that same year of 1961, the first decline in giving as a percentage of income occurred since 1950.

The next year, 1962, a decline in membership as a percent of U.S. population occurred for this group that would continue through the year 2000. While this group of denominations continued to increase in membership until 1968, U.S. population grew at a faster rate. Therefore, while this group represented 20% of U.S. population in 1961, by the year 2000, this group represented 12.8% of U.S. population.

During this 1961-2000 period, the Southern Baptist Convention grew from 9,792,426 to 15,960,308. Meanwhile, the other ten denominations, all of which might be termed mainline Protestant, declined in membership, from 26,683,648 to 20,158,386.

The growth in the number of members in the Southern Baptist Convention offset the mainline Protestant membership loss, so that as a whole, the group's membership was fairly static, measuring 36,661,788 in 1961 and 36,118,694 in 2000. However, U.S. population increased from 183,742,000 in 1961, when the group of 11 denominations represented 20% of the U.S. population, to 282,489,000, when the 11 denominations represented 12.8% of the U.S. population.

It is interesting to note that giving as a percentage of income declined the year before membership as a percent of U.S. population began its decline, and nine years before the 11 denominations experienced a decline in absolute membership, from 37,382,659 in 1968 to 37,128,594 in 1969.

Although giving as a percent of income decreased to 2.3% in 1979 and 1980, it recovered to 2.42% in 1986. It was again down to 2.30% in 1992, but as of 2000 had recovered to 2.56%.

In contrast, membership as a percent of population for the 11 denominations as a group began a decline in 1962 that continued uninterrupted through the year 2000.

Figure 7 presents both per member giving as a percentage of income and membership as a percent of U.S. population, for the composite of eleven Protestant denominations, from 1921 through 2000.

Figure 7: Per Member Giving as a Percent of Income and Membership as a Percent of U.S. Population, 11 Denominations, 1921-2000

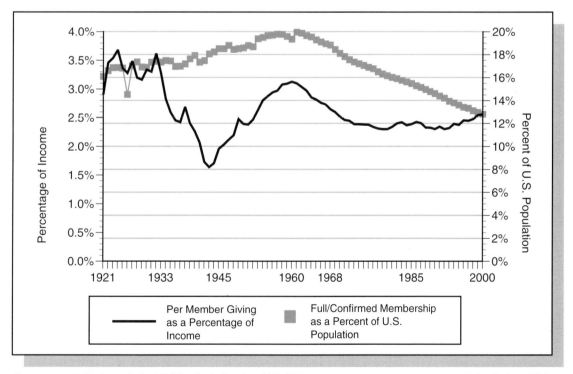

Source: empty tomb analysis; *YACC* adjusted series; U.S. BEA   empty tomb, inc. 2002

Change in Per Member Giving and U.S. Per Capita Disposable Personal Income, in Inflation-adjusted 1996 Dollars. For this group of 11 communions, per member giving in inflation-adjusted 1996 dollars increased half the time during the 1921-1947 period. Per member giving in inflation-adjusted dollars decreased from 1924 to 1925. While it increased from 1925 to 1926 and again in 1927, giving began a seven-year decline in 1928. This seven-year period, from 1928 to 1934, included some of the worst years of the Great Depression. Giving increased again in 1935. Declines in 1939, 1940, 1942, 1946 and 1947 alternated with increases in the other years.

Then, from 1948 through 1968,[2] the members in these 11 communions increased per member giving in inflation-adjusted 1996 dollars each year. During the 1948-1960 interval of 12 years, per member giving averaged an increase of $9.97 a year. Although giving continued to increase for the next few years, it was at the slower rate of $3.56 per year. Overall, in inflation-adjusted 1996 dollars, income grew 57% from 1948 to 1968, while per member giving increased 89%.

Per member giving in inflation-adjusted dollars declined in 1969, 1970 and 1971, followed by two years of increase and two of decline.

The longest sustained period of average annual increases in per member giving in inflation-adjusted dollars during the 90-year period occurred during the most recent 24-year interval, from 1976 to 2000. During this time, income increased an average of $413.42 annually in inflation-adjusted 1996 dollars. Meanwhile, per member giving increased $11.19 on average each year, a higher overall rate than during the 20-year interval of 1948-1968, when the annual increase was $7.41. Giving increased 72% from 1976 to 2000, while income increased 61%. Therefore, giving as a percentage of income was 2.38% in 1976 and 2.56% in 2000.

By reviewing this data in smaller increments of years from 1950 to 2000, as presented in Table 15, the time period in which giving began to decline markedly can be identified.

As indicated in Table 15, during the 1950 to 2000 period, the highest annual increase in per member giving in inflation-adjusted 1996 dollars occurred from 1995-2000. However, the highest annual increase in giving considered as a portion of the annual change in U.S. per capita income occurred in 1950-1955, followed by 1955-1960. In 1995-2000, the annual dollar increase in giving of $27.59 represented only 4% of the average annual increase in U.S. per capita income, compared to the 8% represented by the increased dollars given during 1950-1955 and 1955-1960.

Average annual change in per member giving declined markedly between 1960 and 1964 in these communions. While income was increasing at an annual rate of $299.96 in this four-year period, 226% greater than in the 1955-1960 period, the average annual increase in per member contributions in inflation-adjusted 1996 dollars was $2.38 in 1960-1964, only a third of the $7.25 annual rate of increase in the 1955-1960 period.

The 1960-1964 period predates many of the controversial issues often cited as reasons for declining giving as a percent of income. Also, it was at the end of the 1960-1964 period

---

[2]For the years 1965 through 1967, estimated data is used. See first footnote in this chapter.

Table 15: **Average Annual Increase in U.S. Per Capita Disposable Personal Income and Per Member Giving in 11 Denominations, 1950-2000, Inflation-Adjusted 1996 $**

| Time Period | U.S. Per Capita Income | | | Per Member Giving | | | Avg. Ann. Chg. Giv. as % Avg. Annual Chg. in Income |
	First Year in Period	Last Year in Period	Average Annual Change	First Year in Period	Last Year in Period	Average Annual Change	
1950-1955	$7,954	$8,675	$144.12	$190.09	$249.39	$11.86	8.23%
1955-1960	$8,675	$9,134	$91.92	$249.39	$285.64	$7.25	7.89%
1960-1964 ³	$9,134	$10,334	$299.96	$285.64	$295.16	$2.38	0.79%
1964-1970 ³	$10,334	$12,361	$337.88	$295.00	$311.42	$2.71	0.80%
1970-1975	$12,361	$13,665	$260.66	$311.42	$325.40	$2.80	1.07%
1975-1980	$13,665	$15,546	$376.25	$325.40	$357.57	$6.44	1.71%
1980-1985	$15,546	$17,559	$402.60	$357.57	$419.30	$12.34	3.07%
1985-1990	$17,559	$19,850	$458.15	$419.30	$456.77	$7.49	1.64%
1990-1995	$19,850	$20,750	$180.08	$456.77	$492.94	$7.23	4.02%
1995-2000	$20,750	$23,587	$709.19	$492.94	$603.31	$27.59	3.89%

Details in the above table may not compute to the numbers shown due to rounding.

when membership began to decrease in mainline denominations, ten of which are included in this group. Therefore, additional exploration of that period of time might be merited.

Increases in per member giving were consistently low from 1960-1975. The annual rates of increase of $2.38 per year from 1960 to 1964, $2.71 from 1964 to 1970, and $2.80 from 1970 to 1975, were the lowest in the 1950 to 2000 period. From 1960 to 1970, the increase in dollars given represented less than one percent of the average annual increase in per capita income, while from 1970-1975, it was 1.07%.

In the 1975-1980 period, the average annual increase in giving grew to $6.44, representing 1.71% of the average annual increase in per capita income.

From 1980 to 1985, the average annual increase in giving of $12.34 represented 3.07% of the average annual increase in income during the 1980-1985 period. As a portion of the increase in per capita income, the 3.07% of the 1980 to 1985 period ranked fifth among the ten five-year periods from 1950 to 2000.

The annual average change in giving as a percent of the average annual income increase during 1985 to 1990 fell from the 1980 to 1985 period. The 1990-1995 average change in giving as a percent of the average annual income increase represented more than double the 1985-1990 figure.

For 1995-2000, the average annual change in contributions as a percentage of change in income—while it was an increase over the 1990-1995 period, and while it was the third largest in the 1950-2000 period—was less than half that of the 1950-1960 period.

Per Member Giving as Percentage of Income, 1921, 1933 and 2000. By 2000, U.S. per capita disposable (after-tax) personal income had increased 401% since 1921 in inflation-adjusted 1996 dollars, and 504% since 1933—the depth of the Great Depression.

---

³ Use of the intervals of 1960-1964 and 1964-1970 allows for the use of years for which there is known data, avoiding the use of the 1965 through 1967 years for which estimated data is used in this chapter.

Meanwhile, by 2000, per member giving in inflation-adjusted 1996 dollars had increased 342% since 1921, and 372% since the depth of the Great Depression.

Consequently, per member giving as a percentage of income was lower in 2000 than in either 1921 or 1933. In 1921, per member giving as a percentage of income was 2.9%. In 1933, it was 3.3%. In 2000, per member giving as a percentage of income was 2.6% for the composite of the eleven denominations considered in this section. The percent change in the per member portion of income donated to the church had declined by 12% from the 1921 base, from 2.9% in 1921 to 2.6% in 2000, and by 22% from the 1933 base, from 3.3% in 1933 to 2.6% in 1999.

Appendix A contains a listing of the denominations contained in this analysis.

chapter 5

Church Member Giving and Membership Trends Based on 1968-2000 Data

HIGHLIGHTS

- Between 1993 and 2000, giving to Congregational Finances as a portion of income increased, in contrast to the decline suggested by an exponential projection based on 1968-1985 data.

- The relationship of actual 1986-2000 data to the projections based on 1968-1985 data suggest that, by the middle of this century, giving to Benevolences may represent a reduced portion of income.

- The composite data set communions analyzed in earlier chapters of this volume measured 14.1% of U.S. population in 1968 and 10.9% in 2000, down 23% as a portion of U.S. population from the 1968 base.

- Membership in a set of 37 Protestant denominations and the Roman Catholic Church represented 45% of U.S. population in 1968, and 38% in 2000, a decline of 15% from the 1968 base.

- Eleven mainline Protestant denominations represented 13.2% of the population in 1968, and 7.2% in 2000, a decline of 46% from the 1968 base.

- A set of fifteen evangelical denominations grew 45% as a portion of U.S. population between 1968 and 2000. However, the growth as a portion of population for this group peaked in the mid-1980s, and then began a slow decline through 2000.

- Spending on new construction of religious buildings was higher from 1964 through 1968 than during 1998-2000 on a per capita basis in inflation-adjusted dollars.

NARRATIVE _____

Information as a Tool. The rich historical data series in the *Yearbook of American and Canadian Churches* has, in this volume, been supplemented with and revised by additional denominational data for the 1968-2000 period.

Analysis of this data has been presented in the *State of Church Giving*°series since the early 1990s. When first published, the finding that giving as a portion of income was shrinking was received with surprise and intense interest in many quarters.

Now, the data in chapter 1 of the present volume indicates that, since 1994, giving as a portion of income to Congregational Finances has made what begins to look like a recovery. The upward direction is in contrast to the fairly consistent decline in this category between 1968 and 1993.

It is generally acknowledged that most individuals do not decide how much to give based on academic information such as that contained in these analyses. However, is it possible that institutional leaders at all levels, particularly at the congregational level, are able to make use of trend information to formulate strategies in response to the findings? If so, the data indicating increased giving to Congregational Finances as a portion of income may be reflecting, in part, leadership recognizing a negative trend and taking steps to address it. The fact that the upturn in large part has been for local expenses, with only a slight slowing of the decline to Benevolences, indicates that church leadership may yet be operating with a limited vision of whole-life stewardship.

Nevertheless, facts and figures may be useful to those responsible for promoting the health of the church. The analyses in this chapter are presented in an effort to expand the available information base.

The Meaning of Trends. Statistical regression models are a tool to help leaders plan in response to reported data. Communities use them to know whether to build schools and roads. Hospitals consider trends to know the direction of health care several decades in the future. On a more alarming note, experts warn now of water shortages globally that could lead to conflict in fifty years if the situation is not soon redressed.

Statistical techniques can also be used to suggest both consequences and possibilities regarding church giving and membership patterns as well. Of course, trend data only indicates future directions. Data does not dictate what will happen. Available information, including trend analysis, can help formulate intelligent responses to current analysis. Church leaders and members can help decide, through action or inaction, what the future will look like.

Trend analysis was first included in this series partly in response to developments in national church offices. After talking with a number of denominational officials who were making painful decisions about which programs to cut, in light of decreased Benevolences dollars being received, it seemed useful to see where the present patterns of giving might lead if effective means were not found to alter present behavior. Were current patterns likely to prove a temporary setback, or did the data suggest longer-term implications?

The Current Trend in Church Giving. The first chapter in this report indicates that per member giving as a percentage of income decreased between 1968 and 2000. Further, contributions to the category of Benevolences have been declining proportionately faster than those to Congregational Finances between 1968 and 2000.

The data for the composite denominations analyzed for 1968 through 2000 has been projected in *The State of Church Giving* series, beginning with the edition that included 1991 data.[1] The most recent projection is based on data from 1968 through 2000.

The data for both Benevolences and Congregational Finances can be projected using linear and exponential regression analysis. To determine which type of analysis more accurately describes the data in a category's giving pattern, the data for 1968-1985 was projected using both techniques. Then, the actual data for 1986 through 2000 was plotted. The more accurate projection was judged to be the procedure that produced the trend line most closely resembling the actual 1986-2000 data.

The Trend in Congregational Finances. The 1968-2000 church giving data contained in this report indicates that giving as a percentage of income for Congregational Finances declined from 2.45% in 1968, to 2.24% in 2000, a decline of 9%.

Both linear and exponential regression were used to analyze the data for giving as a percentage of income to Congregational Finances for the 17-year interval of 1968 through 1985. Then the actual data for 1986 through 2000 was plotted. The actual data for

Figure 8: Projected Trends for Composite Denominations, Giving as a Percentage of Income to Congregational Finances, Using Linear and Exponential Regression Based on Data for 1968-1985, with Actual Data for 1986-2000

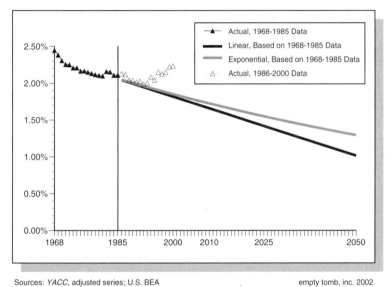

Sources: *YACC*, adjusted series; U.S. BEA   empty tomb, inc. 2002

1986-1992 followed the exponential curve. Since 1993, the giving levels have increased rather than decreased from the 1992 base. The results are shown in Figure 8.

Since data for the most recent years have differed markedly from the previous trend, long-term projections may not be meaningful. The upturn over the last seven years merits continuing observation.

The Trend in Benevolences. Per member contributions to Benevolences as a percentage of income decreased from 0.66% in 1968 to 0.40% in 2000, a percent change in giving as a percentage of income of 39% from the 1968 base.

---

[1]John Ronsvalle and Sylvia Ronsvalle, *The State of Church Giving through 1991* (Champaign, IL: empty tomb, inc., 1993), and subsequent editions in the series. The edition with data through 1991 provides a discussion of the choice to use giving as a percentage of income as a basis for considering future giving patterns.

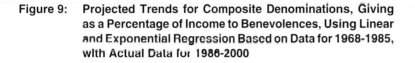

Figure 9: Projected Trends for Composite Denominations, Giving
as a Percentage of Income to Benevolences, Using Linear
and Exponential Regression Based on Data for 1968-1985,
with Actual Data for 1986-2000

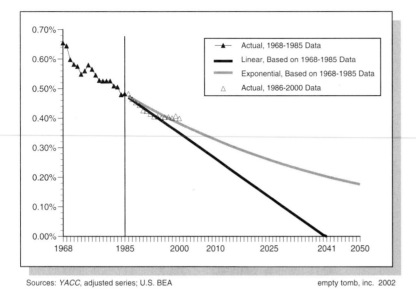

Sources: *YACC*, adjusted series; U.S. BEA   empty tomb, inc. 2002

The data for giving as a percentage of income to Benevolences for the 17-year interval of 1968 through 1985 was also projected using both linear and exponential regression. The actual data for 1986 through 2000 was then plotted. The results are shown in Figure 9.

Reported per member giving as a percentage of income to Benevolences was above the projected value of the linear and exponential regressions for 1986. For 1988-1993, the reported data was at or below the linear trend data. Although giving was at a relative plateau from 1994-1999, it reached the lowest point in the 1968-2000 period in 2000. Nevertheless, the 2000 level was higher than either the linear or exponential trends lines, suggesting a slowing in the rate of decline.

The linear trend based on 1968-2000 data indicated that per member giving as a portion of income to the category of Benevolences will reach 0% of income in the year A.D. 2041. The exponential curve based on 1968-2000 data indicated that giving in 2050 would be 0.18%, down 56% from the 0.40% level in 2000.[2] In both trend lines, by 2050 the amount of income going to support Benevolences, including denominational structures, would be either negligible or severely reduced, if the overall pattern of the last 33 years continues.

Trends in Church Membership as a Percentage of U.S. Population, 1968-2000.[3] Membership data for various church groupings is available for review for the years 1968

---

[2] In the linear regression, the value for the correlation coefficient, or r_{XY}, for the Benevolences data is -.98. The strength of the linear relationship in the present set of 1968-2000 data, that is, the proportion of variance accounted for by linear regression, is represented by the coefficient of determination, or r^2_{XY}, of .95 for Benevolences. In the exponential regression, the value for r_{XY}, for the Benevolences data is -.98, while the strength of the exponential relationship is .96. The Benevolences *F*-observed values of 631.83 for the linear, and 837.03 for the curvilinear, regression are substantially greater than the *F*-critical value of 7.53 for 1 and 31 degrees of freedom for a single-tailed test with an Alpha value of 0.01. Therefore, the regression equation is useful at the level suggested by the r^2_{XY} figure in predicting giving as a percentage of income.

[3] The denominations analyzed in this section include the composite data set whose financial patterns were analyzed in earlier chapters. The data for 29 communions is supplemented by the data of eight denominations included in an analysis of church membership and U.S. population by Roozen and Hadaway in David A. Roozen and Kirk C. Hadaway, eds., *Church and Denominational Growth* (Nashville: Abingdon Press, 1993), 393-395.

through 2000. When the reported data is considered as a percent of U.S. population, the membership data is placed in the larger context of the changing environment in which the church exists. This measurement is similar to giving as a percentage of income that reflects how much a financial donation represents of the resources available to the donor. In the same way, measuring membership as a percentage of U.S. population takes into account the changes in total population as well as in membership.

The State of Church Giving through 1993 included a chapter entitled, "A Unified Theory of Giving and Membership." The hypothesis explored in that discussion is that there is a relationship between a decline in church member giving and membership patterns. One proposal considered in that chapter is that a denomination which is able to involve its members in a larger vision as evidenced in giving patterns will also be attracting additional members.

In the present edition, discussion will be limited to patterns and trends in membership as a percentage of U.S. population.

Membership in the Composite Denominations, 1968-2000. The composite denominations, which span the theological spectrum, included 28,256,265 Full or Confirmed Members in 1968. By 2000, these communions included 30,656,474 members, an increase of 8%.[4] However, during the same 32-year interval, U.S. population increased from 200,745,000 to 282,489,000, an increase of 41%. Therefore, while this church member grouping represented 14.1% of the U.S. population in 1968, it included 10.9% in 2000, a decline of 23% from the 1968 base.

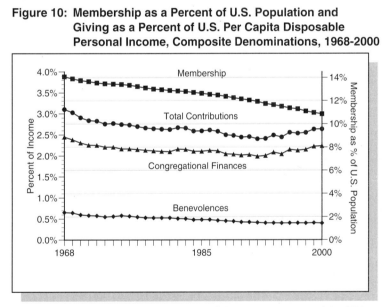

Figure 10: Membership as a Percent of U.S. Population and Giving as a Percent of U.S. Per Capita Disposable Personal Income, Composite Denominations, 1968-2000

Source: empty tomb analysis; *YACC* adjusted series; U.S. BEA   empty tomb, inc. 2002

Figure 10 presents membership as a percent of U.S. population, and giving as a percentage of income, for the composite denominations, 1968-2000.

[4]Of the 30 denominations in the composite data set considered in earlier chapters, financial information was not available for the Friends United Meeting after 1990. Therefore, the composite included a set of 29 denominations. This was true even though the Mennonite Church USA, one of the 29, did not provide complete 2000 financial data in time for the current report, and the Church of God (Anderson, IN), did not have 1998-2000 data. As of this edition, inclusive membership for the Friends United Meeting was obtained for 1991 through 2000. Therefore, in this chapter, the composite set of denominations generally refers to a set of 29 denominations regarding financial data (more precisely, 28 for 1998 and 1999, and 27 for 2000), and 30 denominations for membership analysis. See Appendix B-1 for details. Consult Appendix B-4 for the total Full or Confirmed Membership numbers used for the American Baptist Churches in the U.S.A. See Appendix B-3.3 and Appendix B-4 for the membership data of the other denominations included in subsequent analyses in this chapter that are not one of the composite denominations.

Data Trends in Three Church Groups. Membership data for three subgroups within the historically Christian church in the U.S. is available. Data was analyzed for eleven mainline denominations, fifteen evangelical denominations, and the Roman Catholic Church.

Eleven Mainline Denominations. The declining membership trends have been noticed most markedly in the mainline Protestant communions. Full or Confirmed Membership in eleven mainline Protestant denominations affiliated with the National Council of the Churches of Christ in the U.S.A.[5] decreased as a percentage of U.S. population by 46% between 1968 and 2000, from the 1968 base. In 1968, this group included 26,508,288, or 13.2% of U. S. population. In 2000, the 11 denominations included 20,199,683, or 7.2% of U.S. population, a decline of 46% in the portion of U.S. population with membership in these groups.

Fifteen Evangelical Denominations. Data is also available for a group of fifteen denominations that might be classified on the evangelical end of the theological spectrum.[6] Although one or more of the communions in this grouping might prefer the term "conservative" to "evangelical" as a description, the latter term in its current sociological usage may be useful. These communions included some of the fastest growing denominations in the United States. This group grew 45% in membership, from 15,101,542 in 1968 to 21,952,742, in 2000, while U.S. population grew 41%. As a result, this group measured 7.5% of U.S. population in 1968, and 7.8% in 2000. In the mid-1980s, the group peaked at 8.23% as a portion of U.S. population peaked, and then declined to 7.77% by 2000, a decline of 6% as a portion of U.S. population from the 1986 peak. In 1993, these fifteen evangelical communions surpassed the 11 mainline communions in the portion of U.S. population that they represented.

Figure 11: Membership as a Percent of U.S. Population, 15 Evangelical Denominations, 11 Mainline Denominations, and the Roman Catholic Church, 1968-2000

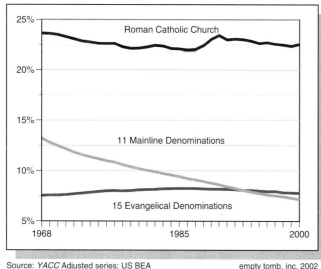

Source: *YACC* Adjusted series; US BEA   empty tomb, inc. 2002

The Roman Catholic Church. The Roman Catholic Church included 47,468,333 members in 1968, or 24% of U.S. population. Although the church's membership grew 34%, to 63,683,030 in 2000, it decreased to 23% as a portion of the faster-growing U.S. population, a decline of 5%.

Figure 11 presents the membership data for these groups of communions.

---

[5]These eleven denominations include nine of the communions in the composite set of denominations as well as The Episcopal Church and The United Methodist Church.
[6]A list of the communions in this set is presented in Appendix A.

Membership in 38 Communions. In 1968, a set of 37 Protestant denominations and the Roman Catholic Church included a total of 90,252,533 members. With the U.S. population at 200,745,000, these Christians constituted 45% of the 1968 U.S. population. By 2000, the group had grown to 107,692,814 members. However, with U.S. population having grown to 282,489,000 in 2000, these Christians comprised 38% of the American population, a percent change of -15% from the 1968 base.

Projected Membership Trends in Eleven Mainline Denominations. As with giving as a percentage of income to Congregational Finances and Benevolences, trend lines using

both linear and exponential regression were developed for the eleven mainline Protestant communions discussed above, using their 1968-1985 membership data. The actual 1986 through 2000 data was also plotted. As shown in Figure 12, the actual 1986-2000 data more closely follows the exponential curve for these denominations. An exponential curve based on the entire 1968-2000 reported data series suggested that these denominations would represent 2.8% of the U.S. population in 2050.

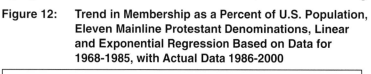

Figure 12: Trend in Membership as a Percent of U.S. Population, Eleven Mainline Protestant Denominations, Linear and Exponential Regression Based on Data for 1968-1985, with Actual Data 1986-2000

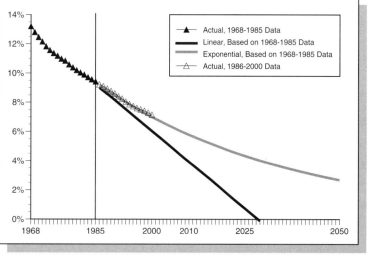

Sources: *YACC*, adjusted series; U.S. BEA   empty tomb, inc. 2002

Projected Membership Trends in the Composite Denominations. Nine of the eleven mainline Protestant denominations discussed above are included in the composite set of denominations that have been considered in earlier chapters of this report. Figure 13 presents membership information as a percent of U.S. population for this group. Regression analysis was carried out on the 1968-1985 membership

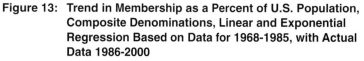

Figure 13: Trend in Membership as a Percent of U.S. Population, Composite Denominations, Linear and Exponential Regression Based on Data for 1968-1985, with Actual Data 1986-2000

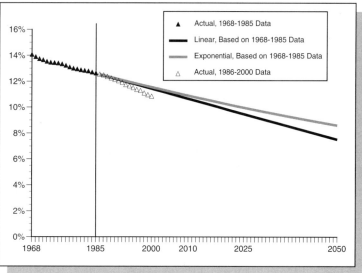

Source: *YACC* adjusted series; U.S. BEA   empty tomb, inc. 2002

data for the composite denominations to determine if the trends in the larger grouping differed from the mainline denomination subset. The results were then compared to the actual 1986 through 2000 membership data for the composite data set.

The composite denominations represented 14.1% of the U.S. population in 1968, and 12.6% in 1985. Linear trend analysis suggests that this grouping would have represented 11.4% of U.S. population in 2000, while exponential regression suggests it would have been 11.5%. In fact, this composite grouping of communions represented 10.9% of the U.S. population in 2000, a smaller figure than that indicated by linear regression, suggesting the trend is closer to that predicted by linear regression than the exponential curve.

If the linear trend continues uninterrupted into the future, these composite denominations would represent 7.5% of the U.S. population in the year 2050.

Buildings. The current level of building activity among churches in the U.S. has attracted attention in various quarters. Is the present church building boom unusual? Once again, data helps evaluate whether the present level of church construction is part of an ongoing trend or varies from past behavior.

Census Bureau data provides information on the new construction of religious buildings. The Census Bureau defines its Religious category as follows: "*Religious* includes houses of worship and other religious buildings. Certain buildings, although owned by religious organizations, are not included in this category. These include education or charitable institutions, hospitals, and publishing houses."[7] According to this data, construction of religious buildings was $1.04 billion dollars in 1964, compared to $8.0 billion in 2000. On a current-dollar aggregate level, more building was going on in the late 1990s than in the mid-1960s.

However, as has been emphasized in previous chapters of this volume, aggregate numbers considered apart from population, inflation, and changes in income, do not give a complete picture.

When inflation was taken into account, the data indicated that the total aggregate $25.2 billion cost of new religious building construction in 1997-2000 was higher than the 1964-1967 cost of $24.4 billion. At $6.9 billion, building in 2000 was highest in the 1964-2000 period, with 1965 second at $6.8 billion in the number of aggregate, inflation-adjusted dollars spent on the construction of new religious buildings.

Again, to obtain the most realistic picture about giving patterns, changes in population and per capita income also need to be factored into the evaluation. In 1965, per capita expenditure in the U.S. on religious buildings was $35 dollars per person in inflation-adjusted 1996 dollars. In 2000, it was $24 dollars. The period 1964 through 1968 posted the highest per capita expenditures on new religious buildings in the 1964-2000 period. The period 1999-2000 was next highest. Of course, a smaller portion of the entire U.S. population may have been investing in religious buildings in the late 1990s than in the mid-1960s. To have the most meaningful comparison, changes in membership as a portion of population would have to be taken into account. Data considered above suggests that membership in historically Christian

---

[7]U.S. Census Bureau, Current Construction Reports, C30/01-5, *Value of Construction Put in Place*: May 2001, U.S. Government Printing Office, Washington, DC 20402, Appendix A, "Definitions," p. A-2.

churches declined as a portion of the U.S. population between 1964 and 2000. However, other religions were added to the religious milieu of the United States during this period. The Census data includes all religious construction, not just Christian churches. So the rough estimate may be fairly useful as a first approximation.

What may be more informative from the perspective of giving patterns, however, is religious construction as a portion of income. Again, the $35 per capita spent on religious buildings in 1965 represented a different portion of income than the $24 spent in 2000. In fact, as a portion of income, Americans spent 0.25% on the construction of new religious buildings in 1965, compared to 0.11% in 2000.

The building activity occurring in the late 1990s has to be evaluated in the context of the general affluence produced by decades of economic expansion in the U.S. The two charts in Figure 14 contrast the annual aggregate dollar value of new religious building construction with the per capita expenditure as a portion of U.S. per capita income for the 1964-2000 period.

Figure 14: Construction of Religious Buildings in the U.S., 1964-2000, Aggregate Inflation-Adjusted 1996 Dollars, and Percent of U.S. Per Capita Disposable Personal Income

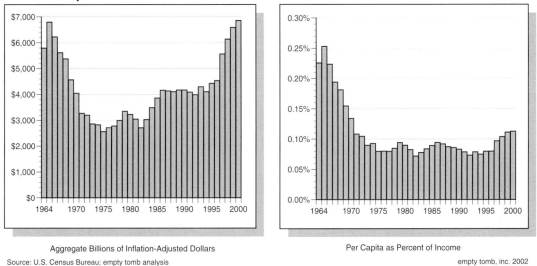

Aggregate Billions of Inflation-Adjusted Dollars

Source: U.S. Census Bureau; empty tomb analysis

Per Capita as Percent of Income

empty tomb, inc. 2002

The Response to the Trends. As in other sectors, trend lines in church giving and membership are designed to provide an additional source of information. Planning, evaluation and creative thinking are some of the types of constructive responses which can be made in light of projections. The information on church member giving and membership trends is offered as a possible planning tool.[8] The trend lines are not considered to be dictating what must happen, but rather as providing important indicators of what might happen if present conditions continue in an uninterrupted fashion. Trends in church giving and membership, if used wisely, may be of assistance in addressing conditions present in the body of Christ in the United States.

---

[8]For additional discussion of the implications of the trends, see Ronsvalle and Ronsvalle, *The State of Church Giving through 1991*, pp. 61-67.

chapter 6

The Potential of the Church

HIGHLIGHTS_____

- If members of historically Christian churches in the United States were giving an average of 10% in 2000, there would have been an additional $139 billion a year going through church channels.

- If church members decided to spend most of this additional money on helping others, in keeping with the Great Commandment to love God and love neighbor, there would have been an additional $83.6 billion for international outreach, and $27.9 billion for domestic outreach, with another $27.9 billion available for related congregational activities.

NARRATIVE_____

What difference does it make that church member giving as a portion of income was 2.64% in the year 2000, instead of at the classic tithe, or 10%?

Of course, it would not be reasonable to expect that every person in every congregation would give 10% of their incomes. But what difference would it make if congregation members, on a congregationwide average, gave 10%? Some would always give less, and some already give more than that level. Would an average of 10% giving really be so very different than present levels?

These questions reflect the culturally invisible state of church giving. The role of religion in general, and the church in particular, is largely taken for granted in U.S. culture. While the media and the public avidly watch portions of points change on the stock market, church giving is not seen as having much significance in the culture.

Yet, as noted in the "Measurement of Charitable Giving" chapter in this volume, religious causes receive the largest share of the charitable dollar. Religious causes focus not only on worship, but also on social services and international activities, as well as education. The vast majority of the religious charitable dollars are donated to congregations, where some portion is then directed to charitable activity beyond the local congregation.

Here is an exercise to try to make the impact of church giving more visible. Imagine U.S. and global society if private charitable activity were cut in half. Picture a massive decline in the ministries often undertaken by religious groups: the homeless; the hungry; the elderly; orphans; refugees; youth; international relief and development. A bleak picture emerges of what society would be like without the activities often taken for granted.

Now imagine what that picture would look like if the present level of private charitable activity, both domestically and globally, were expanded many times. Can we picture a world where infant mortality was an exception in all countries: Where a parent could expect a child not only to live past age five, but also be healthy and educated to make a positive contribution to that country's society, and thereby also to the global community?

The difference between these two pictures, to a great degree, has to do with whether church member giving levels move towards or away from the religiously-recognized standard of giving 10% of one's income.

Potential Giving. Some religious leaders debate whether, in the affluent culture that describes the early twenty-first century U.S., the tithe is too low a standard. Others are concerned because it suggests legalism. However those who support the tithe note that it provides a biblically-based standard, against which church members can compare their own practice of their faith. Moreover, a congregationwide average of ten percent giving would allow for a range in which some might give considerably more than ten percent, while some may not feel they can give, or refuse to consider giving, at that level.

If members of historically Christian churches in the U.S. had been giving at an average of 10% of income in 2000, they would have donated an additional $139.3 billion dollars to their churches.

One may continue this hypothetical discussion by supposing that these additional donations could have been directed not to the internal operations of the congregations, but rather to the broader mission of the church, as represented by Benevolences. Finally, one may suppose that denominations had adopted a proposed formula that 60% of this additional money be designated for international missions—where the greatest need is—and 20% be directed to domestic benevolences.[1]

The amount available for international ministries, had 60% of the $139.3 billion increase been directed to that category, would have been $83.59 billion shared in Jesus' name to provide word and deed witness to global neighbors in need. This amount is more than the

---

[1] UNICEF estimates that approximately 29,000 children under the age of five die *daily* around the globe, mostly from preventable poverty conditions. UNICEF also estimates that 30,000 children under the age of five die *annually* in the United States (Carol Bellamy, *The State of the World's Children 2001* [New York: UNICEF, 2001], 81.) These statistics indicate that the great majority of need is in countries other than the U.S. The 60%/20% formula was used in the authors' work with congregations. For a discussion of their international and domestic strategy approaches, see John Ronsvalle and Sylvia Ronsvalle, *The Poor Have Faces* (Grand Rapids, MI: Baker Books, 1992).

$5 billion[2] additional that has been estimated could stop most of the 10.6 million, global under-five child deaths each year, or the $7 billion additional each year that could provide primary education enrollment for all children. Estimates are that $70 to $80 billion a year additional could ensure access to basic services for the world's population.[3]

Meanwhile, the 20% of the $139.3 billion additional giving that would be available for domestic benevolences, to help local neighbors in need, would have amounted to $27.86 billion.

After the 60% for international ministries, and 20% for domestic ministries, 20% of the increased giving would be a basic increase for related expenses. Part of this portion of the additional Benevolences money could be used for mission education activities within the congregation, including work project trips internationally—as well as to cover additional direct expenses related to raising and distributing the additional funds.

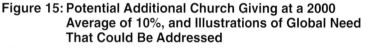

Figure 15: Potential Additional Church Giving at a 2000 Average of 10%, and Illustrations of Global Need That Could Be Addressed

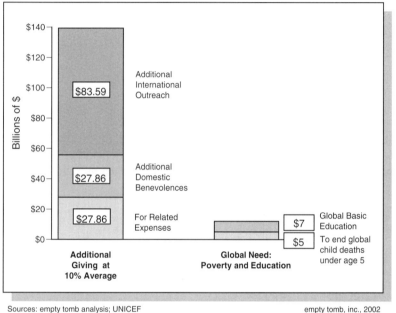

Sources: empty tomb analysis; UNICEF   empty tomb, inc., 2002

Figure 15 presents both the potential giving amounts, and two areas of global need that could be addressed.

Basis for the Calculations. In the chapter in this volume titled "Measuring Charitable Giving in the United States," a revised total giving to religion "Denomination-Based Series Keyed to 1974 Filer Estimate" is offered. In that series, the 2000 estimate for total giving to religion was $59.4 billion.

If giving increased to an average of 10% giving, instead of $59.4 billion, in 2000 $225.2 billion would have been donated to all religions in the U.S. The difference would have been an additional $165.9 billion (rounded) given to religion in the United States that year.

It was also estimated that 84% of the U.S. population identifies with the historically Christian church—those communions and traditions, such as Roman Catholic, Orthodox,

---

[2] James P. Grant, *The State of the World's Children 1990* (New York: Oxford University Press, 1990), 16, estimated $2.5 additional each year could stop most of the under-five global child deaths occurring from preventable poverty conditions. This number has been increased by the authors to account for inflation nad growth in the economy.

[3]Bellamy, *The State of the World's Children 2001*, 81; Carol Bellamy, *The State of the World's Children 1999* (New York: UNICEF, 1999), 85; and Bellamy, *The State of the World's Children 2000*, 37.

mainline Protestant, Pentecostal, evangelical, and Anabaptist, that profess a commitment to the historic tenets of the faith.

This figure of 84% can be applied to the additional $165.9 billion, to calculate the additional activity of the historically Christian Church, had giving been at the 10% level in 2000. These church members would have given $139.3 billion more at an average of 10% giving in 2000.[4]

If giving had increased to an average of 10%, and the additional funding had been directed to Benevolences, then giving would have increased from 0.40% of income to about 7.8%, with Congregational Finances staying at about the same levels.

The Implications of the Hypothetical Scenario. As the nonprofit sector receives more attention from society in general, the role it plays and can play is discussed and debated. One might review the above scenario in order to consider the question of whether the private sector, or more specifically the church, can take on additional responsibilities toward those who are in need in the U.S.

The data suggests that, if giving had increased from the actual 2000 level to an average giving level of 10%, there could have been an additional $139 billion available to assist people in need in the U.S. In theory, therefore, the church could have the resources necessary to impact domestic need, even while working at a significant level to alleviate global need in partnership with international sister churches.

However, it may also be noted that giving as a percentage of income did not increase at the rate that income did between 1968 and 2000, nor had it reached the 10% level by 2000. On the contrary, giving as a percentage of income declined by 15% between 1968 and 2000. More to the point, the portion of income going to Benevolences, the category that would take into account programs that address poverty conditions in the U.S. among other issues, declined by 39% in the 1968 to 2000 period. Further, the monetary potential of the church to address both domestic and global needs has remained culturally invisible in most church circles, as well as secular media discussions.

Any novel writer will confirm that bad characters are easy to make interesting and good characters always are difficult to make anything but boring.

In crafting our society, it seems that it is easier to complain about all that is wrong rather than have a vision for what is possible. Religion is supposed to give members the ability to see beyond themselves to a higher and better order of living. If religion is having a practical impact on those members, potential giving levels will move from an invisible option to a visible reality.

---

[4]An analysis based on information in George H. Gallup, Jr., *Religion in America* (Princeton, NJ: The Princeton Religion Research Center, 1996), 42. This somewhat conservative estimate assumes that the religious giving was given by 100% of the U.S. population. If total religious giving comes only from the 91% of the U.S. population that claims a religious affiliation (see Gallup, p. 35), then the historically Christian component gave 92% of the total (84%/91%). In that case, rather than $139 billion, $151 billion of the total potential $165.9 billion additional would have been given by those who identify with the historically Christian church.

chapter 7

Measuring Charitable Giving in the United States

HIGHLIGHTS

- Current measurement of philanthropy efforts in the United States are inadequate to provide accurate information about charitable giving to a concerned public.

- The second annual Report Card on the Measurement of Philanthropy evaluates major entities involved in the reporting of charitable giving (see Fig. 16).

- Recommendations to improve the measurement of philanthropy include:

  - Reports of philanthropic giving need to be adjusted by population and income.

  - Changes are needed in the Internal Revenue Service Form 990 to provide information about contributions from living individuals as a distinct category. In order to assist this development, the Unified Chart of Accounts needs to provide a meaningful category dedicated to contributions from living individuals.

  - A policy decision is needed to change Form 990, to provide that a nonprofit may choose between the governance categories of faith-based and secular. Groups also need to be able to define themselves through the use of a standard classification system, such as the National Taxonomy of Exempt Entities.

  - A policy decision is needed to measure contributions to recipient categories by source of donations. Form 990 needs to be changed so that reporting recipient organizations define their contributions by source, choosing among individual, bequest, corporations (businesses), and foundations.

  - A permanent commission with a Presidentially-appointed and U.S. Senate-approved chair, similar to one recommended in the 1970s by the Filer Commission, is needed to establish and maintain consistent standards of philanthropy measurement.

Figure 10. Report Card on the Measurement of Philanthropy, Twelve Entities

Evaluation Category	Providers of Public Estimates of Giving				
	Giving USA: AAFRC, Indiana Univ. Center on Phil.	Independent Sector Publications	Philanthropy 400: Chronicle of Philanthropy	NPT 100: NonProfit Times	Statistical Abstract of the United States
Addresses Annual Measurement	A	D	A	A	A
Adjusts for Population & Income	D	A	F	F	D
Report Available for Timely Review	A	F	A	A	A
Distance from For-Profit Counsel	D	A	F	F	A
Consistency over Time	D	F	D	D	A
Treatment of Religion	D	F	F	F	D
Provides Comparable Data	D	F	C	C	F
Revisits Major Questionable Findings	D	D	D	D	D
Availability of Information	D	C	A	A	A
Takes Steps to Maximize Validity	D	F	D	F	F
Summary Grade	**C-**	**D+**	**C-**	**C-**	**C+**

- A peer-reviewed Journal of Philanthropy Measurement would assist with developing and refining standards of philanthropy measurement.

- A validation comparison of AAFRC's widely quoted *Giving USA* series suggested that the estimate for religion, the single largest charitable category, is not accurate.

NARRATIVE

Current measurement of philanthropy efforts in the United States is inadequate to inform a concerned public. As Hayden W. Smith wrote in a 1993 article, "But we must face the truth: no one—repeat, no one—really knows how much money and other property is given to charity in any given year . . . "[1]

The media regularly reports one major professional organization's estimates as fact, other surveys cannot be externally validated, and the available tools to measure philanthropy do not provide a clear gauge of contributions from living individuals.

---

[1]Hayden Smith, "Some Thoughts on the Validity of Estimates of Charitable Giving," *Voluntas*, Vol. 4, No. 2, August 1993, p. 251.

Additional Entities Involved in the Measurement of Philanthropy						
Advisory Committees, GUSA and GAVITUS	Foundations	Form 990 IRS Treasury Dept.	U.S. Government	National Bureau of Economic Research	Urban Institute	Universities (with Nonprofit Programs)
B	C	A	C	F	D	F
C	C	F	F	—	D	—
C	D	—	A	—	D	—
C	A	A	A	—	A	—
D	D	A	A	—	D	—
F	F	F	F	—	F	—
F	C	F	F	—	D	—
D	D	D	D	—	D	—
B	A	D	C	—	C	—
F	F	F	F	—	D	—
D+	**C-**	**C-**	**C-**	**F**	**D+**	**F**

Yet, private contributions involve tens of billions of dollars each year. The nonprofit institutions that they support are estimated to constitute as much as six percent of the U.S. economy, when various sources of income including fees and government grants are taken into account.[2] In addition, the charitable activity that is widespread throughout American society provides assistance to segments of the population whose needs would otherwise be severely, or in some cases completely, underserved. Whether the category is assistance to the poor or giving to the arts in the U.S., it is difficult to obtain a good measure of the condition of this society without an adequate measure of the charitable giving level.

As a first step toward changing this condition, an evaluation scale of those involved with measuring philanthropy was designed to provide an overview of the current situation. In this chapter, a second annual Report Card on the Measurement of Philanthropy evaluates twelve national entities involved in one or more aspects of the measurement of charitable giving.

The overall grade for the measurement of philanthropy in the United States is a C-. This grade combines the resulting numerical values from the 10 categories on which the twelve entities were evaluated.

---

[2]"Nonprofit Information Center"; <http://www.independentsector.org/ Nonprofit%20Information%20Center/nonprofit_size_and_scope.htm>; p. 1 of 8/23/01 4:28 PM printout.

These twelve groups can be generally divided into those that provide public estimates of giving, and the additional groups involved in one or more aspects of the measurement of philanthropy. The following list includes the entities and their overall grades. The details of the evaluation of each entity are presented in the last section of this chapter.

Providers of Public Estimates of Giving:

C- The American Association of Fundraising Counsel Trust for Philanthropy's *Giving USA* reports, researched and written, under contract, at the Indiana University Center on Philanthropy

D+ Independent Sector's *Giving and Volunteering in the United States* series, *Balancing the Scales,* and *The New Nonprofit Almanac and Desk Reference*

C- *The Chronicle of Philanthropy* Philanthropy 400

C- *The NonProfit Times* NPT 100

C+ *The Statistical Abstract of the United States*

Additional Entities Involved in the Measurement of Philanthropy:

D+ Advisory Committees to the *Giving USA* and *Giving and Volunteering in the United States* publications

C- Foundation efforts in the area of the measurement of philanthropy

C- U.S. Government Internal Revenue Service Form 990

C- U.S. Government efforts to secure and disseminate philanthropy information

F National Bureau of Economic Research

D+ Urban Institute efforts, both in cooperation with the U.S. Government and independently

F Universities with philanthropy centers

Grades for each of the twelve groups were given in several categories. The categories and standards of evaluation were as follows.

Annual Measurement. Does the entity address issues related to, and provide regular information on, the annual measurement of philanthropy?

Adjustments for Population and Income. Does the entity address issues related to the adjustment of aggregate philanthropic figures for changes in U.S. population and income?

Report Available for Timely Review. If the entity issues a report, does it make that full report available for review by researchers at the same time that it makes news of the report available to the general public via press releases or other announcements?

Distance from For-Profit Counsel. Does the entity have sufficient independence and distance from the influence and agenda of groups involved in fundraising on a for-profit basis that therefore may have a vested interest in the results of any measurement analysis?

Consistency over Time. Does the entity approach its work with a reasonable degree of consistency over a period of years?

Treatment of Religion. Does the entity treat the category of religion, the single largest charitable category, in a reasonable and comprehensive fashion?

Comparable Data. Does the entity present data in ways that facilitate comparisons with other sources of information, or among its own categories?

Review of Major Questionable Findings. Does the entity review and reevaluate major findings in the entity's published reports that are questioned or challenged by others in the field?

Availability of Data. Does the entity publish or otherwise make its data available to researchers for independent analysis?

Validity of Data. Does the entity take comprehensive steps to insure and maximize the likelihood of valid, integrated data for its measurement of philanthropy?

Grade Standards. Each entity involved with the measurement of philanthropy that was evaluated was issued a grade in each of the relevant categories. The grades for each category were then averaged, and an overall grade issued. An "A" was measured at 95, a "B" at 85, a "C" at 75, a "D" at 65, and an "F" at 55.

RECOMMENDATIONS. Several steps could be taken to improve the reporting of philanthropy in the United States. Some are fairly simple to implement. Others would require more of an investment, both financial and academic.

Funding the Solutions. For these suggestions to be useful, the reader must be assured that they are feasible. To be feasible, these efforts will need to be funded. A budget could be available from either of two sources to underwrite efforts to improve the measurement of philanthropy in the United States.

The first option is the excise tax levied on foundations by the U.S. Government beginning in 1969. The purpose of this tax, according to Pablo Eisenberg of the Georgetown University Public Policy Institute, was "to use the income to regulate tax-exempt organizations and handle the myriad administrative tasks associated with them. But things didn't work out that way. That income has gone into the general treasury." Eisenberg argues that redirecting the tax to the Internal Revenue Service's oversight of nonprofits could not only provide for regulation and supervision, but also help to make the collected data available for purposes of public accountability.[3]

Another potential funding source would be pooled foundations funds for a "foundation research service." A model can be found in the Congressional Research Service, which is designed to provide "comprehensive and reliable analysis, research and information services that are timely, objective, unbiased, and confidential."[4] Since 1987, at least 31 foundations have spent some unspecified millions of dollars on the measurement of philanthropy. Yet, there has been little to no evaluation or accountability that would improve the giving estimates produced by this funding. The foundation research service could provide coordinated objective analysis of reports issued by grantees, including research on issues related to the measurement of philanthropy. The foundation research service could provide evaluation of additional categories of research, particularly those that receive funding from multiple

---

[3]Pablo Eisenberg, "How to Help the IRS Improve Charity Oversight," *The Chronicle of Philanthropy*, October 18, 2001, p. 34.
[4]"CRS Employment Home Page — What's CRS: History and Mission;" <http://lcweb.loc.gov/crsinfo/whatscrs.html#org>; p. 1 of 10/4/01 12:10 PM printout.

foundations. The service could also keep track of whether reports funded by foundations were published in a timely fashion—or whether these reports were published at all.

Adjustment for Population and Income for the General Public Audience. As discussed in chapter one of this volume, the type of measurement of charitable giving defines the type of information that results. If church member contributions are measured in dollars, then the figures provide a limited measure of how much church institutions had to spend. If the contributions are measured as a portion of income, then the figures indicate the value that the church member places on the contribution in the context of the resources available.

In the same way, whether philanthropy measures are reported in aggregate numbers or in per capita numbers defines the quality of information that is being conveyed.

To provide the best measure of charitable giving levels, data should be presented in per capita dollars, and as a portion of after-tax income. These standards account for changes in population and in income. A more accurate picture of the public's level of giving results.

Confusion exists in the measurement and reporting of philanthropy because the audience for the information is not well defined. The needs of the general public are different than the interests of those involved in the profession of fundraising. Consider that religion is the single largest charitable giving category, and attendance at houses of worship is highly correlated with charitable giving behavior.[5] A pastor or lay leader of a congregation will use individual giving levels as a portion of income to "see how they are doing" compared to average individual giving levels. Yet public discussion of philanthropy is routinely conducted in terms of the professional fundraisers' concerns about the aggregate billions of dollars raised.

The fact that the fundraising profession has different interests than the public was expressed by two experts in the field. Ann E. Kaplan, then editor of *Giving USA*, was asked about the value of waiting to issue giving estimates in order to provide more precise information when more reliable data became available. "Ms. Kaplan says that approach is not appealing. 'The longer you wait,' she says, 'the more accurate the data, but when you're fund raising and making public-policy decisions it's hard to wait.' "[6]

The Center on Philanthropy at Indiana University studies the area of philanthropy, and also offers courses to professional fundraisers. The Philanthropic Giving Index is produced by the Center on Philanthropy. This index is a nationwide survey of fundraisers and consultants. One aspect of the Index is to measure the optimism of fundraisers. The Center on Philanthropy is now also researching, writing, and editing *Giving USA* under contract with the American Association of Fundraising Counsel. *The NonProfit Times* interviewed Eugene R. Tempel, executive director of the Center on Philanthropy. The interview referred to the *Giving USA* estimates as a validation of the optimism expressed in the Philanthropic Giving Index. " 'Fundraisers may be optimistic people,' he said, noting that such an outlook helps them keep going after failed solicitations."[7]

---

[5] Arthur D. Kirsch, et al., *Giving and Volunteering in the United States 1999 Edition* (Washington, DC: Independent Sector, 2002), pp. 84-85.
[6] Harvey Lipman, "Report's Numbers Are No True Measure of Charity, Critics Say," *The Chronicle of Philanthropy*, June 3, 1999, p. 30.
[7] Matthew Sinclair, "Giving Attitudes: Survey Shows Drop in Optimism," *The NonProfit Times*, Feb. 2001, p. 32.

While the fundraiser is motivated by having an optimistic report of aggregate billions of dollars raised, unadjusted for population and income, the denominational leader or pastor needs to know if his people are being as faithful in giving as they could be.

Adjusting Media Reports for Population and the Economy. Trade estimates of fundraising may do their constituents a service by providing them with encouragement and overly positive information that fosters their optimism. However, the *Giving USA* series, funded by a professional trade group of for-profit fundraisers, the American Association of Fundraising Counsel, Inc. (AAFRC) Trust for Philanthropy, has been reported to the general public by the media as an objective measure of fundraising levels in the United States.

For example, the headline on its *Giving USA 2002* press release read "Charitable Giving Reaches $212 Billion."[8] This headline was echoed in the related *New York Times* story titled, "Charitable Contributions in 2001 Reached $212 Billion."[9] The *NonProfit Time*'s wrote, "Giving Hit $212 Billion; Individual Donors Led The Way."[10] The headline in the Associated Press story declared, "2001 Charitable Giving Same As 2000."[11]

Only the headline in *The Chronicle of Philanthropy* reflected the entire AAFRC press release as it announced, "Charitable Giving Slides."[12]

The third paragraph on page one of the AAFRC press release read, "The 2001 total is an increase of one-half of one percent (0.5 percent) over the $210.89 billion now estimated for total giving in 2000. Adjusted for inflation, giving in 2001 is a decrease of 2.3 percent compared to the previous year."

The media in general had not done a critical review of AAFRC's public relations efforts that emphasized aggregate billions of dollars raised. If the media had asked AAFRC what happened when changes in the economy and population were taken into account, AAFRC might have pointed to its own published analysis of giving as a percent of Personal Income, which takes changes in both population and the economy into account. Philanthropy as a percent of Personal Income indicated giving was down from 1999 to 2000 and again from 2000 to 2001.[13]

An Associated Press business writer used the aggregate Total Contributions figure from 1972 through 2001 to compare changes from the previous year for both philanthropy and the S&P 500.[14] The graphic accompanying the AP article attributed as sources AAFRC, the

---

[8] AAFRC, "Charitable Giving Reaches $212 Billion," <http://www.aafrc.com/press3.html>; 9/26/02 2:06 PM printout.

[9] Stephanie Strom; "Charitable Contributions in 2001 Reached $212 Billion;" *New York Times*; published June 21, 2002; <http://www.nytimes.com/2002/06/21/national/21CHAR.html?pagewanted=print&position=bottom>;

[10] Matthew Sinclair, "Giving Hit $212 Billion; Individual Donors Led The Way," *The NonProfit Times*, July 1, 2002, p. 1.

[11] Helena Payne, Associated Press Writer; "2001 Charitable Giving Same As 2000;" published June 20, 2002, <http://www.washingtonpost.com/ac2/wp-dyn/A17534-2002Jun20?language=printer>; 12:20 PM; p. 1 of 6/27/02 9:09 PM printout.

[12] Nicole Lewis, "Charitable Giving Slides," *The Chronicle of Philanthropy*, June 27, 2002, p. 27.

[13] Center on Philanthropy at Indiana University, *Giving USA 2002* (New York: AAFRC Trust for Philanthropy, 2002), pp. 178.

[14] Alan Clendenning, "Shaky Market, Economy Leaving Charities in Pinch," an Associated Press story appearing in *The* (Champaign, Ill.) *News-Gazette*, September 22, 2002, p. C-1.

Center on Philanthropy, which AAFRC contracts to produce its giving estimates, and *The Chronicle of Philanthropy*, a trade newspaper that publicizes philanthropy. The AP graphic presented *Giving USA 2002* data in the category that AAFRC emphasizes, that is, aggregate billions of dollars raised. However, in the same *Giving USA 2002* report, the information for Total Contributions as a percent of Gross Domestic Product (GDP) was also available. Thus, the AP writer would have been able to tell the general public, for whom the story was written, not the annual change in how much professional fundraisers raised (aggregate billions donated) but the annual change in how much the American public gave when population and changes in the economy were taken into account (contributions as a percent of GDP). The two series paint very different pictures. The AP graphic indicated that giving declined from one year to the next in nine out of 30 years in the 1972-2001 period, or 30% of the time. However, as a percent of GDP, giving declined 19 of 30 times, or 63%.

Figure 17 presents the change in AAFRC Total Contributions from the previous year in aggregate inflation-adjusted billions of dollars, and as a percent of GDP. The graph format is similar to the one that accompanied the AP story.

Figure 17: AAFRC *Giving USA 2002* Total Contributions, Aggregate Inflation-Adjusted Dollars, and as a Percent of Gross National Product, Percent Change from Previous Year, 1972-2001

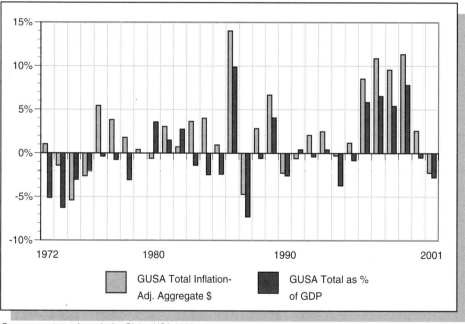

Source: empty tomb analysis, *Giving USA 2002*   empty tomb, inc. 2002

If the media had taken the initiative to compare AAFRC's published individual giving numbers as a portion of U.S. Per Capita Disposable (after-tax) personal income, they would have found that giving declined from 2.30% in 1999 to 2.17% in 2001.

Although the American public thinks of "giving" generally in terms of individual giving, the media does not make a distinction between AAFRC's total contributions numbers, that also include gifts from bequests, corporations and foundations, and individual-only numbers.

Individual giving was estimated to constitute 95 percent of the donations from Individuals and Corporations in 2002. [15] These are the two categories that track giving from living donors, making current decisions about their own resources.

During 2001 and 2002, the media reported about major for-profit corporations, such as Enron, that presented unrealistic pictures of their financial condition by selective presentation. One may hope that a positive outcome of this very sad reality would be an increased sophistication on the part of the media about how numbers are reported in both the for-profit and nonprofit realms.

To obtain a meaningful measure of the public's participation in philanthropy, population and economic factors need to be included and reported in more than a passing mention lost in the preoccupation with aggregate numbers that present an overly rosy picture. Since individual giving is estimated to constitute the bulk of all giving, an analysis of individual giving in light of these factors is very important. Although AAFRC used to provide a breakdown by source of donations (individual, bequest, corporation, foundation) for each recipient sector (such as religion, education, etc.), it has not done so for the past several years. It is not likely to do so again unless the public, likely through the media, holds it accountable.

Media could develop generally accepted standards for the reporting of philanthropy. In calls to ten major newspapers, two syndicated services, and two national newsweeklies, only four had designated philanthropy reporters: *The Dallas Morning News*; *The Washington Post*; *The San Jose Mercury News*; and *The Atlanta Constitution-Journal/* Cox News Service. Clear responsibility could be established for reporting in the area of philanthropy at other media. Reporters could be sensitized to the need for adjustments for changes in population and disposable personal income.

Changes in Form 990. The Internal Revenue Service requires any tax-exempt group registered as a 501(c)(3) charitable organization that normally has more than $25,000 in annual income, and is not an exception under defined criteria, to file a Form 990 each year. Three changes in the information requested by the Internal Revenue Service's Form 990 would assist in improving the measurement of philanthropy in the United States. The recommendations about contributions from living donors, and the self-definition of organizations, are developed more fully under the section on recommendations related to the Urban Institute that follows.

Contributions from Living Donors. Theoretically, the most accurate measure of individual giving possible is from receipts by nonprofit organizations via a revised Form 990, rather than from IRS itemizer returns and estimates of nonitemizer amounts. A policy decision needs to be made that it is important to obtain a sound Form 990 measure of individual giving by living donors. Individual giving, in addition to bequests, corporations (businesses), and foundations, the four categories tracked in the *Giving USA* series, could be one of four options for the organization to choose when reporting contributions by source.

---

[15] empty tomb analysis of data on *Giving USA 2002*, p. 10.

Self-Definition of Purpose and Governance Type. Form 990 needs to be changed so that reporting, recipient organizations define themselves through the use of a numerical system based on a standard classification such as the National Taxonomy of Exempt Entities.

Another change in Form 990 would be the implementation of a self-definition category describing the governance of the organization as either faith-based or secular. Currently, no such self-description is systematically requested. The result is the undercounting of the role of religion in the philanthropic sector, and consequently, in American society as a whole. An organization that is faith-based and provides, for example, human services is offered only the choice of being categorized as "human services" with the religious component ignored.

Contributions by Source. Form 990 does not now, but should, request that organizations provide donation information based on source of contributions. A policy decision is needed to measure contributions to recipient categories (religion, education, etc.) by source of donations. Currently, the standard source categories reported by *Giving USA* are individuals, bequests, corporations (businesses), and foundations. If the 990 were to collect this information from organizations defined by standard recipient categories, the information could serve as a validation for the *Giving USA* series and other survey-based giving data.

Recommendations Related to the Urban Institute. The Urban Institute received a relatively high grade for its involvement in the area of the measurement of philanthropy in the first Report Card, which has since been revised, based on its co-publication of the *New Nonprofit Almanac and Desk Reference.* Several actions could be taken by this group to improve the national collection of giving data.

Changes in the Urban Institute's Unified Chart of Accounts to Account for Donations by Living Individuals. The Urban Institute provides a permanent home for the Unified Chart of Accounts (UCOA),[16] "designed so that nonprofits can…**quickly and reliably translate their financial statements into the categories required by the IRS Form 990**, the federal Office of Management and Budget, and into other standard reporting formats. UCOA also seeks to…promote uniform accounting practices throughout the nonprofit sector" (bold emphasis in original).[17]

1. A critical weakness in the UCOA is its treatment of individual giving. This category is combined with "small businesses" in category "4010-xxx," to be reported on Form 990 Line Number 1a. The UCOA provides that gifts from individuals, whether designated, pledged or undesignated, be included on the same line as gifts from small businesses, including commercial co-ventures. In order to obtain a clear measure of individual giving, Account Number 4010-xxx should be reserved for individuals. "Small businesses" should be moved either to a new or some existing account series, such as "4210-xxx, Corporate and other business grants."

---

[16]Russy D. Sumariwalla and Wilson C. Levis, *Unified Financial Reporting System for Not-for-Profit Organizations: A Comprehensive Guide to Unifying GAAP, IRS Form 990, and Other Financial Reports Using a Unified Chart of Accounts* (San Francisco: Jossey-Bass, 2000), p. 211, Note.
[17]"The Unified Chart of Accounts;" National Center for Charitable Statistics, Urban Institute; <http://nccs.urban.org/ucoa/nccs-ucoa.htm>; p. 1 of 8/20/01 3:18 PM printout.

Part of the rationale for this separation in the reporting of individuals and small businesses is the definition of "small business." Contributions from small businesses are often not the type that can be compared with the IRS *Statistics of Income Bulletin*'s Table 1:—Individual Income Tax Returns "Itemized deductions" for "Charitable contributions." The Small Business Administration indicates that "Approximately 95% of all businesses are eligible for SBA [Small Business Administration] assistance."[18] The Small Business Administration has size standards that include: 500 employees for most manufacturing and mining industries; 100 employees for all wholesale trade industries; $5 million for most retail and service industries;[19] 4 million megawatt hours for energy producing companies; and $100 million in assets for banks or similar institutions.[20]

If the Form 990 is ever going to provide a clear set of data on giving by living individuals, then the data must be separated from this wide spectrum of additional sources of business donations. To assist organizations in classifying donations, incorporated businesses that make deductible charitable contributions could be required to identify in a clear, standardized and regulated fashion that the gift comes from an incorporated business. In this way, the organization can easily attribute the gift to the appropriate bookkeeping/accounting category, which will subsequently be used for Form 990 reporting purposes.

2. Form 1040 (Individual Return) Schedules A and C and Form 1065 (Partnership Return) should also be changed. Currently contributions made through certain businesses, specifically sole proprietorships or partnerships, can be reported on Schedule A for Form 1040. Gifts from such businesses might best be deducted on the business's tax return on Form 1065 rather than the individual's return. A precedent for separating personal and business contributions is found in the treatment of "Car and Truck Expenses" in the "Tax Guide for Small Business." The Tax Guide reads "If you have an expense that is partly for business and partly personal, separate the personal part from the business part."[21] If not changed, then the individual donor should be required to indicate to the organization that the gift will be reported as an individual, rather than business, contribution so that the organization can attribute the gift accordingly.

3. "Contributions through commercial co-ventures" should be moved to the corporate/business UCOA account number. Income from such co-ventures cannot validly be compared with the IRS Statistics of Income Bulletin's Table 1:—Individual Income Tax Returns "Itemized deductions" for "Charitable contributions." Commercial co-ventures can involve millions of dollars to nonprofits in exchange for positive marketing results for the company. While the arrangement may be a legitimate symbiotic relationship, it cannot be compared with the type of philanthropy normally assumed to be defined by the term "individual giving."

---

[18]U.S. Small Business Administration; "Small Business Resource Guide;" "startup pdf;" created Thu, Apr 6, 2000, 9:24 PM; downloaded from: <http://www.sba.gov/starting/startup.pdf>; p. 38.

[19]U.S. Small Business Administration, Office of Size Standards; "Frequently Asked Questions (FAQs);" <http://www.sba.gov/size/indexfaqs.html>; p. 1 of 9/13/01 8:00 AM printout.

[20]U.S. Small Business Administration; "Small Business Size Standards: Matched to North American Industry Classification System (NAICS) Codes Effective December 21, 2000;" <http://www.sba.gov/size/Table-of-Small-Business-Size-Standards-from-final-rule.html>; pp. 4 and 23 of 9/12/01 2:43 PM printout.

[21]Internal Revenue Service, "Tax Guide for Small Business (For Individuals Who Use Schedule C or C-EZ): For use in preparing 2000 Returns," Publication 334, Cat. No. 11063P, p. 26.

Any effort to change the Form 990 to yield an accurate measure of the level of giving from living individuals will be impeded to the extent that the Uniform Chart of Accounts, being championed by the Urban Institute for use by nonprofit organizations as a standard basis for bookkeeping categories, is structurally designed not to collect information specifically about giving by living individuals.

Categorization of organization by self-description of purpose and governance. The Urban Institute's National Center for Charitable Statistics has worked with the U.S. Internal Revenue Service to categorize nonprofit organizations that return Form 990. Further refinements could help to classify organizations using nationally-accepted standards.

In 1993, the National Center for Charitable Statistics was housed at Independent Sector. Virginia Hodgkinson authored a report calling for "a check-off list for charities based on the categories developed by Independent Sector for the National Taxonomy of Exempt Entities, an effort to classify all non-profit organizations registered with the IRS."[22] More specifically, the report recommended, "The Form 990 should be revised to allow for institutions of various functions to report their major purposes and programs, taking into account systems already in place to define such institutions."[23]

A precedent for this type of information gathering is Schedule C (Form 1040) that is used to report "Profit or Loss from Business (Sole Proprietorship)." This form requires a reporting business to select a category from the "Principal Business or Professional Activity Codes" that best describes the business. The codes provide 300 activities under 19 general categories.[24]

The National Taxonomy for Exempt Entities contains ten core categories from which a nonprofit organization could select to identify its main activity.

An important further refinement would provide a more complete picture of philanthropy in America. Before selecting one of the ten core categories, the nonprofit organization would first indicate its form of governance as either "faith-based" or "secular." This identification could provide valuable information to help clarify the role of religion in the area of giving. Form 990 could also require that the organization define itself, first by selecting either faith-based or secular as the category of governance, and then the specific activity described by one or more of the NTEE core codes.

In their book on the Unified Chart of Accounts, Russy D. Sumariwalla and Wilson C. Levis reproduced a graphic originally prepared by United Way of America that depicts how the account classification would appear in practical application.[25] For purposes of the present discussion, that graphic was adapted to include a statement about receipts

---

[22]Jennifer Moore, "Charity Group Backs Overhaul of Tax Form," *The Chronicle of Philanthropy*, November 30, 1993, pp. 34-35.

[23] Virginia Hodgkinson, et al., *A Portrait of the Independent Sector: The Activities and Finances of Charitable Organizations*, (Washington, DC: Independent Sector, 1993), p. 80.

[24]Internal Revenue Service, "Profit or Loss From Business (Sole Proprietorship)," Schedule C (Form 1040) 2000, OMB No. 1545-0074, Cat. No. 11334P, and Internal Revenue Service, "2000 Instructions for Schedule C, Profit or Loss From Business," Cat. No. 24329W, pp. C-7 and C-8.

[25]Sumariwalla and Levis, p. 41.

Figure 18: Account Classification Application with Faith-based/Secular Governance Option Included

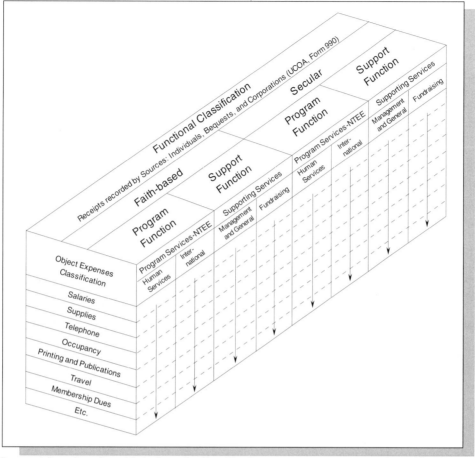

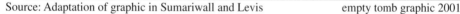

Source: Adaptation of graphic in Sumariwall and Levis   empty tomb graphic 2001

classification, and to describe at what point the choice of faith-based or secular governance would be included in the accounting hierarchy (see Figure 18).

Do Not Count Donations from Private Foundations. This recommendation is made persuasively in a 1993 paper by Hayden Smith. He noted that it is understandable that AAFRC, in its *Giving USA* series, for example, would include contributions to private foundations as charitable giving. Yet he developed the position that it is a mistake to include the donations from foundations in a measure of the current flow of Total Contributions, writing in part:

> However, if we are thinking about the flow of contributions and bequests from outside the charitable community, it is a mistake to include private foundation grants in our measure of total philanthropy, for one simple reason: private foundations themselves are charitable organizations and they are the recipients of gifts and bequests from individuals and families as well as makers of grants to other charities. By including them, we double-count some of the dollars that flow from donors to ultimate donations. . . Perfect validity requests that grants made out of the income generated from the investment of foundation assets, or any transfers of those assets to other charities, should not be included as part of the current flow of charitable giving.[26]

---

[26]Smith, p. 253.

A Commission on Private Philanthropy and Public Needs. A standing United States Commission on Private Philanthropy and Public needs was recommended in the previous volume of *The State of Church Giving* series. Subsequent research found that a recommendation for such a commission by Act of Congress was a finding of the original Commission on Private Philanthropy and Public Needs, also known as the Filer Commission. Details of that proposal are outlined in the Commission's report.[27] Among the recommendations were that the Commission's chair and 12 additional members would be appointed by the President of the United States, all subject to senatorial confirmation. These 13 appointees would name an additional 12 members. The term of the Commission would be permanent. The focus of the Commission was described in the Filer Commission Report as follows.

> Among other purposes and roles of the commission would be continuous collection of data on the sources and uses of the resources of the nonprofit sector; exploring and proposing ways of strengthening private giving and nonprofit activity; providing a forum for public discussion of issues affecting, and for commentary concerning, the nonprofit sector; studying the existing relationships between government and the nonprofit sector and acting as an ombudsman in protecting the interests of the sector as affected by government.[28]

The Commission could also assist in developing standards for the reporting of philanthropy data, facilitating changes in Form 990 to yield giving data by living individuals, and assisting in the dissemination of Form 990 data in an effort to increase the public accountability of nonprofit organizations. The Commission ought to involve academic economists of the highest caliber, who are well versed in national economic accounting and the development of the National Income and Products Accounts of the United States, including those who would have a link to the Council of Economic Advisors, and the Internal Revenue Service Form 990, as well as those who could influence the National Bureau of Economic Research to assist with the improvement of the measure of philanthropy.

Journal of Philanthropy Measurement. A peer-reviewed journal on the topic of philanthropy measurement could raise the reporting standards in this field of study. The journal could include a focus on obtaining sound annual estimates of philanthropy in the United States. The Hauser Center for Nonprofit Organizations housed at Harvard University's John F. Kennedy School of Government would be one logical place in which to house such a journal. The Hauser Center was designed to take a broader view of the field of philanthropy. As reported in the May 1, 1997 issue of *The Chronicle of Philanthropy*, "Harvard officials say that after they examined the existing academic centers in the field, they felt that many were parochial in their approach."[29]

Other Recommendations. Several other options could also assist in improving the measurement of philanthropy in the United States. A brief description of each follows.

NBER. The National Bureau of Economic Research would provide a valuable service were it to elevate the study of the nonprofit sector to a standing program, instead of only issuing occasional papers.

---

[27]Commission on Private Philanthropy and Public Needs, *Giving in America: Toward a Stronger Voluntary Sector: Report of the Commission on Private Philanthropy and Public Needs* (n.p.: Commission on Private Philanthropy and Public Needs, 1975), pp. 191-193.
[28]Commission on Private Philanthropy and Public Needs, p. 27.
[29]*The Chronicle of Philanthropy*, May 1, 1997, p. 10.

USBEA. The U.S. Department of Commerce, Bureau of Economic Analysis National Income and Product Accounts could expand analysis of the nonprofit sector.

GIVING ESTIMATES BY GIVING USA. By far, the most commonly quoted estimates of giving are produced by the American Association of Fundraising Counsel Trust for Philanthropy and published in its *Giving USA* series.

A Comparison of Estimates for Aggregate Giving to Religion. The largest category in philanthropy, as measured in *Giving USA* and other information sources, is religion. In 2001, according to *Giving USA 2002*, religion received 36.7% of all contributions, with Education receiving the next largest amount at 15.0%.[30] Therefore, any estimate of giving would be affected by the quality of the measurement of giving to religion.

The watershed Commission on Private Philanthropy and Public Needs of the 1970s, commonly referred to as the Filer Commission, produced an estimate of giving to religion. That report estimated that in 1974, giving to religion was $11.7 billion.[31] This estimate was relatively close to the AAFRC estimate for 1974 of $11.84 billion.[32]

In theory, one could follow a methodology for religion similar to that AAFRC used for the categories of education and health, in this case keying 1974 data to the Filer Commission estimate, and then calculate estimates for the years 1968 to 1973, and 1975 to 2000, based on an external source of data. The external source of data could be the same that AAFRC used to revise its 1987 through 1996 and 2000 religion data: a set of denominations that publish data in the *Yearbook of American and Canadian Churches* series. This revised approach would remedy the estimates for those years, presumably from about 1977 to 1985 based on the data patterns, when AAFRC did not calculate a figure for religion, but rather considered it a "residual" category, having the religion category absorb the difference between AAFRC's estimate of total contributions and the sum of AAFRC's estimates for the other recipient categories.[33]

The starting base in this approach could be the Filer Commission estimate of $11.7 billion for 1974. The amount of change from year to year, calculated for 1968 to 1973 and also 1975 to 2000, could be the annual percentage change in the composite denomination set analyzed in other chapters of this report.[34] This calculation yields a total of $8.01 billion given to religion in 1968, and $59.36 billion in 2000. These figures contrast with the AAFRC estimate of $8.42 billion in 1968 and $77.44 billion in 2000. Table 16 presents this data.

Comparing these two estimate series, one may observe that the two series are within a few per-centage points of each other for two years on either side of 1974, the year of the Filer estimate to which the denominational-based series is keyed. AAFRC methodology

---

[30]Center on Philanthropy at Indiana University, *Giving USA 2002* (New York: AAFRC Trust for Philanthropy, 2002), p. 17.

[31]Gabriel Rudney, "The Scope of the Private Voluntary Charitable Sector," Research Papers Sponsored by The Commission on Private Philanthropy and Public Needs, Vol. 1, History, Trends, and Current Magnitudes, (Washington, DC: Department of the Treasury, 1977), p. 136.

[32] *Giving USA 2002*, 171.

[33]For a more detailed discussion of the methodology employed by AAFRC to develop estimates presented in the *Giving USA* series, see previous editions in the *State of Church Giving* series.

[34]For this comparison, the composite data set of denominations was adjusted for missing data.

Table 16: Giving to Religion, AAFRC Series[35] and Denomination-Based Series, 1968-2000, Aggregate Billions of Dollars and Percent Difference

Year	AAFRC Series (Billions $)	Denomination-Based Series Keyed to 1974 Filer Estimate (Billions $)	Percent Difference between AAFRC and Denomination-Based Series
1968	$8.42	$8.01	5%
1969	$9.02	$8.33	8%
1970	$9.34	$8.67	8%
1971	$10.07	$9.13	10%
1972	$10.10	$9.78	3%
1973	$10.53	$10.69	-2%
1974	$11.84	$11.70	1%
1975	$12.81	$12.74	1%
1976	$14.18	$13.87	2%
1977	$16.98	$15.02	13%
1978	$18.35	$16.41	12%
1979	$20.17	$18.15	11%
1980	$22.23	$20.08	11%
1981	$25.05	$22.14	13%
1982	$28.06	$24.00	17%
1983	$31.84	$25.61	24%
1984	$35.55	$27.71	28%
1985	$38.21	$29.40	30%
1986	$41.68	$31.09	34%
1987	$43.51	$32.42	34%
1988	$45.15	$33.68	34%
1989	$47.77	$35.46	35%
1990	$49.79	$36.98	35%
1991	$50.00	$38.37	30%
1992	$50.95	$39.43	29%
1993	$52.89	$40.50	31%
1994	$56.43	$43.37	30%
1995	$58.07	$44.19	31%
1996	$61.90	$47.70	30%
1997	$64.68	$49.42	31%
1998	$68.24	$52.28	31%
1999	$71.24	$55.10	29%
2000	$77.44	$59.36	30%

does not indicate when religion became a residual recipient category, although the differences in the data series suggests a major change in AAFRC methodology took place between 1976 and 1977.

In 1982, while the denominational-based estimate series continues to change at a consistent rate, the AAFRC estimate series begins to expand more rapidly from year to year. The percentage difference grew from 17% in 1982 to 35% in 1989-1990. In 2000,

---

[35]Center on Philanthropy, *Giving USA 2002*, p. 171, and *Giving USA 1999* (New York: AAFRC Trust for Philanthropy, 1999), p. 132.

the difference was 30%. AAFRC updates the aggregate *Giving USA* numbers each year by a percent from the previous year, and thus the later years continue to build on the data years when religion was a residual category, absorbing that portion of the estimated Total Contributions amount that could not be placed in another category.

A Comparison of Per Capita Giving as a Percent of Income to Religion. The aggregate data in Table 16 was divided by U.S. population to produce a per capita figure for both the AAFRC giving to religion series and the denomination-based series keyed to the Filer estimate. The two series were then converted to giving as a percentage of U.S. disposable personal income. Figure 19 displays a decline and then upturn in the AAFRC series, while the denomination-based series reflects the pattern in the composite denomination set. When the denomination-based series is taken as a portion of disposable (after-tax) personal income, in 1968 charitable giving was 1.28%, while in 2000, it was 0.83%, a decline of 35% in the portion of U.S. per capita disposable personal income contributed to religion.

An analysis was developed by consultant Joseph Claude Harris.[36] Harris had taken a sample of Catholic parishes. Using that data in combination with denominational data from the *Yearbook of American and Canadian Churches*, he developed an estimate for "All Denominations and the Catholic Church" for 1991-1999. His individual contributions data, adjusted for population, follows the Filer-Adjusted series, as shown in Figure 19.

Per Capita Giving to Additional Recipient Categories, 1968-2000. Considering giving on a per capita basis as a percentage of income to various recipient categories in addition to

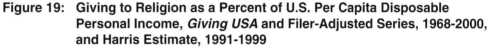

Figure 19: Giving to Religion as a Percent of U.S. Per Capita Disposable Personal Income, *Giving USA* and Filer-Adjusted Series, 1968-2000, and Harris Estimate, 1991-1999

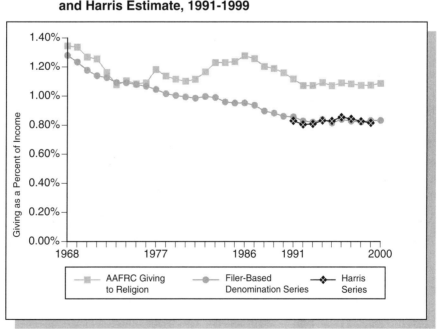

Sources: AAFRC; *YACC* adjusted series; U.S. BEA   empty tomb, inc. 2002

[36]Joseph Claude Harris, "A Summary of Church Contributions.xls," Seattle, WA, Date Written March 7, 2001; Date Revised April 7, 2001. Letter and Spreadsheet to empty tomb, inc., July 10, 2001.

religion may provide a different picture than presented by the aggregate AAFRC data for these categories. A comparison is presented in Table 17.

It should be noted that the recipient categories presented by AAFRC do not make a distinction by source of contribution. AAFRC does state that the majority of donations to religion comes from individuals. However, in recent years AAFRC does not provide figures within each of the various recipient categories as to the amount of donations from each source, the four being: individuals, bequests, corporations, and foundations. Therefore, the comparison in Table 17 is only approximate. The information does, however, suggest that population and income are important factors to be taken into consideration when discussing trends in charitable giving.

Table 17 presents the AAFRC published data for the recipient categories of: religion; education; health; human services; arts, culture, and humanities; and public/society benefit.[37] Since data for the recipient categories of environment/wildlife and international affairs is

Table 17: AAFRC Giving to Recipient Categories, 1968 and 2000, Aggregate, Current and Inflation-Adjusted 2001 Dollars (Billions of Dollars), and Per Capita as a Percent of U.S. Disposable Personal Income, with Percent Change 1968-2000

	Religion			Education		
	Aggregate (Billions $)		Per Capita	Aggregate (Billions $)		Per Capita
	Current $	Inf.-Adj. '01 $	% Income	Current $	Inf.-Adj. '01 $	% Income
1968	$8.42	$42.85	1.34%	$2.38	$12.11	0.38%
2000	$77.44	$79.65	1.09%	$31.67	$32.57	0.44%
% Change	820%	86%	-19%	1231%	169%	17%

	Health			Human Services		
	Aggregate (Billions $)		Per Capita	Aggregate (Billions $)		Per Capita
	Current $	Inf.-Adj. '01 $	% Income	Current $	Inf.-Adj. '01 $	% Income
1968	$2.08	$10.59	0.33%	$2.31	$11.76	0.37%
2000	$18.82	$19.36	0.26%	$17.99	$18.50	0.25%
% Change	805%	83%	-20%	679%	57%	-32%

	Arts, Culture and Humanities			Public/Society Benefit		
	Aggregate (Billions $)		Per Capita	Aggregate (Billions $)		Per Capita
	Current $	Inf.-Adj. '01 $	% Income	Current $	Inf.-Adj. '01 $	% Income
1968	$0.60	$3.05	0.10%	$0.43	$2.19	0.07%
2000	$11.50	$11.83	0.16%	$11.59	$11.92	0.16%
% Change	1817%	287%	69%	2595%	445%	137%

provided only for years beginning with 1987, these categories are not included. The category of giving to foundations has current dollar data only back to 1978, and likewise is not considered in this table. The category of unallocated is also not included.

From this table, it is apparent once again that giving to religion received the highest level of charitable giving support. Aggregate giving in both current and inflation-adjusted dollars increased. However, as a portion of U.S. per capita disposable personal income, the amount of giving to religion decreased by 19%. Table 17 uses AAFRC's revised *Giving 2002* estimate of giving to religion series.

All the categories in Table 17 showed an increase in terms of aggregate giving in both current and inflation-adjusted dollars. However, giving as a percentage of income provides additional information. Per capita giving as a portion of income to education increased by 17% during this period, compared to an increase of 169% in inflation-adjusted aggregate dollars. However, giving to health declined 20%, and giving to human services declined 32%, rather than an inflation-adjusted aggregate increase of 83% and 57% to health and human services, respectively.

Two recipient categories that show an increase were arts, culture and humanities, and the category of public/society benefit. While neither group represented more than 0.2% of per capita giving as a portion of income in 2000, these two categories posted increases of 69% and 137% respectively, between 1968 and 2000, in contrast to the other categories in the table.

Figure 20, on the next two pages, depicts two views of five recipient categories: education; health; human services; arts, culture, and humanities; and public/society benefit. The view in the left column presents the aggregate AAFRC data as it is presented in the *Giving USA* series, in both current and inflation-adjusted 2000 dollars. The view in the right column for each recipient category presents an additional view: the AAFRC data was converted to a per capita basis as a percentage of U.S. per capita disposable personal income. It may be observed that the two approaches present different pictures of charitable giving patterns.

GRADING SYSTEM METHODOLOGY AND DETAIL. The preceding discussion has considered various aspects of the measurement of philanthropy, and recommendations to improve it.

---

[37]Data for 1968 was obtained from Ann E. Kaplan, ed., *Giving USA 1999* (New York: AAFRC Trust for Philanthropy, 1999), pp. 134-135. Data for 2000 was obtained from *Giving USA 2002*, pp. 171-173. In Table 17, the per capita figures for 1968 and 2000, and, using the CPI, the 1968 aggregate, inflation-adjusted figures for 1968, were calculated by empty tomb, inc.

Figure 20. AAFRC Recipient Category Data, 1968-2000

Giving to Education

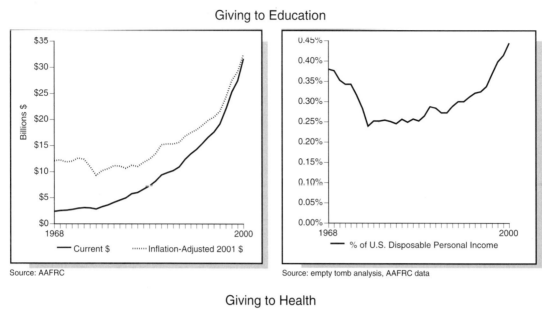

Source: AAFRC

Source: empty tomb analysis, AAFRC data

Giving to Health

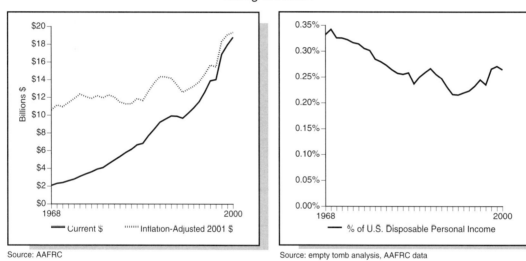

Source: AAFRC

Source: empty tomb analysis, AAFRC data

Giving to Human Services

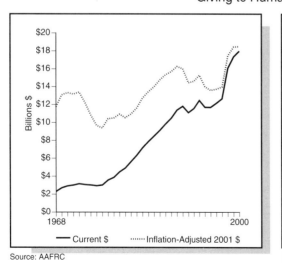

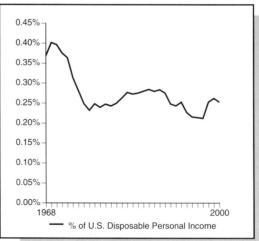

Source: AAFRC

Source: empty tomb analysis, AAFRC data

Figure 20: AAFRC Recipient Category Data, 1968-2000, Continued

The Report Card on the Measurement of Philanthropy was designed to provide an overview of the quality of present efforts to measure charitable giving in the United States.

Each grade level from A to F was given a numerical value. Each of the twelve specific entities were graded in each relevant category. The numerical value of all the categories for which an entity was graded were then averaged to produce an overall grade for that entity.

For each of the twelve entities, Table 19 presents the Overall Grade, and lists the Evaluation Category, Grade, and Evaluation Comments that combined to provide the Overall Grade.

Table 18:   Report Card on the Measurement of Philanthropy Detail

Providers of Public Estimates of Giving

AAFRC Trust for Philanthropy *Giving USA* series Overall Grade: C-		
Evaluation Category	Grade	Evaluation Comments
Annual Measurement	A	AAFRC issues an annual *Giving USA* report.
Adjustments for Population and Income	D	The predominant emphasis in the *Giving USA* series' press release headline and text, and *Giving USA* tables, graphics, and text is on aggregate dollar amounts and percent changes in aggregate dollar amounts, which do not account for changes in population and after-tax income. The result is an artificially optimistic estimate of changes in giving.
Report Available for Timely Review	A	The *Giving USA 2002* Annual Report was available at essentially the time of the related AAFRC June 20, 2002 press release. Thus, the grade for this category improved to A in 2002 from 2001's D.
Distance from For-Profit Counsel	D	*Giving USA* is an industry publication. While it may be a desirable professional fundraising tool, it has not also served the purpose of providing an objective estimate of giving for use by the general public. The desire for latest year data has led to an emphasis on, and the development of, a series of models to produce estimates for the latest year. The result is both an annual estimate that is generally revised in subsequent years, combined with a lack of a comprehensive overview of philanthropy measurement. However, the revision for 1997-2000 data showing that the original estimates are lower than the revised estimates, in contrast to the previous pattern, leads to an improved D in 2002 from the F grade in 2001.
Consistency over Time	D	The emphasis on developing a latest year projection has led to the use of a changing mixture of variables with no published systematic basis for the revisions made in rapid succession. For an undisclosed period of time in the 1980s, Religion was a "residual category." More recently, Religion for the years 1986 through the most recent year has been adjusted, but earlier years, when Religion was the residual category, have not yet been.
Treatment of Religion	D	While *Giving USA* revised its Education and Health series, keying them to the Filer Commission estimates, it has not treated Religion in a similarly consistent manner. Also, it does not take into account that many groups included in other recipient categories are faith-based in governance. Therefore, the picture of giving to religion is at the same time distorted and incomplete.
Comparable Data	D	*Giving USA* considers philanthropy by Source categories, and separately, by Recipient categories. Only rarely in the past has it provided a breakdown within Recipient categories by Source. It would be useful to know the amount of giving by source to each Recipient category.
Review of Major Questionable Findings	D	*Giving USA* has revised some of its historical series but has not reviewed others. The "residual category" years for religion is one example. Another important example of questionable data that has not been addressed is a 27% change in Human Services from 1997 to 1998. Data for the largest Human Services organizations in The Chronicle of Philanthropy 400 list indicated these groups grew only 7% that year. A request to review the data producing the estimate was denied by the previous *Giving USA* editor on the basis of confidentiality. Subsequent editions of *Giving USA* did not indicate an internal review of that data.

Availability of Data	D	Each issue of *Giving USA* provides discussion and also a series of data tables based on the information in their study. However, as noted in the previous category comments, a request to the previous editor for the data that served as the basis for the 1997-1998 Human Services giving estimates was refused based on a stated need of AAFRC to keep the data confidential.
Validity of Data	D	*Giving USA* has not published an adequate validation comparison study between its estimates and other available information.

Independent Sector *Giving and Volunteering in the United States*, *Balancing the Scales*, and *The New Nonprofit Almanac and Desk Reference.*

Overall Grade: D+

Evaluation Category	Grade	Evaluation Comments
Annual Measurement	D	Independent Sector's *Giving and Volunteering in the United States* was published biannually from 1988 to 1996. A 1999 edition was published in 2002.
Adjustments for Population and Income	A	Independent Sector adjusts for population by using the number of households in the United States. It also adjusts for income.
Report Available for Timely Review	F	Independent Sector distributed a press release about *Giving and Volunteering in the United States, 1999 edition* in 1999. Media reports appeared that fall. *The Statistical Abstract* listed a reference source indicating the document was published in 2000. Repeated contacts with Independent Sector resulted in varying publication due dates. The 1999 edition was available in May 2002.

The Independent Sector Web site announced major findings in a November 4, 2001 release of its new "comprehensive study," measuring giving in 2000, the "comprehensive report" for which would "be available in the spring of 2002."[38] September 2002 correspondence indicates an October 2002 availability date.

In its publication, *America's Religious Congregations: Measuring their Contribution to Society*, published in 2000, Independent Sector has footnotes referring to their full report, *Balancing the Scales*. The reference in their resource list reads, "published by Independent Sector, Washington, DC, 2001." However, correspondence from February 2001 through May 2002 indicated the document had not yet been published. |
| Distance from For-Profit Counsel | A | Independent Sector's "2000 Annual Report" described Independent Sector's membership as including "700 of the nation's leading foundations, prominent and far-reaching nonprofits of all sizes, and corporations with strong commitments to community involvement." The organization has sufficient independence and distance from the influence and agenda of those who have a vested interest in the outcome of any measurement of philanthropy. |

---

[38]"Independent Sector Survey Measures the Everyday Generosity of Americans;" Embargoed until November 4, 2001; <http://www.independentsector.org/media/GV01PR.html>; printed 11/25/01 2:30 PM.

Independent Sector *Giving and Volunteering in the United States, Balancing the Scales*, and *The New Nonprofit Almanac and Desk Reference*, continued		
Consistency over Time	F	Independent Sector's *Giving and Volunteering in the United States* series has generally maintained a comparable series of data in its published editions—1988, 1990, 1992, 1994 and 1996. However, the *Giving and Volunteering in the United States 1999* edition available in 2002, for the first time in the series, did not include the category of "Religion," with its subcategories including Catholics, All Protestants, Baptists, Lutherans, Methodists, Presbyterians, Jewish, All Other Religions, in its table of "Demographic Characteristics of Volunteers and Contributing Households." Given the increasingly visible role of religion in America, this inconsistency along with that noted in the following comment, led to the downgrade to F in 2002 from the 2001 rating of B.
		Independent Sector, referring to the forthcoming Giving and Volunteering in the United States 2001 edition, reported that, due to a "change in methodology," it will be "difficult to compare these new findings to our earlier studies."[39]
Treatment of Religion	F	The *Giving and Volunteering in the United States (GAVITUS)* survey instrument has, for the most part, provided for the measurement of several significant issues regarding religion, such as the relationship between membership and worship attendance, and charitable giving and volunteering. However, in terms of actual giving estimates, the *GAVITUS* survey could be improved.
		For example, the 1990, 1992, 1994 and 1996 *GAVITUS* "Type of Organization" Attachment used by the interviewers provided the option for a breakdown between "Nonprofit, Religious" and "Nonprofit, Nonsectarian" in the types of organizations. However, the report does not provide a table that breaks down Use categories, such as International or Human Services, into these two categories. A detailed analysis of the potential distortion of not including such a distinction in such areas as International and Human Services was provided in *The State of Church Giving through 1991 (SCG91)*. Also in *SCG91*, the recommendation was made to include the option of distinguishing between gifts to "church, synagogue or mosque" and other religious organizations. This distinction would provide the basis for external validation of the survey instrument by enabling the comparison of survey responses with available church giving data.
		The *GAVITUS 1999* failure to include Religion in its table of "Demographic Characteristics of Volunteers and Contributing Households" leads to a 2002 grade of F in comparison to the 2001 rating of D. Previous editions in the *State of Church Giving* series had recommended that the sample sizes be expanded to be statistically reliable.

---

[39]The press release for the new Independent Sector survey, *Giving and Volunteering in the United States 2001*, presenting figures for reporting households that are 51% higher than two years earlier, includes a change in methodology that will make "it difficult to compare these new findings to our earlier studies," [a series beginning in 1988] according to Dr. Sara E. Melendez, President and CEO of Independent Sector. "Independent Sector Survey Measures the Everyday Generosity of Americans;" <http://www.independentsector.org/media/GV01PR.html>; embargoed until November 4, 2001; printed 11/25/01 2:30 PM.

		In 2002, Independent Sector published *Faith and Philanthropy: The Connection Between Charitable Behavior and Giving to Religion* that was "based on analysis from Independent Sector's *Giving and Volunteering in the United States* 2001 national survey" (p.4). *Faith and Philanthropy* does not provide a breakdown by various major denominations or denominational families as has been the case in the 1990, 1992, 1994 and 1996 *GAVITUS.* Reported gifts to denominations provide one of the better opportunities for validation studies of giving survey data because (1) of the relatively large size of some denominational memberships, and (2) denominations annually compile and publish their congregations' giving reports.
Comparable Data	F	While Independent Sector uses household contributions as a standard, AAFRC's *Giving USA* uses aggregate. When the Independent Sector data is multiplied by the number of households in the United States to obtain an aggregate number to compare with *Giving USA*, the difference between the two estimates was $56 billion for 1998 data. That the Independent Sector household data represented the entire United States was stated in its own press releases. Further, its methodology, while acknowledging that the sample did not target the wealthy, states, "Weighting procedures were used to ensure that the final sample was representative of the adult population in the United States in terms of age, race/ethnicity, education, marital status, size of household, region of country and household income."[40] One may assume, therefore, that multiplying its average household contribution by the number of households in the United States would yield an aggregate estimate for contributions in the United States. This calculation yielded an estimate of $78.3 billion, compared to a *Giving USA* estimate of $134.1 billion in 1998.[41] An unexplained development in Independent Sector's process was a comment on the Independent Sector Web site. While the Key Findings section reproduced the Key Findings section of the *GAVITUS* 1999 edition, another sentence was added that stated, "from 1995 to 1998, after inflation, the average household contribution decreased by 1.2%.*" The note to the asterisk stated, "At present both Independent Sector and AAFRC's *Giving USA* 1999 estimate $135 billion in total individual giving for 1997."[42] No basis for Independent Sector's estimate was provided.
Review of Major Questionable Findings	D	External validation tests of Independent Sector data suggest a great volatility in the level of contributions from one survey to another, compared to the relatively stable trends of other data.[43] These findings have not been adequately acknowledged or addressed in subsequent surveys.

---

[40]Susan K.E. Saxon-Harrold et al., "Household Giving in America;" "Giving and Volunteering in the United States: Executive Summary;" (Washington, DC: Independent Sector, 1999), p. 16.

[41]For a detailed comparison of the two estimates, see John Ronsvalle and Sylvia Ronsvalle, *The State of Church Giving through 1998* (Champaign, IL: empty tomb, inc., 2000), pp. 61-68.

[42]"Household Giving in America;" "Giving and Volunteering in the United States: Findings from a National Survey;" published 1999; <http://www.independentsector.org/GandV/s_keyf.htm>; p. 2 of 1/26/01 9:41 AM printout.

[43]Ronsvalle, *The State of Church Giving through 1998*, pp. 68-73.

Independent Sector *Giving and Volunteering in the United States, Balancing the Scales*, and *The New Nonprofit Almanac and Desk Reference*, continued		
Availability of Data	C	Independent Sector has the *GAVITUS* data not available for purchase.
		While Independent Sector was rated A in 2001 for the availability of its data to researchers for independent analysis, its rating was downgraded to C in 2002 as a function of inadequate specificity in its documentation and/or publication of source data for some of the tables and technical notes in *The New Nonprofit Almanac and Desk Reference* (Jossey-Bass, 2002) which Independent Sector co-published with the Urban Institute in 2002. This weakness is observed in relation to the critically important area of giving by individuals. *The New Nonprofit Almanac* Table 3.3 and Sources notes on page 59, Table 3.6 on page 64, with the accompanying technical note on pages 218-219, neither list methodological or formulaic detail, nor provide or reference documentation and rationale for *The New Nonprofit Almanac's* shift from the AAFRC's *Giving USA* individual giving series for the 1986-1998 period, while following the *Giving USA* series from 1964-1985. Both *The New Nonprofit Almanac* and the AFFRC *Giving USA*[44] series adjust for non-itemizer giving.
		The New Nonprofit Almanac Table 3.2, "Distribution of Private Contributions by Recipient Area: AAFRC Trust for Philanthropy Estimates, 1968-1998," compares eight "Recipient" areas. A Note states, "Giving to some categories prior to 1985 cannot be compared to giving since 1985 because of different statistical tabulation and analysis procedures."[45] This lack of specificity renders major portions of the Table unintelligible.
		The last column of the same Table 3.2 is labeled "Unclassified" and is referenced to "AAFRC Trust for Philanthropy, 1999." Yet, AAFRC's *Giving USA 1999* has the Recipient category of "Unallocated" for 1968-1998 along with the Recipient category of "Gifts to Foundations" for the years 1978-1998.
Validity of Data	F	As noted above, external validation tests, comparing Independent Sector *GAVITUS* data with other sources, indicated a volatility in the Independent Sector data that was not present in the other sources. Steps to reduce this variation were not taken as of the 1999 edition.

The Chronicle of Philanthropy Philanthropy 400 Overall Grade: C-		
Evaluation Category	Grade	Evaluation Comments
Annual Measurement	A	This report is issued annually.
Adjustments for Population and Income	F	The Philanthropy 400 does not address issues related to the adjustment of philanthropic giving in U.S. population and income.
Report Available for Timely Review	A	The report is published in full in *The Chronicle of Philanthropy*.
Distance from For-Profit Counsel	F	*The Chronicle of Philanthropy* is supported directly by advertising from for-profit fundraising groups.

---

[44] Ann Kaplan, ed., *Giving USA 1999* (New York: AAFRC Trust for Philanthropy, 1999), p. 148-149.

[45] Murray S. Weitzman, Nadine T. Jalandoni, Independent Sector, and Linda M. Lampkin, Thomas H. Pollak, Urban Institute, *The New Nonprofit Almanac and Desk Reference* (New York: John Wiley & Sons/Jossey-Bass, 2002), p. 57.

Consistency over Time	D	The report is published annually using the same categories. However, the report is fundamentally flawed in that it presents a changing list of organizations from one year to the next as a basis for determining any change in giving patterns.
Treatment of Religion	F	The Philanthropy 400 does not treat religion in a reasonable and comprehensive way. For example, religious denominations are excluded.
Comparable Data	C	The Philanthropy 400 uses publicly available reports. However, it does not present data that facilitates comparisons either internally (using faith-based/secular categories) or externally (using standardized recipient or source categories).
Review of Major Questionable Findings	D	Although concerns about not using a consistent set of organizations for year-to-year comparisons have been published,[46] the Philanthropy 400 has not adequately addressed the issue.
Availability of Data	A	The Philanthropy 400 data is published and available for independent analysis.
Validity of Data	D	The Philanthropy 400 does not take comprehensive steps to maximize the likelihood of the valid, integrated measurement of philanthropy. Further, the Philanthropy 400 sits in the larger context of a lack of an integrated critical analysis by *The Chronicle of Philanthropy* of the overall measurement of giving among the various available estimates. The rating for this category improved in 2002 to D from the F grade in 2001 as a function of *The Chronicle of Philanthropy*'s reporting of AAFRC's *Giving USA 2002* results. While, of the major media that were reviewed, none bannered *Giving USA* results adjusted for population and income, *The Chronicle of Philanthropy* clearly headlined the decrease in giving for 2001, in spite of a general trend in philanthropic circles to report overly optimistic findings. The headline of a *Chronicle of Philanthropy* article by Nicole Lewis stated clearly, "Charitable Giving Slides." [47]

The NonProfit Times NPT 100 Overall Grade: C-		
Evaluation Category	Grade	Evaluation Comments
Annual Measurement	A	The report is issued annually.
Adjustments for Population and Income	F	The NPT 100 does not address issues related to the adjustment of philanthropic giving for changes in U.S. population and income.
Report Available for Timely Review	A	The report is published in full in *The NonProfit Times*.
Distance from For-Profit Counsel	F	*The NonProfit Times* is supported directly by advertising from for-profit fundraising groups.
Consistency over Time	D	The report is published annually using the same categories. However, the report is fundamentally flawed in that it presents a changing list of organizations from one year to the next as a basis for determining any change in giving patterns.
Treatment of Religion	F	The NPT 100 does not treat religion in a reasonable and comprehensive way. For example, religious denominations are excluded.

---

[46]John Ronsvalle and Sylvia Ronsvalle, *The State of Church Giving through 1997* (Champaign, IL: empty tomb, inc., 1999), pp. 62-63, and Ronsvalle, *The State of Church Giving through 1998*, pp. 73-74.
[47] Nicole Lewis, "Charitable Giving Slides," *Chronicle of Philanthropy*, June 27, 2002, p. 27.

The NonProfit Times NPT 100, continued		
Comparable Data	C	The NPT 100 uses publicly available reports. However, it does not present data that facilitates comparisons either internally (using faith-based/secular categories) or externally (using standardized recipient or source categories).
Review of Major Questionable Findings	D	Although concerns about not using a consistent set of organizations for year-to-year comparisons have been published,[48] The NPT 100 has not adequately addressed the issue.
Availability of Data	A	The NPT 100 data is published and available for independent analysis.
Validity of Data	F	The NPT 100 does not take comprehensive steps to maximize the likelihood of the valid, integrated measurement of philanthropy. Further, the NPT 100 sits in the larger context of a lack of an integrated critical analysis by *The NonProfit Times* of the overall measurement of giving among the various available estimates.

Statistical Abstract of the United States **Overall Grade: C+**		
Evaluation Category	Grade	Evaluation Comments
Annual Measurement	A	The *Statistical Abstract of the United States* annually presents tables containing data for the measurement of philanthropy.
Adjustments for Population and Income	D	Philanthropic data is not presented in a way that adjusts for changes in total U.S. population and income.
Report Available for Timely Review	A	The tables in the *Statistical Abstract* present complete data with references.
Distance from For-Profit Counsel	A	The *Statistical Abstract* has sufficient independence and distance from the influence and agenda of those who have a vested interest in the outcome of any measurement of philanthropy.
Consistency over Time	A	The *Statistical Abstract* approaches its work with a reasonable degree of consistency over the years.
Treatment of Religion	D	The *Statistical Abstract* does not treat religion in a reasonable and comprehensive fashion, primarily due to weaknesses in its source materials.
Comparable Data	F	The *Statistical Abstract* does not adequately present philanthropic data in a way that facilitates comparisons between the data sources it presents. *GAVITUS* data for households reporting charitable contributions is used, rather than all households; the reported data cannot be aggregated by using the number of households in the U.S. available elsewhere in the *Statistical Abstract*.
Review of Major Questionable Findings	D	The *Statistical Abstract* presents philanthropic data which is questionable primarily due to weaknesses in its source materials.
Availability of Data	A	The *Statistical Abstract* tables reproduce data from other sources that is then available for independent analysis.
Validity of Data	F	The *Statistical Abstract* does not take comprehensive steps to maximize the likelihood of valid, integrated measurement of philanthropy.

---

[48]Ronsvalle, *The State of Church Giving through 1997*, pp. 62-63, and Ronsvalle, *The State of Church Giving through 1998*, pp. 73-74.

Additional Entities Involved in the Measurement of Philanthropy

Advisory Committees to the *Giving USA* and *Giving and Volunteering in the United States*[49]

Overall Grade: D+

Evaluation Category	Grade	Evaluation Comments
Annual Measurement	B	The advisory committees are related to the annual *Giving USA* publication and the occasional *Giving and Volunteering in the United States* (*GAVITUS*) publications.
Adjustments for Population and Income	C	*Giving USA* emphasizes aggregate data while *GAVITUS* does adjust for population and income.
Report Available for Timely Review	C	The *Giving USA 2002* Annual Report was available at essentially the time of the related AAFRC June 20, 2002 press release. Thus, the grade for this category improved to C in 2002 from 2001's F.

In 2001 neither advisory committee had successfully influenced the respective publications to release the report in a coordinated fashion with the publication of press announcements. |
| Distance from For-Profit Counsel | C | The *Giving USA* committee does not have distance from for-profit counsel. The *GAVITUS* committee does have distance from for-profit counsel. |
| Consistency over Time | D | While the advisory committee has not assisted *Giving USA* to produce consistent data over the years, the *GAVITUS* committee's failure to provide *GAVITUS 1999* consistency in Religion leads to a 2002 grade of D in comparison to the 2001 rating of C. |
| Treatment of Religion | F | Neither advisory committee has successfully pressed to solve the long-standing problems in estimating giving to religion.

The *GAVITUS 1999* failure to include Religion in its table of "Demographic Characteristics of Volunteers and Contributing Households" leads to a 2002 grade of F in comparison to the 2001 rating of D. |
| Comparable Data | F | Neither advisory committee has successfully pressed to solve the long-standing problems in providing comparable data between the estimates. |

Advisory Committees to the *Giving USA* and *Giving and Volunteering in the United States*, continued

[49]The *Giving USA* 1987-2002 advisory committees included, for one or more years, representatives of: the American Association of Fundraising Counsel (AAFRC) Trust for Philanthropy, The Aspen Institute, Association for Healthcare Philanthropy, Boston College, The Brookings Institution, Center for Responsive Governance, City University of New York, The Conference Board, Council for Advancement and Support of Education, Council for Aid to Education, Council on Foundations, ePhilanthropy Foundation, The Ford Foundation, The Foundation Center, Georgetown University Center for the Study of Voluntary Organizations and Service, Independent Sector, Indiana University, Indiana University/ Purdue University-Indianapolis, Johns Hopkins University, Marts & Lundy, Inc., National Bureau of Economic Research, National Council of the Churches of Christ in the U.S.A., The Nonprofit Sector Research Fund, Princeton Survey Research Associates, Raybin Associates, Inc., U.S. Treasury Department, United Way of America/International, University of Michigan, The Urban Institute, Yale University.

The Independent Sector *Giving and Volunteering in the United States* advisory committees for one or more years of the 1990-1999 editions or the Executive Summary for 1999 had representatives from: the American Association of Fund-Raising Counsel (AAFRC) Trust for Philanthropy, The Aspen Institute, Boston College, Canadian Centre for Philanthropy, College of St. Catherine, Council on Foundations, The Ford Foundation, The Gallup Organization, George Washington University, Georgetown University, Johns Hopkins University, London School of Economics, The Minneapolis Foundation, the National Alliance of Business, The National Volunteer Center, *The NonProfit Times*, Northwestern University, Princeton University, Rockefeller Brothers Fund, United Way of America, University of Maryland, College Park, University of Massachusetts at Amherst, University of Minnesota, The Urban Institute, Volunteers of America, and the Weber Reports.

Review of Major Questionable Findings	D	Neither advisory committee has successfully pressed to address major questions about the findings of the respective publications.
Availability of Data	R	The *Giving USA* committee has not insured that data is available for review. The *GAVITUS* committee has carried out its work in such a way that the data is available for independent analysis.
Validity of Data	F	Neither committee has successfully pressed to implement comprehensive steps that would help to maximize the likelihood of valid, integrated measurement of philanthropy.

Foundation Efforts in the Area of Measurement of Philanthropy[50] **Overall Grade: C-**		
Evaluation Category	Grade	Evaluation Comments
Annual Measurement	C	Foundations are involved in funding reports through other entities. However, foundations have not systematically addressed issues related to the annual measurement of philanthropy.
Adjustments for Population and Income	C	Foundations have not worked to insure that all major measures of philanthropy adjust for population and income.
Report Available for Timely Review	D	Major reports that receive foundation funding are not available for researchers at the same time press releases are issued. The *Giving USA 2002* Annual Report was available at essentially the time of the related AAFRC June 20, 2002 press release. Thus, the grade for this category improved to D in 2002 from 2001's F.
Distance from For-Profit Counsel	A	Foundations have sufficient independence and distance from the influence and agenda of those who have a vested interest in the results of any measurement of philanthropy.

---

[50]Foundations that have funded the *Giving and Volunteering the United States* series (edition year in parentheses) include The Atlantic Philanthropies (1999), The Chevron Companies (1994), The Ford Foundation (1990, 1992, 1994, 1996, 1999 Executive Summary, 1999), GE Foundation (1994), William Randolph Hearst Foundation (1990), IBM Corporation (1990), W.K. Kellogg Foundation (1992, 1994, 1996, 1999 Executive Summary, 1999), Knight Foundation (1990), Lilly Endowment Inc. (1990, 1992, 1999 Executive Summary, 1999), Robert McCormick Charitable Trust (1990), Metropolitan Life Foundation (1996, 1999 Executive Summary, 1999, Faith and Philanthropy 2002), Charles Stewart Mott Foundation (1992, 1994, 1996, 1999 Executive Summary, 1999), Rockefeller Brothers Fund (1992), Dr. Scholl Foundation (1992).

The Ford Foundation and Lilly Endowment Inc. funded the Independent Sector Measures Survey, published as *America's Religious Congregations: Measuring Their Contribution to Society* (Washington, DC: Independent Sector, November 2000), funded by the Lilly Endowment Inc., and *Balancing the Scales*, as yet unpublished, although referenced in *America's Religious Congregations* (p. 2) as containing "more comprehensive information and complete methodology."

Foundations that have funded the *Nonprofit Almanac* most recent series (publication year in parentheses) include The Atlantic Philanthropies (2002), The Chevron Companies (1996), The Ford Foundation (1996, 2001 In Brief, 2002), Robert Wood Johnson Foundation (2002), Ewing Marion Kauffman Foundation (2002), W.K. Kellogg Foundation (1996, 2002), Lilly Endowment (2001 In Brief, 2002), Andrew W. Mellon Foundation (1996), Charles Stewart Mott Foundation (1996, 2002), "Anonymous donors" (1996), "corporate, foundation, and nonprofit embers of Independent Sector" (2002).

The Lilly Endowment, Charles Stewart Mott Foundation, Rockefeller Brothers Fund, and William Randolph Hearst Foundation funded the Russy D. Sumariwalla, Wilson C. Levis, *Unified Financial Reporting System for Not-for-Profit Organizations: A Comprehensive Guide to Unifying GAAP, IRS Form 990, and Other Financial Reports Using a Unified Chart of Accounts* (San Francisco: Jossey-Bass, 2000).

In addition, representatives of the Council on Foundations and The Foundation Center have been Advisory Council members of AAFRC's *Giving USA* series.

Consistency over Time	D	While some aspects of reports funded by foundations provide a level of consistent categories over time, foundations on the whole do not approach this area with attention to consistency. *GAVITUS 1999*'s omission of the Religion category and subcategories leads to a 2002 grade of D in comparison to the 2001 rating of C.
Treatment of Religion	F	Foundations have not worked to insure that the annual measurement of religion is conducted in a reasonable and comprehensive fashion. *GAVITUS 1999*'s omission of the Religion category and subcategories leads to a 2002 grade of F in comparison to the 2001 rating of D.
Comparable Data	C	The funding of research produces data. However, foundations have not funded the presentation of data in ways that sufficiently facilitate comparisons, either between sources or within the same source.
Review of Major Questionable Findings	D	Foundations have not funded efforts that have adequately reviewed and addressed major questionable findings in national philanthropy estimates.
Availability of Data	A	Foundations generally emphasize the need for dissemination and making data available.
Validity of Data	F	Foundations have not taken comprehensive steps to maximize the likelihood of valid, integrated measurement of philanthropy. There are not adequate mechanisms in place to follow up on the coordinated implementation of, and comprehension of, the various streams of research that have been funded.

U.S. Government Internal Revenue Service Form 990

Overall Grade: C-

Evaluation Category	Grade	Evaluation Comments
Annual Measurement	A	Form 990 annually addresses issues related to the measurement of philanthropy.
Adjustments for Population and Income	F	The IRS Form 990 does not request a breakout of giving by living donors such that a measurement could be more precisely adjusted for population and income.
Report Available for Timely Review	—	
Distance from For-Profit Counsel	A	The IRS Form 990 has sufficient independence and distance from the influence and agenda of those who have a vested interest in the outcome of any measurement of philanthropy.
Consistency over Time	A	Form 990 provides a reasonable degree of consistency over time.
Treatment of Religion	F	Form 990 does not ask whether an organization is constituted as, governed as, or defines itself as "faith-based" or "secular." As a result, parachurch activity cannot be adequately evaluated. The result is an overly secularized view of nonprofit activity.
Comparable Data	F	Form 990 data collection is critically flawed in terms of providing comparable data, in that it does not request information about donations from living individuals, nor does it allow an organization to identify its governance as "faith-based" or "secular."

U.S. Government Internal Revenue Service Form 990, continued		
Review of Major Questionable Findings	D	Form 990 has not addressed the need for the implementation of a classification system that includes a clear determination of faith based or secular organizations, or donations by living individuals.
Availability of Data	D	The IRS has not computerized Form 990 so that summary data is available to donors, researchers and the media for independent analysis. Such computerization has been discussed beginning with the Filer Commission papers published in 1977.[51]
Validity of Data	F	The IRS has not taken comprehensive steps to maximize the likelihood of valid, integrated measurement of philanthropy. The full commitment of the federal government, including the Internal Revenue Service and the Office of Management and Budget, as well as the American Institute of Certified Public Accountants, would need to be marshaled to revise Form 990 to yield a sound measure of individual giving by living donors.

U.S. Government Efforts to Secure and Disseminate Philanthropy Information Overall Grade: C-		
Evaluation Category	Grade	Evaluation Comments
Annual Measurement	C	The U.S. Government is involved in the annual Form 990 collection, and in the *Statistical Abstract* tables on philanthropy. However, the U.S. Government does not systematically address issues related to the annual measurement of philanthropy.
Adjustments for Population and Income	F	The U.S. Government does not adequately address issues of the measurement of philanthropy adjusted for population and income.
Report Available for Timely Review	A	Through the *Statistical Abstract*, the U.S. Government annually disseminates philanthropy data.
Distance from For-Profit Counsel	A	The U.S. Government has sufficient independence and distance from the influence and agenda of those who have a vested interest in the outcome of any measures of philanthropy.
Consistency over Time	A	The U.S. Government approaches the area with a reasonable degree of consistency over the years.
Treatment of Religion	F	The U.S. Government has not encouraged the treatment of religion in a reasonable and comprehensive fashion.
Comparable Data	F	The U.S. Government has not facilitated or encouraged the development of comparable data.
Review of Major Questionable Findings	D	While the U.S. Government revises its publications, it has not addressed major questionable findings, such as the lack of data for contributions from living individuals, or the distinction between faith-based and secular organizations.
Availability of Data	C	The U.S. Government provides information to researchers but could improve.
Validity of Data	F	The U.S. Government has not taken comprehensive steps to maximize the likelihood of valid, integrated measurement of philanthropy. This fact is particularly true in the category of donations from living individuals.

---

[51]Burton A. Weisbrod and Stephen H. Long, "The Size of the Voluntary Nonprofit Sector: Concepts and Measures," *History, Trends, and Current Magnitudes*, Vol. 1 in the series, *Research Papers Sponsored by The Commission on Private Philanthropy and Public Needs*, (Washington, DC: Department of the Treasury, 1977), p. 360, n. 17.

National Bureau of Economic Research		
Overall Grade: F		
Annual Measurement	F	The National Bureau of Economic Research does not address issues related to the annual measurement of philanthropy in a regular way through one of its standing programs.
Adjustments for Population and Income	—	
Report Available for Timely Review	—	
Distance from For-Profit Counsel	—	
Consistency over Time	—	
Treatment of Religion	—	
Comparable Data	—	
Review of Major Questionable Findings	—	
Availability of Data	—	
Validity of Data	—	
Validity of Data	—	

Urban Institute Efforts, Both in Cooperation with the U.S. Government and Independently		
Overall Grade: D+		
Evaluation Category	Grade	Evaluation Comment
Annual Measurement	D	In 2001, even though the Urban Institute did not publish an estimate of philanthropy, the Urban Institute received an A for this category because of its infrastructure work that could reasonably result in improved annual measures of philanthropy. That is, through its work with the U.S. Government and Form 990, as well as the Center's work with the Unified Chart of Accounts and its National Center for Charitable Statistics, the Urban Institute addressed issues related to the annual measurement of philanthropy.
		In 2002, the rating for this category was downgraded to a D because Urban Institute explicitly involved itself with the occasional publication of specific measures of philanthropy by virtue of co-publishing *The New Nonprofit Almanac and Desk Reference* (Jossey-Bass, 2002) with Independent Sector. [52]

---

[52] Murray S. Weitzman, Nadine T. Jalandoni, Independent Sector, and Linda M. Lampkin, Thomas H. Pollak, Urban Institute, *The New Nonprofit Almanac and Desk Reference* (New York: John Wiley & Sons/Jossey-Bass, 2002).

Urban Institute Efforts, Both in Cooperation with the U.S. Government and Independently, continued		
Adjustments for Population and Income	D	Rated in 2002 for the first time based on the co-publication of *The New Nonprofit Almanac and Desk Reference* (Jossey-Bass, 2002) with Independent Sector, Urban Institute's D rating reflects two countervailing realities as illustrated by the following examples. Individual giving data adjusts for changes in population and income in *The New Nonprofit Almanac* Table 3.4. However, the accompanying Figure 3.4 graphs per capita individual income only in the overly positive categories of constant 1997 dollars and current dollars, excluding individual giving as a percentage of personal income presented in Table 3.4. Chapter 3, "Trends in Private Giving" introductory remarks do not adjust for changes in population and income. Chapter 4 considers subsector performance, again without adjusting for population or income in graphics addressing change over time. A further contribution to the D grade comes from the March 12, 2002 press release for *The New Nonprofit Almanac*. The release stated, "In addition to the growth in the number of organizations, the total annual revenue of the independent sector increased from $317 billion in 1987 to an estimated $665 billion in 1997."[53] Adjustment for population and income was neither included nor, as a result, emphasized in the press release.
Report Available for Timely Review	D	Rated in 2002 for the first time based on the co-publication of *The New Nonprofit Almanac and Desk Reference* with Independent Sector, Urban Institute's D rating stems from Independent Sector's release of *The New Nonprofit Almanac In Brief—2001*[54] on July 18, 2001[55] and Independent Sector and Urban Institute releasing *The New Nonprofit Almanac and Desk Reference* on March 12, 2002.[56]
Distance from For-Profit Counsel	A	The Urban Institute has sufficient independence and distance from the influence and agenda of those who have a vested interest in the outcome of any measurement of philanthropy.
Consistency over Time	D	Rated in 2002 for the first time based on the co-publication of *The New Nonprofit Almanac and Desk* Reference[57] with Independent Sector, Urban Institute's D rating is based on the shift from an emerging focus on a Form 990-based measure of individual giving to the lending of its organization reputation to the promulgation and furtherance of a number of well-entrenched shortcomings in the measurement of philanthropy.
Treatment of Religion	F	The Urban Institute does not treat religion in a reasonable and comprehensive fashion, primarily due to weaknesses in the classification system for which it carries major responsibility.

[53] Independent Sector; "New Nonprofit Almanac Gives Detailed Information on Size and Scope of Sector: Joint Independent Sector and Urban Institute Resource Provides New Insights Into How Nonprofits Work;" published March 12, 2002; <http://www.independentsector.org/media/NA01PR.html>; p. 1 of 9/26/02 5:09 PM printout.
[54] *The Nonprofit Almanac in Brief—2001: Facts and figures from the forthcoming New Nonprofit Almanac and Desk Reference* and *Giving and Volunteering in the United States*, 1999, (Washington, DC: Independent Sector, 2001).
[55] Independent Sector; "Number of Charities Grows 74% in Just Over Decade: New Independent Sector Report Counts 1.6 Million Nonprofit Organizations, Including 734,000 Charities;" published July 18, 2001; <http://www.independentsector.org/media/InBriefPR.html>; p. 1 of 8/14/01 10:37 AM printout.
[56] Independent Sector; "New Nonprofit Almanac Gives Detailed Information on Size and Scope of Sector: Joint Independent Sector and Urban Institute Resource Provides New Insights Into How Nonprofits Work;" published March 12, 2002; <http://www.independentsector.org/media/NA01PR.html>; p. 1 of 9/26/02 5:09 PM printout.
[57] Weitzman, et al., *The New Nonprofit Almanac and Desk Reference*.

Comparable Data	D	Rated in 2002 for the first time based on the co-publication of *The New Nonprofit Almanac and Desk Reference* (Jossey-Bass, 2002) with Independent Sector, Urban Institute's D rating reflects the fact that considerably more intentional and higher quality work is necessary to address the need for a critical approach to the limitations in comparability between data from Independent Sector, the American Association of Fund-Raising Counsel's (AAFRC) *Giving USA*, and U.S. IRS Form 990—employing standardized National Taxonomy of Exempt Entities major group categories.
Review of Major Questionable Findings	D	Rated in 2002 for the first time based on the co-publication of *The New Nonprofit Almanac and Desk Reference* (Jossey-Bass, 2002) with Independent Sector, Urban Institute's D rating reflects the fact that the Urban Institute reported but did not review the questionable American Association of Fund-Raising Counsel's *Giving USA* finding that there was a 27% change in Human Services from 1997 to 1998.
Availability of Data	C	While the Urban Institute was rated A in 2001 for publishing the data it has so that it is available to researchers for independent analysis, its rating was downgraded to C in 2002. This change was a function of inadequate specificity in its documentation and/or publication of source data for some of the tables and technical notes in *The New Nonprofit Almanac and Desk Reference* (Jossey-Bass, 2002) which the Urban Institute co-published with Independent Sector in 2002. This weakness is observed in relation to the critically important area of giving by individuals. *The New Nonprofit Almanac* Table 3.3 and Sources notes on page 59, Table 3.6 on page 64, with the accompanying technical note on pages 218-219, neither list methodological or formulaic detail, nor provide or reference documentation and rationale for *The New Nonprofit Almanac's* shift from the AAFRC's *Giving USA* individual giving series for the 1986-1998 period, while following the *Giving USA* series from 1964-1985. Both *The New Nonprofit Almanac* and the AFFRC *Giving USA*[58] series adjust for non-itemizer giving. *The New Nonprofit Almanac* Table 3.2, "Distribution of Private Contributions by Recipient Area: AAFRC Trust for Philanthropy Estimates, 1968-1998," compares eight "Recipient" areas. A Note states, "Giving to some categories prior to 1985 cannot be compared to giving since 1985 because of different statistical tabulation and analysis procedures."[59] This lack of specificity renders major portions of the Table unintelligible. The last column of the same Table 3.2 is labeled "Unclassified" and is referenced to "AAFRC Trust for Philanthropy, 1999." Yet, AAFRC's *Giving USA 1999* has the Recipient category of "Unallocated" for 1968-1998 along with the Recipient category of "Gifts to Foundations" for the years 1978-1998.
Validity of Data	D	A fundamental flaw in the Urban Institute's Unified Chart of Accounts (UCOA) is that it does not provide a measure of individual giving distinct from business giving. Urban Institute has also not acknowledged and provided for the distinction between faith-based and secular governance categories within recipient categories to provide for an accurate measure of religion. Urban Institute would need to make a policy decision to seek cooperation between the U.S. Government and the American Institute of Public Accountants to revise both Form 990 and the UCOA to make the necessary changes to produce a sound measurement of philanthropy by source and recipient categories.

---

[58] Ann Kaplan, ed., *Giving USA 1999* (New York: AAFRC Trust for Philanthropy, 1999), p. 148-149.
[59] Murray S. Weitzman, Nadine T. Jalandoni, Independent Sector, and Linda M. Lampkin, Thomas H. Pollak, Urban Institute, *The New Nonprofit Almanac and Desk Reference* (New York: John Wiley & Sons/Jossey-Bass, 2002), p. 57.

Universities with Philanthropy Centers[60]		
Overall Grade: F		
Evaluation Category	Grade	Evaluation Comments
Annual Measurement	F	Universities do not systematically address issues related to the annual measurement of philanthropic giving. This is seen in part by the fact that published material suggests that academics enlisted to assist with the American Association of Fundraising Counsel's *Giving USA* annual reports have focused unduly on the for-profit fundraising industry's agenda of providing most recent year estimates through *Giving USA*, rather than the type of comprehensive, in-depth, scholarly analysis of philanthropy engaged in by academics enlisted by the Commission on Private Philanthropy and Public Needs in the mid-1970s.
Adjustments for Population and Income	—	
Report Available for Timely Review	—	
Distance from For-Profit Counsel	—	
Consistency over Time	—	
Treatment of Religion	—	
Comparable Data	—	
Review of Major Questionable Findings	—	
Availability of Data	—	
Validity of Data	—	

[60]At "Research: Academic Centers Focusing on the Study of Philanthropy;" Independent Sector; <http://www.indepsec.org/programs/research/centers>; published 2000; pp. 1-3 of 8/23/01 4:35 PM printout, 35 "Academic Centers Focusing on the Study of Philanthropy" were listed. These included: Boston College, Case Western University, [City] University of New York, Duke University, George Mason University, Harvard University, Indiana University/Purdue University, Loyola University, New York University, Northwestern University, Seton Hall University, Southern Methodist University, Texas Christian University, Tufts University, University of California-Berkeley, University of California-San Francisco, University of Maryland, University of Missouri-Kansas City, University of Pennsylvania, Virginia Polytechnic Institute and State University, and Yale University.

chapter 8

Two Solutions for the Vacuum of Leadership in the Church in the U.S.

HIGHLIGHTS

Giving trends between 1968 and 2000 are evidence that church members have not had a good enough reason to increase, rather than decrease, the portion of income they spend on the church.

This situation exists because there is a vacuum of leadership in the church.

A proposed solution to negative giving trends includes two parts. The goal of both parts is to leverage general church member giving to scale in keeping with members' potential giving levels, and in keeping with needs around the globe, particularly those of children.

The first facet of the proposed solution involves a decision to mobilize. A blue-ribbon commission would be formed. This commission would be asked: (1) to gain coordinated support across the whole spectrum of the historically Christian church in the U.S. for a "positive agenda for affluence" that will encourage church members to increase giving; (2) secure $1.25 billion annually for 10 years from wealthy donors to match new money raised by congregations to support additional mission activities; and (3) promote nationally the positive agenda and the matching idea.

The second facet of the proposed solution to negative church member giving patterns is the development of a dynamic Web-based feedback system. The system could be used independently by any denomination for its own mission projects. The software for the Web-based feedback system would: (1) provide a way to list mission projects that qualify for the matching funds; (2) allow individual congregations to know how much money is needed for a particular project; and (3) provide regular and project-specific feedback to congregations that donated to a particular mission activity.

NARRATIVE

The 1968-2000 giving trends analyzed in other chapters of this volume make clear that church member giving did not increase at a rate that kept up with incomes that were expanding between the years 1968 and 2000. As a result, the percentage of income donated to the church was smaller in the year 2000 than in 1968.

A variety of issues contributed to the lack of growth in church giving as a percentage of income. One key contributing factor is the vacuum of church leadership. At any level of the church, leaders were not calling for increased giving from church members for any purpose other than institutional maintenance. The 1968-2000 giving tables indicate that this maintenance agenda did not appeal to church members enough to cause them to invest more of their resources in the church. Therefore, giving levels moved away from the goal of a congregation-wide average of ten percent, rather than toward the standard of the tithe.

In keeping with the maintenance agenda, Congregational Finances, focusing on the needs of current members, absorbed the vast majority of the increased dollars that were given between 1968 and 2000.

During the long U.S. economic expansion, which was continuing in the year 2000, giving as a portion of income could have returned to the level of the late 1960s or even to Depression-era levels, both of which were higher than the percent of income given in 2000. It would also have been possible to surpass those earlier donation levels, moving decisively toward the tithe on a congregation-wide scale.

One major factor helped to create these declining trends. Giving levels did not increase because there has been a vacuum of trusted leadership calling on church members to reverse present trends for a purpose that members feel is worthy of their investment.[1]

As noted in the earlier Trends chapter of this volume, the current condition of church giving need not define future patterns. Specific steps could be taken, if church leadership were to emerge and focus on giving to others as a priority.

Figures 21 and 22 describe two aspects of a proposed solution to address this vacuum of leadership. One element of the proposed solution calls for a decision to mobilize. The second part of the solution is the development of a dynamic feedback system to encourage real partnership between church members in the U.S. and their denominational mission activities.

Proposed Solution Part A: Decision to Mobilize. Figure 21 presents one aspect of the proposed solution to the present vacuum of leadership regarding church giving patterns.

The summary of this solution is "Decision to Mobilize."

National church leaders need to make a decision to mobilize church members such that increased giving to the church will be a positive side effect of members' desire to take action.

---

[1] For a discussion of dynamics related to this vacuum of leadership in the church, see John Ronsvalle and Sylvia Ronsvalle, "Systems and Subsystems Analysis: A Case Study," *The State of Church Giving through 1998* (Champaign, Ill.: empty tomb, inc., 2000), pp.°77-95, or at <http://www.emptytomb.org/SystemsSubsystems.pdf>.

Figure 21:   Vacuum of Leadership Proposed Solution Part A:
Decision to Mobilize

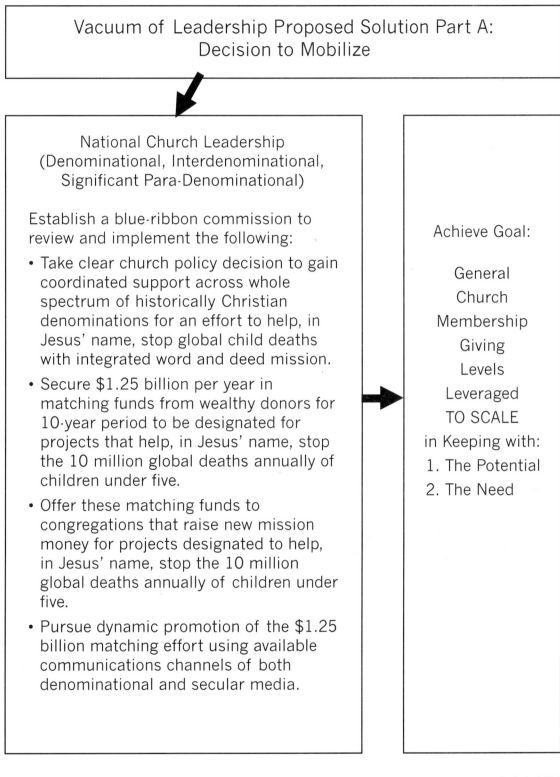

**Vacuum of Leadership Proposed Solution Part A:
Decision to Mobilize**

National Church Leadership
(Denominational, Interdenominational,
Significant Para-Denominational)

Establish a blue-ribbon commission to review and implement the following:

• Take clear church policy decision to gain coordinated support across whole spectrum of historically Christian denominations for an effort to help, in Jesus' name, stop global child deaths with integrated word and deed mission.

• Secure $1.25 billion per year in matching funds from wealthy donors for 10-year period to be designated for projects that help, in Jesus' name, stop the 10 million global deaths annually of children under five.

• Offer these matching funds to congregations that raise new mission money for projects designated to help, in Jesus' name, stop the 10 million global deaths annually of children under five.

• Pursue dynamic promotion of the $1.25 billion matching effort using available communications channels of both denominational and secular media.

Achieve Goal:

General
Church
Membership
Giving
Levels
Leveraged
TO SCALE
in Keeping with:
1. The Potential
2. The Need

empty tomb, inc. 2002

93

In the present discussion, the idea of "national church leaders" has a broad definition. It certainly will include denominational leaders. It is likely that this definition will also include leaders of interdenominational groups. In addition, given the present functioning of the church in the U.S., there may be significant para-denominational groups that should be involved in mobilizing church members. These para-denominational groups probably have no formal affiliation with the denominational church structures in the U.S. Yet, they maintain a national presence that could help to mobilize all church members.

Of course, the idea of mobilizing church members to increase giving is much easier to say than to do. Present relatively low giving levels exist in spite of various efforts to increase donations to the church. Nonprofit and for-profit groups, both denominationally-affiliated and independent, produce libraries full of technique manuals and campaign outlines intended to address the giving issue. The giving data for 1968-2000 suggest that a different approach is needed to change the long-established low levels of giving.

The proposed solution includes the forming of a blue-ribbon commission made up of respected representatives of denominational, interdenominational and para-denominational groups. While this panel would be only advisory to national denominational structures, the opinions of its members should carry enough practical authority that the recommendations will carry weight in national church leadership circles.

The present solution proposes that the commission represent the "historically Christian church," as a matter of both conviction and efficiency.[2] In that setting, a basic core set of beliefs may be assumed. That set of beliefs may have to be narrowly defined. However, it should be possible for this group to focus on what they have in common, instead of the common emphasis of differences that separate them. Given the challenge of securing agreement among the broad spectrum of Christian traditions in the U.S., even when they share the same religious texts, the commission would be limited to historically Christian churches.

Traditionally, there has been no forum that fosters a broad national dialogue among these varied Christian communions.

The empty tomb, inc. Stewardship Project National Advisory Committee bridged some, but not all, of these boundaries from 1992-1995. Those participating in the Stewardship Project National Advisory Committee represented the Roman Catholic church, seven communions that would be termed mainline Protestant communions, and seven that might be termed evangelical communions. Several of the committee members expressed surprise at the degree of similarity in experience among the otherwise disparate groups when the discussion focused on the effective practice of financial stewardship. The experience of the National Advisory Committee demonstrated that a broad spectrum of Christians could interact about clearly defined common interests, and pursue the common good of the body of Christ

---

[2] The definition of "historically Christian" includes that combination of believers with a historically acknowledged confession of the faith, including Roman Catholic, other Catholic, mainline Protestant, Orthodox, Evangelical, Pentecostal/Charismatic, Baptist, Anabaptist, and Fundamental communions..

as a whole. These fifteen national stewardship officials gathered twice during the three years of the project and were able to agree on seven conclusions about stewardship as it is practiced in the U.S.[3]

More recently, another group, named "Christian Churches Together in the U.S.A.," has begun an intentional dialogue among Christians. In April 2002, representatives of 20 denominations in the U.S., as well as two interdenominational and two para-denominational groups, signed a draft statement for this emerging body. The statement reads:

> Christian Churches Together in the U.S.A. gathers together those churches and Christian communities which acknowledging God's revelation in Christ, confesses the Lord Jesus Christ as God and Savior according to the Scripture, and in obedience to God's will and in the power of the Holy Spirit commit themselves to seek a deepening of their communion with Christ and with one another; to fulfill their mission to proclaim the Gospel by common witness and service in the world for the glory of the one God, Father, Son and Holy Spirit.[4]

The communions signing the statement included representatives of the Roman Catholic Church, as well as Orthodox, mainline Protestant and evangelical Protestant communions. A group such as Christian Churches Together in the U.S.A. could be a broad enough entity to establish the type of blue-ribbon commission called for in the presently proposed solution.

In whatever manner that leaders are gathered to form the blue-ribbon commission, the commission will need sufficient practical authority that its recommendations will be seriously considered by the broad array of denominational leaders in the United States.

It is proposed that the commission not study the issue of giving, but rather be given the charge to review and implement several action steps that set the stage for increased church member giving.

Policy Decision. The first step for the commission would be to take a clear church policy decision to gain support across the whole spectrum of the historically Christian church for a common objective. To use one of the recommendations from the empty tomb, inc. Stewardship Project National Advisory Committee, the commission would secure support from a broad spectrum of church leaders for an agreed-upon "positive agenda for affluence." This positive agenda would not replace the many agenda items being pursued by church

---

[3] The conclusions were presented in *Behind the Stained Glass Windows: Money Dynamics in the Church* (Baker Books, 1996), p. 293. As noted at the meeting, the conclusions were not "word-smithed" but rather were designed to promote further dialogue. The conclusions were:
1. Owning the gap between beliefs and practice.
2. Recognizing creative tension between reality and vision.
3. Need for conversion/formation, which is part of the process.
4. Leadership needs conversion and formation in personal stewardship and to be given a level of confidence and courage in terms of corporate leadership.
5. A whole-life response to the Great Commandment of Jesus (Mark 12:29-31), to be disciples who are stewards.
6. The church needs a positive agenda for the great affluence in our society.
7. Healthy churches produce generous people

[4] "Christian Churches Together in the U.S.A.: An Invitation to a Journey," Chicago, IL, April 6, 2002.

leaders independently and in cooperation with others. The positive agenda identified by the commission, and supported by church leaders, would be a rallying point around which actions to reverse giving trends could focus. An agenda for affluence that includes an action component would provide both a measurable goal, and a clear general concept with which leaders could agree.

The action focus recommended in this proposed solution to address the present vacuum of leadership is to stem the child death rate globally. More specifically, the suggested focus is an effort to help, in Jesus' name, stop global child deaths through integrated word and deed mission.[5]

Why global child deaths? Several points recommend this particular theme of global child deaths.

First, the need is compelling enough to attract the immediate attention of all church members. One problem in any effort to increase giving among church members is the difficulty of capturing church members' imaginations. The church's message of service to others competes with the most sophisticated advertising and communication industry in the world promoting a message of "self." In an era of "sound bites," any agenda on which church leaders hope to build increased financial discipleship must immediately touch the hearts and grab the attention of church members. The deaths of children is an issue that is instantly clear to busy church members with varying levels of commitment to the church.

Second, research by the authors concluded that most church members in the U.S. have been educated to "crisis fundraising." Any pastor will tell you that it is easier to raise money for a leaky roof than for the general operating budget. In fact, this aspect of stewardship practice in the U.S. is very negative. Church members are not discipled, or taught to observe the teachings of their faith, about integrating faith and money. Rather, members are educated to pay the bills of the congregation or to address an emergency. Given the reality of the present state of stewardship, the plight of dying children is a "silent emergency" as the late James Grant termed it. Therefore, as a starting point, this positive agenda for affluence presents a compelling need that will be easily understood by church members who presently equate the need to give with an emergency.

Third, this particular goal is a good choice because there is already a consensus about it among a broad spectrum of church leaders in the U.S. The work of the commission can build on that consensus. In 2001, a national survey of 202 historically Christian communions in the U.S. resulted in a 41% response rate. Of those responding, 81% agreed with the statement, "Church members in the United States should increase giving through their churches in an effort to stop the millions of annual preventable global child deaths in Jesus' name." Leaders agreed from denominations that are African-American, Anabaptist, Baptist, Evangelical, Fundamental, Mainline Protestant, Orthodox, other Catholic, Pentecostal, and Roman Catholic.

---

[5] The importance of the integration of word and deed is discussed in John Ronsvalle and Sylvia Ronsvalle, "The Theological Implications of Church Member Giving Patterns," *The State of Church Giving through 1995* (Champaign, IL: empty tomb, inc., 1997), pp. 83-96, also available at <http://www.emptytomb.org/research.implications.html>.

It should be noted that of those who agreed, two expressed concern that the phrase "in Jesus' name" be grammatically moved so as to avoid any confusion in the phrasing. Thus, a national policy decision to promote "an effort to help, in Jesus' name, stop global child deaths" has an already demonstrated broad base of support among church leaders in the U.S.[6]

Finally, the particular focus on stopping global child deaths builds on a long tradition of outreach within the historically Christian church that has become more relevant in light of recent events. Church outreach in word and deed, through basic health clinics, education institutions, hunger and disaster relief, all pre-date the post-September 11, 2001 consensus that poverty must be addressed in order to prevent future terrorism.

After the horrible tragedy of 9/11, world leaders acknowledged a relationship between poverty and terrorist activity. In March 2002, global leaders gathered in Monterrey, Mexico for a United Nations summit on poverty. One conclusion from that meeting was that there is an association between desperate poverty and terrorist actions. An Associated Press article about the "Monterrey Consensus" stated, "Leaders of poor countries from Tunisia to Venezuela and rich countries from France to the United States all agreed that terrorism will not be eliminated without a major push to help the world's poorest. Three billion people— half the world's population—live on less than $2 a day."[7]

In a second article on the topic, President George W. Bush was quoted as stating, "We fight against poverty because hope is an answer to terrorism."[8]

Church structures based in the U.S. have long been on the front lines in many of the world's poorest areas, fighting poverty not to end terrorism, but to demonstrate the good news of Jesus Christ in word and deed. In light of post-9/11 perspectives, these ongoing works take on new significance. Many of these church-related outreaches impact the well-being of children. As one United Methodist Board of Global Ministries official wrote to the authors, "Just about every program UMCOR supports assists children directly or indirectly."

Yet, an important point about these ongoing activities of church mission agencies has not been generally understood. The value of these activities is evident to those in direct contact with the people in need. It is also clear to those poor people receiving the benefits of these activities, and to the denominational and agency supervisors who receive reports about these activities. What most church leaders have not understood is that church members in the U.S. could benefit greatly from a more complete understanding of the church's helping works. That fact is particularly painful because church members in the U.S. are in great need of healing in their attitudes toward faith and money; knowing more about these church efforts to impact global need could be an agent of transformation for these members . Without

---

[6] For a full discussion of this survey, see "National Church Leaders Response Form" in John Ronsvalle and Sylvia Ronsvalle, *The State of Church Giving through 1999* (Champaign, IL: empty tomb, inc., 2001), pp. 79-119. A synopsis is available at <http://www.emptytomb.org/research.html#Response Form>.

[7] Niko Price, "World Leaders to Give More to Poor," the Associated Press AP-NY-03-22-02 1430EST, printed from AOL News on March 22, 2002.

[8] Sandra Sobieraj, "Bush Vows to Help Globes Poor," the Associated Press AP-NY-03-22-02 1459EST, printed from AOL News on March 22, 2002.

a compelling need to raise their vision, most church members are abandoned to the self-centeredness resulting from a steady diet of consumer advertising promoting overindulgence. Within the Christian tradition, many verses sound like an oxymoronic idea: It is the rich, and not the poor, who are in greater need. That concept challenges the basic assumption of a culture built on "more" equaling "better." Yet the Roman philosopher Juvenal, documenting the latter days of a decaying empire, made an observation that may also speak to early 21st century American culture when he wrote, "Luxury, more deadly than war, broods over the city." It may be harder to successfully handle affluence than to overcome strife, including poverty.

If the Christian Scriptures are accurate, then church members who have attained a level of comfort beyond basic needs are in potential spiritual trouble.[9] To ask those members only to pay for keeping the church institutional structure functioning is to fail them at a point of their own need. The excellent work conducted by church mission agencies that addresses both the physical and spiritual needs of global neighbors, particularly needs of children, could be a vital tool to help focus church members in the U.S. on "others" rather than "self." The process of giving to a gripping and vital cause becomes a strategy for spiritual growth rather than an institutional maintenance activity. It may not only be more blessed to give than to receive. It may also be absolutely necessary for the spiritual health of church members in the U.S. to discover a more constructive use of a larger portion of their resources than increased and sustained personal consumption.

Precisely because most, if not all, Christian communions already have efforts in place to address the needs of children around the globe, the agreement sought by the blue-ribbon commission would actually be a recognition and affirmation of what is already taking place. This fact means that the blue-ribbon commission would not be designing a new distribution agency. Rather, the commission's task would be to ask church leaders to recognize and acknowledge the common agenda already being pursued to a relatively limited extent among the denominations in the U.S., and to affirm at a priority level the value of increasing the level of church member support for each denomination's own related activities.

Thus, an effort of helping, in Jesus' name, to stop global child deaths is recommended as the focus for a policy decision to gain coordinated support across the whole spectrum of historically Christian churches in the U.S.

Secure $1.25 billion Per Year in Matching Funds. A general practical consensus increases in value as it moves from theory to action. Agreeing that church members should increase giving to help, in Jesus' name, stop global child deaths does not help church members in the U.S. grow in faith, nor does it help the dying children, unless that agreement translates into increased giving.

Therefore, the next facet of this proposed solution to the vacuum of church leadership is that the blue-ribbon commission should secure matching funds from wealthy individual donors. These funds will then be offered to congregations that raise new mission money, in addition to their current budgets, to support mission projects that focus on the basic, life-sustenance needs of children.

---

[9] For a discussion of this point, see Ronsvalle, "Theological Implications."

The amount of matching money available needs to be significant enough to communicate a serious attempt to impact global need in Jesus' name. The amount of $1.25 billion a year was arrived at as follows.

In 1990, James Grant, then executive director of UNICEF, estimated that "a programme to prevent the great majority of child deaths and child malnutrition in the decade ahead might reach approximately $2.5 billion per year by the late 1990s."[10] Progress has been made and the death rate is no longer an estimated 40,000 children under five dying each day around the globe, most from preventable poverty conditions. However, a current daily total of 29,000 is still too high for those who claim loyalty to a compassionate and merciful God through Jesus Christ.

Given that a degree of monetary inflation and growth in the economy has occurred over the past decade, one might estimate that the $2.5 billion a year necessary in the 1990s would have doubled by the present decade. That would mean that $5 billion a year is needed in this decade to decrease the rate of global child deaths significantly. If the commission were to raise $1.25 billion, and match it with another $1.25 billion from congregations, then churches in the U.S. would be salting global conditions by providing $2.5 billion, or perhaps half the estimated money needed each year for ten years to address this goal.

 It is important to note that, under this proposal, the blue-ribbon commission would not replace individual denominations in distributing the additional money. This proposal does not include a new distribution agency. Church members would be donating the money directly to their local congregations, and the congregations would be using their established distribution channels to support the mission projects of their choice by forwarding the matching money. The commission's job would be that of an incentive and promotion agency, and not that of a distribution agency.

Offer the Matching Funds to Congregations. The blue-ribbon commission that raises $1.25 billion a year would offer to match, dollar for dollar, "new money" raised by congregations to support projects of the congregation's choice that focus on children's needs. This matching offer moves the "positive agenda for affluence" from theory to practice.

The donors from whom the $1.25 billion was secured would be given the opportunity to "leverage" their giving. The term "leverage" applies in the following way. If a donor provided $1 directly to a project that addresses the needs of dying children, the project would have $1 to spend. In contrast, through the commission's matching efforts, every $1 in matching funds that a donor provides doubles its impact. The mission project would receive both the $1 from the matching money donor and $1 from a congregation. Further, the donor would be encouraging members in the congregations that receive matching money to increase giving to missions. The donor would be helping needy children overseas with the financial gift, and strategically involving church members in the U.S. in an integration of their faith with practice. One might say that not only are the dollars doubled through the financial matching arrangement, but the impact is doubled as well, affecting both church members in the U.S. and the children helped through the mission projects.

---

[10] James P. Grant, *The State of the World's Children 1990* (New York: Oxford University Press, 1990), p 16.

There are two groups of church members who are particularly under-challenged by present stewardship practices, and who could benefit from the significant challenge presented by the $1.25 billion matching proposal.

One group includes higher-income congregation members who do not feel that the congregation is doing anything important enough to merit the large donations of which they are capable. These congregation members are often approached for lead gifts by secular universities, medical institutions, and when a congregation undertakes a capital campaign. However, the level of *regular* giving to the congregation's operating budget is not on a par with the well-to-do person's ability. Sometimes, this member is concerned lest she "overwhelm" the congregation with the large level of donation of which she is capable. Sometimes he does not want to encourage a "welfare" mentality so that other congregation members become dependent on his giving. However, another reason voiced by some of these more wealthy members is that the congregation is not doing anything important enough, or at a large enough scale, to merit the level of support that the member could give. Many of these individuals are willing to give significantly when presented with a challenge they consider valid. The problem may be that the congregation's institutional maintenance agenda does not provide a compelling reason for them to give to their congregation in keeping with their capability. These people may be attracted by the idea of doubling their donation for a specific project, and of pursuing a measurable goal in coordination with a national agenda that provides some hope of having an impact on an obvious need.

The second group that could benefit very much from this part of the solution is much larger than the first. Initial limited evidence supports a broad estimate that 30-50% of resident members give little or nothing of record to their congregations. Present giving patterns establish that these people are not going to contribute to the general operations or current mission of the church. According to the numbers, they have not done so, although they have been given every opportunity to participate. If these uninvolved, or under-involved, members would begin to provide even relatively small amounts of new mission money to impact need through their congregations, the immediate results would be dynamic. Encouraging these people to give to an undeniable need, such as a national effort to help, in Jesus' name, stop global child deaths, may provide a fresh way for members uninvolved in financial discipleship to integrate their faith with their behavior in a measurable fashion, that is, through their regular giving to church.

Pursue Dynamic Promotion of the Matching. Those who are currently uninvolved in the financial life of their congregations have inertia on their side. Moving from little involvement to greater involvement is more difficult than increasing present giving levels in someone who already has made the decision to give. That is why church leaders generally turn to people who already give to ask them to give more, rather than expending the substantial effort involved in asking people who don't give to give a little.

Thus, the blue-ribbon commission should include people who are gifted in using communication channels to promote both the positive agenda for affluence—an effort to help, in Jesus' name, stop global child deaths—and the matching opportunity. As one national denominational official observed in a formative discussion of the proposed solution, "What you are talking about is a national public relations campaign."

The commission could use great ingenuity in creating national momentum to raise members' sights beyond their own immediate concerns. The solution for reversing negative giving patterns is to provide members with an agenda they perceive as worthy of their support. To invest in a plan, members will need to know about the plan. Promoting the agenda, the value of it, and the benefits of increased faithfulness to church members, would also be a vital responsibility of the commission. To assume that church members recognize their own need to give is naïve. The positive agenda for affluence will be pursued in a nation that spends billions of dollars convincing its citizens of needs those citizens did not know they had before seeing the advertisements. One might argue that Jesus feeding the 5,000 or healing a leper marketed the message of the Gospel, as well as benefited those being fed or healed. To change giving patterns, an intentional effort to creative a positive atmosphere for changing those giving patterns will be a very necessary component.

Proposed Solution Part B: Feedback System. Figure 22 presents the second aspect of the proposed solution to the present vacuum of leadership regarding church giving patterns.

The summary of this solution is "Feedback System."

One important fact defines the need for this part of the solution. That is, people want to know what their money is doing.

In the empty tomb, inc. Stewardship Project national survey, 89% of the responding pastors agreed with the statement, "Most church members want to know 'what their money is buying' when sent out of the congregation."[11]

Donor reactions to a non-church agency's handling of money also confirm this observation. National headlines began to appear about the management of the dollars contributed in the aftermath of the destruction that occurred on 9-11-2001. The Red Cross received a great outpouring of donations. In the months that followed, however, the Red Cross came under public criticism and scrutiny for the way those contributions were handled. A year later, officials reflected on how the situation could have been handled more constructively. "Red Cross officials say the increased scrutiny has taught them several lessons about dealing with donors. Donors want to know when enough money has been collected, and exactly how new contributions will be used, says Skip Seitz, senior vice president for growth and integrated development."[12]

This conclusion is not good news for most denominations. Given that donors want information about their donations, denominations are confronted with a serious structural problem.

As described in the "Systems and Subsystems Analysis: A Case Study" chapter of *The State of Church Giving through 1998*,[13] most denominations do not provide detailed project-specific feedback to congregations that contribute to their mission activities. In some cases,

---

[11] John Ronsvalle and Sylvia Ronsvalle, *Behind the Stained Glass Windows: Money Dynamics in the Church* (Grand Rapids, MI: Baker Books, 1996), pp. 89-90.

[12] Elizabeth Greene and Brad Wolverton, "Learning the Lessons of September 11: Charities Reassess How They Handled Aid," *The Chronicle of Philanthropy*, September 5, 2002, p. 11.

[13] Ronsvalle, "Systems and Subsystems," *The State of Church Giving through 1998*, pp. 77-95.

Figure 21:   Vacuum of Leadership Proposed Solution Part B:
Feedback System

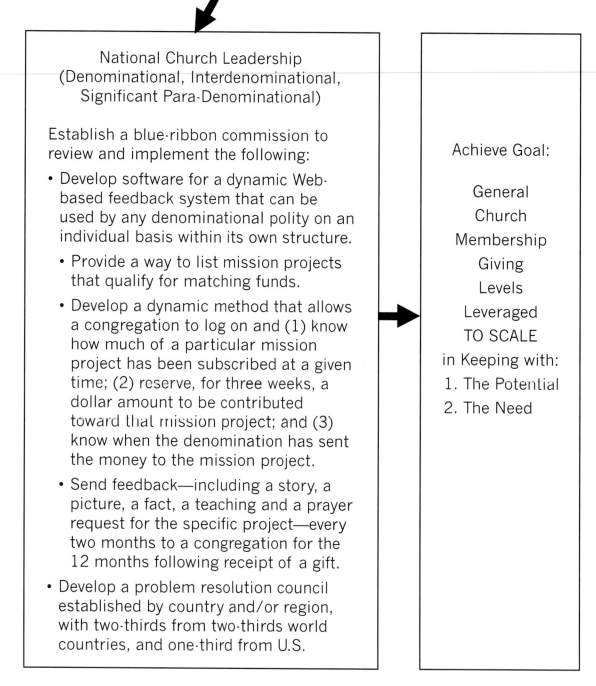

Vacuum of Leadership Proposed Solution Part B:
Feedback System

National Church Leadership
(Denominational, Interdenominational,
Significant Para-Denominational)

Establish a blue-ribbon commission to
review and implement the following:

- Develop software for a dynamic Web-
  based feedback system that can be
  used by any denominational polity on an
  individual basis within its own structure.

  - Provide a way to list mission projects
    that qualify for matching funds.

  - Develop a dynamic method that allows
    a congregation to log on and (1) know
    how much of a particular mission
    project has been subscribed at a given
    time; (2) reserve, for three weeks, a
    dollar amount to be contributed
    toward that mission project; and (3)
    know when the denomination has sent
    the money to the mission project.

  - Send feedback—including a story, a
    picture, a fact, a teaching and a prayer
    request for the specific project—every
    two months to a congregation for the
    12 months following receipt of a gift.

- Develop a problem resolution council
  established by country and/or region,
  with two-thirds from two-thirds world
  countries, and one-third from U.S.

Achieve Goal:

General

Church

Membership

Giving

Levels

Leveraged

TO SCALE

in Keeping with:

1. The Potential
2. The Need

empty tomb, inc. 2002

even a congregation that requests specific information will not be able to obtain it from the denominational structure. This lack of communication is in direct conflict with the donors' desire to know what contributed dollars are doing.

In times past, a denomination might expect congregations to forward money for mission projects with no expectation of specific feedback. The attitude of the 1950s might be summarized as people being content to give because it was the right thing to do. However, the environment has changed considerably. The level of denominational loyalty of the 1990s did not compare favorably with that of previous decades. Of those pastors responding to the Stewardship Project survey, 96% disagreed with the statement, "Most congregations have as strong a denominational identity as they did forty years ago."[14]

Thus, it dearly concerns denominations that other groups will offer individuals and congregations communication services not offered by a denomination. For example, two former officials of the World Bank have established a Web-based "marketplace" for the support of international projects. "Potential donors are able to communicate with a project leader as soon as a project description is posted." The Web host, developmentspace.com, charged seven percent of the money donated for its services when it first began.[15]

Several different Web-based options are now also available for use by local United Way campaigns. For example, United-eWay provides a software program which, according to promotional materials, creates an "enhancement" to existing efforts so that "employees are given choice in how to give, how much to give and where to invest their contributions."[16]

Para-denominational groups have long had the reputation of being responsive to their donors' need for detailed information. This level of service is necessary since para-denominational groups do not have a historical support base that denominations have traditionally counted on. That lack of an established base has encouraged para-denominational groups to pursue entrepreneurial approaches that recognize the donors' desire for information. With the denominational loyalty base eroding, denominations will have to develop some of the same communication skills as other charitable organizations, or risk seeing their level of support diminish.

While some may argue that the decline of denominations is a natural structural evolution, that view may be shortsighted. First, some denominational structures were formed for the efficient use of congregational mission funds. Mission boards, both domestic and foreign, were the first structures formed as denominations took shape. The same efficiencies exist today. If these structures erode, it may be a decade or two before their past value is recognized and their loss mourned. At that point, it may be very difficult to build them again. Meanwhile, the global works that benefited from their existence will stall and in some cases end.

Second, much of the philanthropy education that takes place in the United States takes place in religious congregations. For example, the Independent Sector series on giving has

---

[14] Ronsvalle, *Behind the Stained Glass Windows*, p. 335.

[15] Nicole Wallace, "Web Site to Aid International Projects," *The Chronicle of Philanthropy*, May 16, 2002, p. 33.

[16] "United-eWay: Revolutionizing the World of Charitable Giving, <http://www.united-eay.org/>; 8/22/02, 8:51 AM printout.

repeatedly found a correlation between regular worship attendance and the level of charitable giving.[17] It is conceivable that, without a denominational structure calling attention to issues beyond internal needs, most congregations would continue to encourage support of mission activities beyond members' own needs. It is possible that each congregation might choose one or another para-denominational mission group to support. These diverse mission activities would not be part of a larger coordinated multi-congregational strategy but rather would reflect the individual tastes of the congregation.

However, the trends of giving between 1968 and 2000 heavily favored Congregational Finances over Benevolences, even with regular denominational requests for support. What would happen without denominational efforts to raise the vision of the congregation on a regular basis? Since congregations are such a vital component of philanthropy education in the United States, a further turning inward, with the definition of "charity" being reduced to present members' needs, would have a broad impact on charitable behavior in the U.S. as a whole, and not just in weakening the religious life of the congregations.

For these and other reasons, it is vitally important that denominations respond to the need for improved communication to address congregation members' desire for information about what their mission dollars are doing.

It may be noted that the second part of the present proposed solution was in formation before the authors became aware of other Web-based giving opportunities. The fact that the details of the present proposed solution are similar to services now being offered by other groups suggests that these ideas are addressing commonly acknowledged needs of donors.

Software for a Dynamic Web-based Feedback System. The blue-ribbon commission would also foster the development of software for a dynamic Web-based system to provide feedback about mission projects. The design of the system would be generic enough that any denomination could use it with its own congregations, for the denomination's own mission projects. The software would assist the denomination in addressing donors' desire for project-specific information about mission activities.

The dynamic feedback system would also provide a creative inductive teaching tool. Adults learn on a need-to-know basis. National news recognizes this fact. For example, few Americans knew where Afghanistan was until U.S. soldiers were sent there. Then maps of that part of the globe appeared regularly in TV and print media news reports. Yet church leaders often spend great amounts of time, energy and dollars on didactic education, telling church members what they ought to know rather than responding to what members express a desire to know.

Further, the denominational emphasis on undesignated mission dollars to support the entire structure rather than a specific project runs counter to congregation members' interests. The basic operations of the denomination—and the congregation—can be promoted as the foundation on which valued outreach is built. But only if the congregation and the denomination are providing outreach that is recognized as valuable by the members. In spite of the denominations' present preference for undesignated giving, designated giving

---

[17] Arthur D. Kirsch, et al., *Giving and Volunteering in the United States, 1999 Edition* (Washington, DC: Independent Sector, 2002), pp. 83-84.

to specific mission projects remains popular at the congregational level. Yet, in most denominations, when a congregation contributes to a particular mission activity, there is little specific feedback. Even in denominations that provide for designations to a specific mission project, perhaps over and above general denominational support, no feedback mechanism provides the congregation with desired information. Did the money arrive? What is happening in the project? The congregation may be sent a subscription to a mission magazine that may—or may not—in any twelve-month period contain an article about the country in which the mission project is located. Since there may be many denominational mission projects in a given country, an article about a particular country may—or may not—contain a reference to the specific project that the congregation supports. And certainly, the article will not indicate when the congregation's money arrived, and whether the project has been fully funded.

Technology now makes it easier to provide information to congregations. Feedback can serve as positive reinforcement for the behavior of supporting mission projects, and thus, increased giving at the congregational level.

The software for the Web-based feedback system should include several features.

List of mission projects. The software should allow a denomination to list its mission projects. In addition, the software should allow a special designation for those projects that qualify for the blue-ribbon commission's matching grants.

Funding Status information. The software should allow a congregation to log onto the denomination's Web site and obtain information about the funding status of particular mission projects. How much of a particular mission project's budget has been subscribed? By regularly updating this information, a denomination can avoid the dreaded situation of having some very popular mission projects oversubscribed while other less dynamic but just as valuable projects are under-funded. In fact, a denomination could use this system to analyze which worthy projects need more attention. The denomination could focus its promotion efforts on those projects that are under-funded, as well as use the undesignated mission funds that the denomination receives to insure that all mission projects receive the support they deserve.

In a related matter, the congregation could use the Web to "reserve" for a limited period of time, perhaps up to three weeks, a set amount of dollars it intends to contribute toward an under-subscribed project. This reservation system would prevent a congregation from sending money to a denomination, earmarked for a project, only to have the money returned because in the meantime another congregation has fully funded that project.

Another operating status fact could be keyed to the individual congregation's record, perhaps obtainable by password. The congregation could log on and confirm both, when the denominational office received the money for the project, and when the denomination sent the money on to the mission project. The extent to which it may be a common occurrence is not widely known. However, the authors became aware of a delay between money arriving in a U.S. denominational office, earmarked for an international mission project, and then being forwarded from the U.S. denominational office to the international mission project.

In the interim, the U.S. denominational office was earning significant amounts of interest on the donated money. While that strategy may be viewed as wise stewardship of funds from the national office's perspective, it delayed the help that was meant to be given to the international project, and it weakened any momentum built up in the donating congregation. A Web-based status window could help to insure speedy transfer of funds to the project in need, with the accompanying benefit of speedy feedback to the donating congregation members.

Feedback mechanism. The software could also be programmed to automatically provide feedback to each congregation that donated to a particular mission project. The reports might be every other month for twelve months from the date of the most recent donation. The reports could contain a fact about the need the mission project is addressing, a story related to the project, a photo, a teaching or insight prepared perhaps by a mission project leader in that country, and a prayer request for that project. Each denomination has a limited number of mission projects, even if the projects number in the hundreds or, in some cases, thousands. Yet, those in the field who are working on the project that is receiving the financial support could be asked to provide the feedback information via e-mail. This need for feedback information could be part of the agreement for continued financial support. The software could be designed to accept the information from the international mission project staff, and to forward it automatically to any congregation that is registered as having contributed to that project in the last twelve months.

Individualization is increasing in general advertising. For some years, magazines have contained advertising pages that are personalized with the name on the magazine's address label. Airlines regularly update frequent flyer accounts and mail the reports to the individual account holder within weeks of a trip. Denominations have a limited number of congregations to service—certainly fewer than airlines have frequent flyer accounts. Creative use of technology could provide a denominationally-brokered system to build a true partnership between the congregation members donating dollars and mission project staff who can broaden the vision of those congregation members.

Problem Resolution Council. When congregation members obtain more information about mission projects, those members may also become aware of problems related to specific mission projects. A structure that may give congregation members confidence is a problem resolution council that could be formed by each denomination, or perhaps by the commission.

Most denominations already are part of an international structure. Denominations in the U.S. have counterparts in other countries. The churches in some of the other countries have changed from being mission-receiving churches to mission-funding churches. Others have received mission support for many years. A problem resolution council could include denominational representatives from the mission-sending and the mission-support-receiving countries.

The composition of the problem resolution council would be important. It is suggested that two-thirds of the representatives would come from what are termed "two-thirds world" countries, and one-third from the U.S. and other mission-sending countries. This composition reflects the reality that money often confers power. For an authentic exchange of ideas and resolution of problems, that power would have to be neutralized. The Mennonite Global Sharing Fund has implemented a coordinating council based on a similar composition, including representatives of the Mennonite World Conference Churches.

The value of a problem resolution council is that it addresses a valid concern of denominational mission officials. Sometimes, standards and expectations are different in other countries than in the U.S. When money is involved, misunderstandings can occur. If a congregation is receiving dynamic feedback about a specific mission project, then the congregation may learn of a financial problem with that project. Some denominational officials feel they are "protecting" the congregation from this painful knowledge. However, congregation members cannot grow in their understanding, their sophistication, and their authentic discipleship, if they are isolated from global realities. Also, by allowing the few negative experiences to prevent dynamic feedback, congregations are not permitted to learn from the many good experiences that occur in mission activity, the very experiences that convince denominational officials of the value of the international work. A problem resolution council would provide a mechanism to deal with misunderstandings between the mission project and the denominational agency. Having this structure in place removes one reason, however valid, to keep congregations uninformed about the reality of global mission.

Conclusion. One self-help axiom defines "crazy" as doing the same thing over and over while expecting different results. Denominations have been experiencing a decline in the portion of income donated from congregations. Even when church members increase the number of dollars given to their congregations, over 90% of those inflation-adjusted dollars stay in the congregation to meet the needs of current members. The giving trend from 1968 to 2000 suggests a fresh approach is needed.

A vacuum of leadership among church leaders has resulted in these declining trends in giving.

A solution to address declining giving patterns has two aspects. One is to decide to mobilize church members to increase church member giving through a focus on a positive agenda for affluence. This agenda would be compelling enough to raise members' sights above their own needs. A strategy of matching new money for mission projects that address, in Jesus' name, global child deaths, could help mobilize church members.

The second part of the solution is to provide dynamic feedback to congregation members about what their donated money is doing. The days are gone when congregations forwarded large amounts to denominations because it was the right thing to do. Software for a dynamic Web-based feedback system could build an authentic partnership between congregation members, the denomination, and the mission projects being funded.

The goal of both parts of the solution is to move church membership to giving levels that are on a scale with both donors' potential for giving, and the scope of the need.

APPENDIXES

APPENDIX A: *List of Denominations*

Church Member Giving, 1968-2000, Composite Set

American Baptist Churches in the U.S.A.
Associate Reformed Presbyterian Church
  (General Synod)
Brethren in Christ Church
Christian Church (Disciples of Christ)
Church of God (Anderson, Ind.) (through 1997)
Church of God General Conference (Oregon, IL and
  Morrow, GA.)
Church of the Brethren
Church of the Nazarene
Conservative Congregational Christian Conference
Cumberland Presbyterian Church
Evangelical Congregational Church
Evangelical Covenant Church
Evangelical Lutheran Church in America
  The American Lutheran Church (merged 1987)
  Lutheran Church in America (merged 1987)
Evangelical Lutheran Synod
Evangelical Mennonite Church
Fellowship of Evangelical Bible Churches
Free Methodist Church of North America
Friends United Meeting (through 1990)
General Association of General Baptists
Lutheran Church-Missouri Synod
Mennonite Church USA (through 1999)
  Mennonite Church (merged 1999 data)
  Mennonite Church, General Conference (merged
    1999 data)
Moravian Church in America, Northern Province
North American Baptist Conference
The Orthodox Presbyterian Church
Presbyterian Church (U.S.A.)
Reformed Church in America
Seventh-day Adventist Church, North American
  Division of
Southern Baptist Convention
United Church of Christ
Wisconsin Evangelical Lutheran Synod

Church Member Giving, 1999–2000

The Composite Set Denominations included in the
  1968-2000 analysis with data available for both
  years, plus the following:
African Methodist Episcopal Zion Church
Allegheny Wesleyan Methodist Connection (Original
  Allegheny Conference)

Apostolic Faith Mission Church of God
Baptist General Conference
Bible Fellowship Church
Church of Christ (Holiness)U.S.A.
Church of the Lutheran Brethren of America
Church of the Lutheran Confession
Churches of God General Conference
The Episcopal Church
The Evangelical Church
International Church of the Foursquare Gospel
International Pentecostal Church of Christ
Presbyterian Church in America
The Romano Byzantine Synod of the Orthodox
  Catholic Church
The United Methodist Church
The Wesleyan Church

By Organizational Affiliation: NAE, 1968-2000

Brethren in Christ Church
Church of the Nazarene
Conservative Congregational Christian Conference
Evangelical Congregational Church
Evangelical Mennonite Church
Fellowship of Evangelical Bible Churches
Free Methodist Church of North America
General Association of General Baptists

By Organizational Affiliation: NCC, 1968-2000

American Baptist Churches in the U.S.A.
Christian Church (Disciples of Christ)
Church of the Brethren
Evangelical Lutheran Church in America
Moravian Church in America, Northern Province
Presbyterian Church (U.S.A.)
Reformed Church in America
United Church of Christ

Eleven Denominations, 1921-2000

American Baptist (Northern)
Christian Church (Disciples of Christ)
Church of the Brethren
The Episcopal Church
Evangelical Lutheran Church in America
  The American Lutheran Church
    American Lutheran Church

The Evangelical Lutheran Church
  United Evangelical Lutheran Church
  Lutheran Free Church
  Evangelical Lutheran Churches, Assn. of
Lutheran Church in America
  United Lutheran Church
    General Council Evangelical Lutheran Ch.
    General Synod of Evangelical Lutheran Ch.
    United Synod Evangelical Lutheran South
  American Evangelical Lutheran Church
  Augustana Lutheran Church
  Finnish Lutheran Church (Suomi Synod)
Moravian Church in America, Northern Province
Presbyterian Church (U.S.A.)
  United Presbyterian Church in the U.S.A.
  Presbyterian Church in the U.S.A.
  United Presbyterian Church in North America
  Presbyterian Church in the U.S.
Reformed Church in America
Southern Baptist Convention
United Church of Christ
  Congregational Christian
  Congregational
  Evangelical and Reformed
    Evangelical Synod of North America/German
    Reformed Church in the U.S.
The United Methodist Church
  The Evangelical United Brethren
  The Methodist Church
    Methodist Episcopal Church
    Methodist Episcopal Church South
    Methodist Protestant Church

Trends in Membership,
11 Mainline Protestant Denominations,
1968-2000

American Baptist Churches in the U.S.A.
Christian Church (Disciples of Christ)
Church of the Brethren
The Episcopal Church
Evangelical Lutheran Church in America
Friends United Meeting
Moravian Church in America, Northern Prov.
Presbyterian Church (U.S.A.)
Reformed Church in America
United Church of Christ
The United Methodist Church

Trends in Membership,
15 Evangelical Denominations,
1968-2000

Assemblies of God
Baptist General Conference
Brethren in Christ Church
Christian and Missionary Alliance
Church of God (Cleveland, Tenn.)
Church of the Nazarene
Conservative Congregational Christian Conference
Evangelical Congregational Church
Evangelical Mennonite Church
Fellowship of Evangelical Bible Churches
Free Methodist Church of North America
General Association of General Baptists
Lutheran Church-Missouri Synod
Salvation Army
Southern Baptist Convention

Trends in Membership,
37 Denominations, 1968-2000

11 Mainline Protestant Denominations (above)
15 Evangelical Denominations (above)
11 Additional Composite Denominations:
Associate Reformed Presbyterian Church (General
  Synod)
Church of God (Anderson, Ind.)
Church of God General Conference (Oregon, Ill
  and Morrow, Ga..)
Cumberland Presbyterian Church
Evangelical Covenant Church
Evangelical Lutheran Synod
Mennonite Church
North American Baptist Conference
The Orthodox Presbyterian Church
Seventh-day Adventist Church, North American
  Division of
Wisconsin Evangelical Lutheran Synod

APPENDIX B SERIES: *Denominational Data Tables*

Introduction

The data in the following tables is from the *Yearbook of American and Canadian Churches* (*YACC*) series unless otherwise noted. Financial data is presented in current dollars.

Data in italics indicates a change from the previous edition in *The State of Church Giving* (*SCG*) series.

The Appendix B tables are described below.

Appendix B-1, Church Member Giving, 1968-2000: This table presents aggregate data for the denominations which comprise the data set analyzed for the 1968 through 2000 period.

Elements of this data are also used for the analyses in chapters two through seven.

In Appendix B-1, the data for the Presbyterian Church (U.S.A.) combined data for the United Presbyterian Church in the U.S.A. and the Presbyterian Church in the United States for the period 1968 through 1982. These two communions merged to become the Presbyterian Church (U.S.A.) in 1983, data for which is presented for 1983 through 2000.

Also in Appendix B-1, data for the Evangelical Lutheran Church in America (ELCA) appears beginning in 1987. Before that, the two major component communions that merged into the ELCA—the American Lutheran Church and the Lutheran Church in America—are listed as individual denominations from 1968 through 1986.

In the Appendix B series, the denomination listed as the Fellowship of Evangelical Bible Churches was named the Evangelical Mennonite Brethren Church prior to July 1987.

For 1999, the Mennonite Church (Elkhart, IN) provided information for the Mennonite Church USA. This communion is the result of a merger passed at a national convention in July 2001 between the Mennonite Church and the Mennonite Church, General Conference. The latter's 1968-1998 data has been added to the composite set series. The Mennonite Church USA figures for 1999 combine data for the two predecessor communions.

The 1999 and 2000 data for the Southern Baptist Convention used in the 1968-2000 analysis includes only data for those State Conventions that provided a breakdown of Total Contributions between Congregational Finances and Benevolences for that year. For the Eleven Denominations 1921-2000 analysis, 1999 and 2000 Southern Baptist Convention Total Contributions are $7,772,452,961 and $8,437,177,940, respectively. For the Eleven Denominations 1921-2000 analysis, and the Membership Trends analysis, 1999 and 2000 Southern Baptist Convention Membership is 15,581,756 and 15,960,308, respectively.

Data for the American Baptist Churches in the U.S.A. has been obtained directly from the denominational office as follows. In discussions with the American Baptist Churches Office of Planning Resources, it became apparent that there had been no distinction made between the membership of congregations reporting financial data, and total membership for the denomination, when reporting data to the *Yearbook of American and Canadian Churches*. Records were obtained from the denomination for a smaller membership figure that reflected only those congregations reporting financial data. While this revised membership data provided a more useful per member giving figure for Congregational Finances, the total Benevolences figure reported to the *YACC*, while included in the present data set, does reflect contributions to some Benevolences categories from 100% of the American Baptist membership. The membership reported in Appendix B-1 for the American Baptist Churches is the membership for congregations reporting financial data, rather than the total membership figure provided in editions of the *YACC*. However, in the sections that consider membership as a percentage of population, the Total Membership figure for the American Baptist Churches is used.

Appendix B-2, Church Member Giving for 44 Denominations, 1999-2000: Appendix B-2 presents the Full or Confirmed Membership, Congregational Finances and Benevolences data for the seventeen additional denominations included in the 1999-2000 comparison.

Appendix B-3, Church Member Giving for Eleven Denominations, 1921-2000: This appendix presents additional data which is not included in Appendix B-1 for the Eleven Denominations.

The data from 1921 through 1928 in Appendix B-3.1 is taken from summary information contained in the *Yearbook of American Churches, 1949 Edition*, George F. Ketcham, ed. (Lebanon, PA: Sowers Printing Company, 1949, p. 162). The summary membership data provided is for Inclusive Membership. Therefore, giving as a percentage of income for the years 1921 through 1928 may have been somewhat higher had Full or Confirmed Membership been used. The list of denominations that are summarized for this period is presented in the *Yearbook of American Churches, 1953 Edition*, Benson Y. Landis, ed. (New York: National Council of the Churches of Christ in the U.S.A., 1953, p. 274).

The data from 1929 through 1952 is taken from summary information presented in the *Yearbook of American Churches, Edition for 1955*, Benson Y. Landis, ed. (New York: National Council of the Churches of Christ in the U.S.A., 1954, pp. 286-287). A description of the list of denominations included in the 1929 through 1952 data summary on page 275 of the *YACC Edition for 1955* indicated that the Moravian Church, Northern Province is not included in the 1929 through 1952 data.

The data in Appendix B-3.2 for 1953 through 1964 was obtained for the indicated denominations from the relevant edition of the *YACC* series. Giving as a percentage of income was derived for these years by dividing the published Total Contributions figure by the published Per Capita figure to produce a membership figure for each denomination. The Total Contributions figures for the denominations were added to produce an aggregated Total Contributions figure. The calculated membership figures were also added to produce an aggregated membership figure. The aggregated Total Contributions figure was then divided by the aggregated membership figure to yield a per member giving figure which was used in calculating giving as a percentage of income.

Data for the years 1965 through 1967 was not available in a form that could be readily analyzed for the present purposes, and therefore data for these three years was estimated by dividing the change in per capita Total Contributions from 1964 to 1968 by four, the number of years in this interval, and cumulatively adding the result to the base year of 1964 and the succeeding years of 1965 and 1966 to obtain estimates for the years 1965 through 1967.

In most cases, this procedure was also applied to individual denominations to avoid an artificially low total due to missing data. If data was not available for a specific year, the otherwise blank entry was filled in with a calculation based on surrounding years for the denomination. For example, this procedure was used for the American Baptist Churches for the years 1955 and 1996, the Christian Church (Disciples of Christ) for the years 1955 and 1959, and the Evangelical United Brethren, later to merge into The United Methodist Church, for the years 1957, 1958 and 1959. Data for the Methodist Church was changed for 1957 in a similar manner.

Available Total Contributions and Full or Confirmed Members data for The Episcopal Church and The United Methodist Church for 1969 through 2000 is presented in Appendix B-3.3. These two communions are included in the Eleven Denominations. The United Methodist Church was created in 1968 when the Methodist Church and the Evangelical United Brethren Church merged. While the Methodist Church filed summary data for the year 1968, the Evangelical United Brethren Church did not. Data for these denominations was calculated as noted in the appendix. However, since the 1968 data for The Methodist Church would not have been comparable to the 1985 and 2000 data for The United Methodist Church, this communion was not included in the more focused 1968-2000 analysis.

Appendix B-4, Trends in Giving and Membership: This appendix presents denominational membership data used in the membership analyses presented in chapter five that is not available in the other appendices. Unless otherwise indicated, the data is from the *YACC* series.

APPENDIX B-1: *Church Member Giving 1968-2000*

Key to Denominational Abbreviations: Data Years 1968-2000

Abbreviation	Denomination
abc	American Baptist Churches in the U.S.A.
alc	The American Lutheran Church
arp	Associate Reformed Presbyterian Church (General Synod)
bcc	Brethren in Christ Church
ccd	Christian Church (Disciples of Christ)
cga	Church of God (Anderson, IN)
cgg	Church of God General Conference (Oregon, IL and Morrow, GA)
chb	Church of the Brethren
chn	Church of the Nazarene
ccc	Conservative Congregational Christian Church
cpc	Cumberland Presbyterian Church
ecc	Evangelical Congregational Church
ecv	Evangelical Covenant Church
elc	Evangelical Lutheran Church in America
els	Evangelical Lutheran Synod
emc	Evangelical Mennonite Church
feb	Fellowship of Evangelical Bible Churches
fmc	Free Methodist Church of North America
fum	Friends United Meeting
ggb	General Association of General Baptists
lca	Lutheran Church in America
lms	Lutheran Church-Missouri Synod
mch	Mennonite Church
mgc	Mennonite Church, General Conference
mus	Mennonite Church USA
mca	Moravian Church in America, Northern Province
nab	North American Baptist Conference
opc	The Orthodox Presbyterian Church
pch	Presbyterian Church (U.S.A.)
rca	Reformed Church in America
sda	Seventh-day Adventist, North American Division of
sbc	Southern Baptist Convention
ucc	United Church of Christ
wel	Wisconsin Evangelical Lutheran Synod

Appendix B-1: Church Member Giving 1968-2000 (continued)

	Data Year 1968			Data Year 1969			Data Year 1970		
	Full/Confirmed Members	Congregational Finances	Benevolences	Full/Confirmed Members	Congregational Finances	Benevolences	Full/Confirmed Members	Congregational Finances	Benevolences
abc	1,179,848 a	95,878,267 a	21,674,924 a	1,153,785 a	104,084,322	21,111,333	1,231,944 a	112,668,310	19,655,391
alc	1,767,618	137,260,390	32,862,410	1,771,999	143,917,440	34,394,570	1,775,573	146,268,320	30,750,030 a
arp	28,312 a	2,211,002 a	898,430 a	28,273	2,436,936 a	824,628 a	28,427 a	2,585,974 a	806,071 a
bcc	8,954	1,645,256	633,200 a	9,145	1,795,859	817,445	9,300 a	2,037,330 a	771,940 a
ccd	994,683	105,803,222	21,703,947	936,931	91,169,842	18,946,815	911,964	98,671,692	17,386,032
cga	146,807	23,310,682	4,168,580	147,752	24,828,448	4,531,678	150,198	26,962,037	4,886,225
cgg	6,600	805,000	103,000	6,700	805,000	104,000	6,800	810,000	107,000
chb	187,957	12,975,829	4,889,727	185,198	13,964,158	4,921,991	182,614	14,327,896	4,891,618
chn	364,789	59,943,750 a	14,163,761 a	372,943	64,487,669 a	15,220,339 a	383,284	68,877,922 a	16,221,123 a
ccc	15,127	1,867,978	753,686	16,219	1,382,195	801,534	17,328	1,736,818	779,696
cpc	87,044 a	6,247,447 a	901,974 a	86,435 a	7,724,405 a	926,317 a	86,683 a	7,735,906 a	1,011,911 a
ecc	29,582 a	3,369,308 a	627,731 a	29,652 a	3,521,074 a	646,187 a	29,437 a	3,786,288 a	692,422 a
ecv	66,021	14,374,162 a	3,072,848	67,522	14,952,302 a	3,312,306	67,441	15,874,265 a	3,578,876
elc	ALC & LCA	ALC & LCA	ALC & LCA	ALC & LCA	ALC & LCA	ALC & LCA	ALC & LCA	ALC & LCA	ALC & LCA
els	10,886 a	844,235 a	241,949 a	11,079	1,003,746	315,325	11,030	969,625	242,831 a
emc	2,870 a	447,397	232,331	NA	NA	NA	NA	NA	NA
feb	1,712 a	156,789 a	129,818 a	3,324	389,000	328,000	3,698	381,877	706,398
fmc	47,831 a	12,032,016 a	2,269,677 a	47,954 a	13,187,506 a	2,438,351 a	64,901	9,641,202	7,985,264
fum	55,469	3,564,793	1,256,192	55,257	3,509,509	1,289,026	53,970	3,973,802	1,167,183
ggb	65,000	4,303,183 a	269,921 a	NA	NA	NA	NA	NA	NA
lca	2,279,383	166,337,149	39,981,858	2,193,321	161,958,669	46,902,225	2,187,015	169,795,380	42,118,870
lms	1,877,799	178,042,762	47,415,800	1,900,708	185,827,626	49,402,590	1,922,569	193,352,322	47,810,664
mch	85,682 a	7,078,164 a	5,576,305 a	85,343	7,398,182	6,038,730	83,747 a	7,980,917 a	6,519,476 a
mgc	36,337 a	2,859,340 a	2,668,138 a	35,613	2,860,555 a	2,587,079 a	35,536	3,091,670	2,550,208
mus	MCH & MGC	MCH & MGC	MCH & MGC	MCH & MGC	MCH & MGC	MCH & MGC	MCH & MGC	MCH & MGC	MCH & MGC
mca	27,772	2,583,354	444,910	27,617	2,642,529	456,182	27,173	2,704,105	463,219
nab	42,371 a	5,176,669 a	1,383,964 a	55,100	6,681,410	2,111,588	55,080	6,586,929	2,368,288
opc	9,197	1,638,437	418,102	9,276	1,761,242	464,660	9,401 a	1,853,627 a	503,572 a
pch	4,180,093	375,248,474	102,622,450	4,118,664	388,268,169	97,897,522	4,041,813	401,785,731	93,927,852
rca	226,819 b	25,410,489 b	9,197,642 b	224,992 b	27,139,579 b	9,173,312 b	223,353 b	29,421,849 b	9,479,503 b
sda	395,159 a	36,976,280	95,178,335	407,766	40,378,426	102,730,594	420,419	45,280,059	109,569,241
sbc	11,332,229 a	666,924,020 a	128,023,711 a	11,487,708	709,246,590	133,203,885	11,628,032	753,510,973	138,480,329
ucc	2,032,648 a	152,301,536	18,869,136	1,997,898	152,791,512	27,338,543	1,960,608	155,248,767	26,934,289
wel	259,954 a	19,000,023 a	6,574,308 a	265,069	20,786,613	6,417,042	271,117	22,582,545	6,810,612
Total	27,852,553	2,126,617,403	569,208,785	27,739,243	2,200,900,513	595,653,797	27,880,455	2,310,504,138	599,176,138

a Data obtained from denominational source.
b empty tomb review of RCA directory data.

Appendix B-1: Church Member Giving 1968-2000 (continued)

	Data Year 1971			Data Year 1972			Data Year 1973		
	Full/Confirmed Members	Congregational Finances	Benevolences	Full/Confirmed Members	Congregational Finances	Benevolences	Full/Confirmed Members	Congregational Finances	Benevolences
abc	1,223,735 a	114,673,805	18,878,769	1,176,092 a	118,446,573	18,993,440	1,190,455 a	139,357,611	20,537,388
alc	1,775,774	146,324,460	28,321,740	1,773,414	154,786,570	30,133,850	1,770,119	168,194,730	35,211,440
arp	28,443 a	2,942,577 a	814,703 a	28,711 a	3,329,446 a	847,665 a	28,763 a	3,742,773 a	750,387 a
bcc	9,550	2,357,786	851,725	9,730	2,440,400	978,957	9,877	2,894,622 a	1,089,879 a
ccd	884,929	94,091,862	17,770,799	881,467	105,763,511	18,323,685	868,895	112,526,538	19,800,843
cga	152,787	28,343,604	5,062,282	155,920	31,580,751	5,550,487	157,828	34,649,592	6,349,695
cgg	7,200	860,000	120,000	7,400	900,000	120,000	7,440	940,000	120,000
chb	181,183	14,535,274	5,184,768	179,641	14,622,319 c	5,337,277 c	179,333	16,474,758	6,868,927
chn	394,197	75,107,918 a	17,859,332 a	404,732	82,891,903 a	20,119,679 a	417,200	91,318,469 a	22,661,140 a
ccc	19,279 a	1,875,010 a	930,485 a	20,081 a	1,950,865 a	994,453 a	20,712 a	2,080,038 a	1,057,869 a
cpc	86,945 a	7,729,131 a	1,009,657 a	88,200 a	8,387,762 a	1,064,831 a	88,203 a	9,611,201 a	1,220,768 a
ecc	29,682 a	4,076,576 a	742,293 a	29,434 a	4,303,406 a	798,968 a	29,331 a	4,913,214 a	943,619 a
ecv	68,428	17,066,051 a	3,841,887	69,815	18,021,767 a	4,169,053	69,922	18,948,864 a	4,259,950
elc	ALC & LCA	ALC & LCA	ALC & LCA	ALC & LCA	ALC & LCA	ALC & LCA	ALC & LCA	ALC & LCA	ALC & LCA
els	11,426 a	1,067,650 a	314,335 a	11,532	1,138,953	295,941 a	12,525	1,296,326	330,052 a
emc	NA	NA	NA	NA	NA	NA	3,131	593,070	408,440
feb	NA	NA	NA	NA	NA	NA	NA	NA	NA
fmc	47,933 a	13,116,414 a	2,960,525 a	48,400 a	14,311,395 a	3,287,000 a	48,763 a	15,768,216 a	3,474,555 a
fum	54,522	3,888,064	1,208,062	54,927	4,515,463	1,297,088	57,690	5,037,848	1,327,439
ggb	NA	NA	NA	NA	NA	NA	NA	NA	NA
lca	2,175,378	179,570,467	43,599,913	2,165,591	188,387,949	45,587,481	2,169,341	200,278,486	34,627,978
lms	1,945,889	203,619,804	48,891,368	1,963,262	216,756,345	50,777,670	1,983,114	230,435,598	54,438,074
mch	88,522	8,171,316	7,035,750	89,505	9,913,176	7,168,664	90,967	9,072,858	6,159,740
mgc	36,314	3,368,100	2,833,491	36,129	3,378,372	3,219,439	36,483	3,635,418	3,392,844
mus	MCH & MGC	MCH & MGC	MCH & MGC	MCH & MGC	MCH & MGC	MCH & MGC	MCH & MGC	MCH & MGC	MCH & MGC
mca	26,101	2,576,172	459,447	25,500	2,909,252	465,316	25,468	3,020,667	512,424
nab	54,997	7,114,457	2,293,692	54,441	7,519,558	2,253,158	41,516	6,030,352	1,712,092
opc	9,536 a	2,054,448 a	533,324 a	9,741 a	2,248,969 a	602,328 a	9,940 a	2,364,079 a	658,534 a
pch	3,963,665	420,865,807	93,164,548	3,855,494	436,042,890	92,691,469	3,730,312 d	480,735,088 d	95,462,247 d
rca	219,915 b	32,217,319 b	9,449,655 b	217,583 b	34,569,874 b	9,508,818 b	212,906 b	39,524,443 b	10,388,619 b
sda	433,906	49,208,043	119,913,879	449,188	54,988,781	132,411,980	464,276	60,643,602	149,994,942
sbc	11,824,676	814,406,626	160,510,775	12,065,333	896,427,208	174,711,648	12,295,400	1,011,467,569	193,511,983
ucc	1,928,674	158,924,956	26,409,521	1,895,016	165,556,364	27,793,561	1,867,810	168,602,602	28,471,058
wel	275,500	24,365,692	7,481,644	278,442	26,649,585	8,232,320	283,130	29,450,094	8,650,699
Total	27,959,086	3,062,967,758	628,448,369	28,044,721	2,612,739,407	667,736,226	28,170,850	2,873,608,726	714,393,625

a Data obtained from denominational source.

b empty tomb review of RCA directory data.

c YACC Church of the Brethren figures reported for 15 months due to fiscal year change: adjusted here to 12/15ths.

d The Presbyterian Church (USA) data for 1973 combines United Presbyterian Church in the U.S.A. data for 1973 (see YACC 1975) and an average of Presbyterian Church in the United States data for 1972 and 1974, since 1973 data was not reported in the YACC series.

Appendix B-1: Church Member Giving 1968-2000 (continued)

	Data Year 1974			Data Year 1975			Data Year 1976		
	Full/Confirmed Members	Congregational Finances	Benevolences	Full/Confirmed Members	Congregational Finances	Benevolences	Full/Confirmed Members	Congregational Finances	Benevolences
abc	1,176,989 a	147,022,280	21,847,285	1,180,793 a	153,697,091	23,638,372	1,142,773 a	163,134,092	25,792,357
alc	1,764,186	173,318,574	38,921,546	1,764,810	198,863,519	75,666,809	1,768,758	215,527,544	76,478,278
arp	28,570	3,935,533 a	868,284 a	28,589	4,820,846 a	929,880 a	28,581	5,034,270 a	1,018,913 a
bcc	10,255	3,002,218	1,078,576	10,784	3,495,152	955,845	11,375	4,088,492	1,038,484
ccd	854,844	119,434,435	20,818,434	859,885	126,553,931	22,126,459	845,058	135,008,269	23,812,274
cga	161,401	39,189,287	7,343,123	166,259	42,077,029	7,880,559	170,285	47,191,302	8,854,295
cgg	7,455	975,000	105,000	7,485	990,000	105,000	7,620	1,100,000	105,000
chb	179,387	18,609,614	7,281,551	179,336	20,338,351	7,842,819	178,157	22,133,858	8,032,293
chn	430,128	104,774,391	25,534,267 a	441,093	115,400,881	28,186,392 a	448,658	128,294,499	32,278,187 a
ccc	21,661 a	2,452,254 a	1,181,655 a	22,065 a	2,639,472 a	1,750,364 a	21,703 a	3,073,413 a	1,494,355 a
cpc	87,875 a	9,830,198 a	1,336,847 a	86,903 a	11,268,297 a	1,445,793 a	85,541 a	10,735,854 a	1,540,692 a
ecc	29,636 a	4,901,100 a	1,009,726 a	28,886 a	5,503,484 a	1,068,134 a	28,840 a	6,006,621 a	1,139,209 a
ecv	69,960	21,235,204 a	5,131,124	71,808	23,440,265 a	6,353,422	73,458	25,686,916 a	6,898,871
elc	ALC & LCA	ALC & LCA	ALC & LCA	ALC & LCA	ALC & LCA	ALC & LCA	ALC & LCA	ALC & LCA	ALC & LCA
els	13,097	1,519,749	411,732 a	13,489 a	1,739,255	438,875 a	14,504	2,114,998	521,018 a
emc	3,123	644,548	548,000	NA	NA	NA	3,350	800,000	628,944
feb	NA	NA	NA	NA	NA	NA	NA	NA	NA
fmc	49,314 a	17,487,246 a	3,945,535 e	50,632	19,203,781 a	4,389,757 a	51,565	21,130,066 a	4,977,546 a
fum	NA	NA	NA	56,605	6,428,458	1,551,036	51,032	6,749,045	1,691,190
ggb	NA	NA	NA	NA	NA	NA	NA	NA	NA
lca	2,166,615	228,081,405	44,531,126	2,183,131	222,637,156	55,646,303	2,187,995	243,449,466	58,761,005
lms	2,010,456	249,150,470	55,076,955	2,018,530	266,546,758	55,896,061	2,026,336	287,098,403	56,831,860
mch	92,930 a	13,792,266	9,887,051	94,209	15,332,908	11,860,385	96,092 a	17,215,234	12,259,924
mgc	35,534	4,071,002 a	4,179,003 a	35,673 a	3,715,279 a	3,391,943 a	36,397	4,980,967	4,796,037 a
mus	MCH & MGC	MCH & MGC	MCH & MGC	MCH & MGC	MCH & MGC	MCH & MGC	MCH & MGC	MCH & MGC	MCH & MGC
mca	25,583	3,304,388	513,685	25,512	3,567,406	552,512	24,938	4,088,195	573,619
nab	41,437	6,604,693	2,142,148	42,122	7,781,298	2,470,317	42,277	8,902,540	3,302,348
opc	10,186 a	2,627,818 a	703,653 a	10,129 a	2,930,128 a	768,075 a	10,372	3,288,612 a	817,589 a
pch	3,619,768	502,237,350	100,966,089	3,535,825	529,327,006	111,027,318	3,484,985	563,106,353	125,035,379
rca	210,866 b	41,053,364 b	11,470,631 b	212,349 b	44,681,053 b	11,994,379 b	211,628 b	49,083,734 b	13,163,739 b
sda	479,799	67,241,956	166,166,766	495,699	72,060,121	184,689,250	509,792	81,577,130	184,648,454
sbc	12,513,378	1,123,264,849	219,214,770	12,733,124	1,237,594,037	237,452,055	12,917,992	1,382,794,494	262,144,889
ucc	1,841,312	184,292,017	30,243,223	1,818,762	193,524,114	32,125,332	1,801,241	207,486,324	33,862,658
wel	286,858	32,683,492	10,002,869	293,237	35,889,331	11,212,937	297,862	40,017,991	11,300,102
Total	28,222,603	3,126,736,701	792,460,654	28,467,724	3,372,046,407	903,416,383	28,579,165	3,690,898,682	963,799,509

a Data obtained from denominational source.

b empty tomb review of RCA directory data.

Appendix B-1: Church Member Giving 1968-2000 (continued)

	Data Year 1977			Data Year 1978			Data Year 1979		
	Full/Confirmed Members	Congregational Finances	Benevolences	Full/Confirmed Members	Congregational Finances	Benevolences	Full/Confirmed Members	Congregational Finances	Benevolences
abc	1,146,084 [a]	172,710,063	27,765,800	1,008,495 [a]	184,716,172	31,937,862	1,036,054 [a]	195,986,995	34,992,300
alc	1,772,227	231,960,304	54,085,201	1,773,179	256,371,804	57,145,861	1,768,071	284,019,905	63,903,906
arp	28,371 [a]	5,705,295 [a]	1,061,285 [a]	28,644	6,209,447 [a]	1,031,469 [a]	28,513	6,544,759 [a]	1,125,562 [a]
bcc	11,915 [a]	4,633,334 [a]	957,239 [a]	12,430 [a]	4,913,311	1,089,346 [a]	12,923	5,519,037	1,312,046
ccd	817,288	148,880,340	25,698,856	791,633	166,249,455	25,790,367	773,765	172,270,978	27,335,440
cga	171,947	51,969,150	10,001,062	173,753	57,630,848	11,214,530	175,113	65,974,517	12,434,621
cgg	7,595	1,130,000	110,000	7,550	1,135,000	110,000	7,620	1,170,000	105,000
chb	177,534	23,722,817	8,228,903	175,335	25,397,531	9,476,220	172,115	28,422,684	10,161,266
chn	455,100	141,807,024	34,895,751 [a]	462,124	153,943,138	38,300,431 [a]	473,726	170,515,940 [a]	42,087,862 [a]
ccc	21,897 [a]	3,916,248 [a]	1,554,143 [a]	22,364 [a]	4,271,435 [a]	1,630,565 [a]	23,481 [a]	4,969,610 [a]	1,871,754 [a]
cpc	85,227 [a]	11,384,825 [a]	1,760,117 [a]	84,956 [a]	13,359,375 [a]	1,995,388 [a]	85,932 [a]	13,928,957 [a]	2,192,562 [a]
ecc	28,712 [a]	6,356,730 [a]	1,271,310 [a]	28,459 [a]	6,890,381 [a]	1,454,826 [a]	27,995 [a]	7,552,495 [a]	1,547,857 [a]
ecv	74,060	28,758,357 [a]	7,240,548	74,678	32,606,550 [a]	8,017,623	76,092	37,118,906 [a]	9,400,074
elc	ALC & LCA	ALC & LCA	ALC & LCA	ALC & LCA	ALC & LCA	ALC & LCA	ALC & LCA	ALC & LCA	ALC & LCA
els	14,652	2,290,697	546,899 [a]	14,833	2,629,719	833,543 [a]	15,081	2,750,703	904,774 [a]
emc	NA	NA	NA	3,634	1,281,761	794,896	3,704	1,380,806	828,264
feb	NA	NA	NA	3,956	970,960	745,059	NA	NA	NA
fmc	52,563	23,303,722 [a]	5,505,538 [a]	52,698 [a]	25,505,294 [a]	5,869,970 [a]	52,900 [a]	27,516,302 [a]	6,614,732 [a]
fum	52,599	6,943,990	1,895,984	53,390	8,172,337	1,968,884	51,426	6,662,787	2,131,108
ggb	72,030	9,854,533	747,842	NA	NA	NA	73,046	13,131,345	1,218,763
lca	2,191,942	251,083,883	62,076,894	2,183,666	277,186,563	72,426,148	2,177,231	301,605,382	71,325,097
lms	1,991,408	301,064,630	57,077,162	1,969,279	329,134,237	59,030,753	1,965,422	360,989,735	63,530,596
mch	96,609	18,540,237	12,980,502	97,142	22,922,417	14,124,757 [a]	98,027	24,505,346	15,116,762
mgc	35,575 [a]	5,051,708 [a]	4,619,590 [a]	36,775 [a]	5,421,568 [a]	5,062,489 [a]	36,736	6,254,850 [a]	5,660,477 [a]
mus	MCH & MGC	MCH & MGC	MCH & MGC	MCH & MGC	MCH & MGC	MCH & MGC	MCH & MGC	MCH & MGC	MCH & MGC
mca	25,323	4,583,616	581,200	24,854	4,441,750	625,536	24,782	4,600,331	689,070
nab	42,724	10,332,556	3,554,204	42,499	11,629,309	3,559,983	42,779	13,415,024	3,564,339
opc	10,683 [a]	3,514,172	931,935	10,939	4,107,705	1,135,388	11,306 [a]	4,683,302	1,147,191
pch	3,430,927	633,187,916	130,252,348	3,382,783	692,872,811	128,194,954	3,321,787	776,049,247	148,528,993
rca	210,637 [b]	53,999,791 [b]	14,210,966 [b]	211,778 [b]	60,138,720 [b]	15,494,816 [b]	210,700 [b]	62,297,526 [b]	16,750,408 [b]
sda	522,317	98,468,365	216,202,975	535,705	104,044,989	226,692,736	553,089	118,711,906	255,936,372
sbc	13,078,239	1,506,877,921	289,179,711	13,191,394	1,668,120,760	316,462,385	13,372,757	1,864,213,869	355,885,769
ucc	1,785,652	219,878,772	35,522,221	1,769,104	232,593,033	37,789,958	1,745,533	249,443,032	41,100,583
wel	301,944	44,492,259	11,639,834	303,944	50,255,539	12,960,885	306,264	54,983,467	14,230,208
Total	28,713,781	4,026,403,255	1,022,156,020	28,531,973	4,415,123,919	1,092,967,628	28,723,970	4,887,889,743	1,213,633,756

[a] Data obtained from denominational source.
[b] empty tomb review of RCA directory data.

Appendix B-1: Church Member Giving 1968-2000 (continued)

	Data Year 1980			Data Year 1981			Data Year 1982		
	Full/Confirmed Members	Congregational Finances	Benevolences	Full/Confirmed Members	Congregational Finances	Benevolences	Full/Confirmed Members	Congregational Finances	Benevolences
abc	1,008,700 a	213,560,656	37,133,159	989,322 a	227,931,461	40,046,261	983,580 a	242,750,027	41,457,745
alc	1,763,067	312,592,610	65,235,739	1,758,452	330,155,588	96,102,638	1,758,239	359,848,865	77,010,444
arp	28,166 a	6,868,650 a	1,054,229 a	28,334 a	7,863,221 a	1,497,838 a	29,087 a	8,580,311 a	1,807,572 a
bcc	13,578 a	6,011,465 a	1,490,334 a	13,993	6,781,857	1,740,711	14,413 a	7,228,612 a	1,594,797 a
ccd	788,394	189,176,399	30,991,519	772,466	211,828,751	31,067,142	770,227	227,178,861	34,307,638
cga	176,429	67,367,485	13,414,112	178,581	78,322,907	14,907,277	184,685	84,896,806	17,171,600
cgg	NA	NA	NA	5,981	1,788,298	403,000	5,781 a	1,864,735 a	418,000 a
chb	170,839	29,813,265	11,663,976	170,267	31,641,019	12,929,076	168,844	35,064,568	12,844,415
chn	483,101	191,536,556	45,786,446 a	490,852	203,145,992	50,084,163 a	497,261	221,947,940	53,232,461 a
ccc	24,410 a	6,017,539 a	2,169,298 a	25,044 a	8,465,804	2,415,233	26,008	9,230,111	2,574,569
cpc	86,941 a	15,973,738 a	2,444,677 a	87,493 a	16,876,846 a	2,531,539 a	88,121 a	17,967,709 a	2,706,361 a
ecc	27,567 a	8,037,564 a	1,630,993 a	27,287 a	8,573,057 a	1,758,025 a	27,203 a	9,119,278 a	1,891,936 a
ecv	77,737	41,888,556 a	10,031,072	79,523	45,206,565 a	8,689,918	81,324	50,209,520 a	8,830,793
elc	ALC & LCA	ALC & LCA	ALC & LCA	ALC & LCA	ALC & LCA	ALC & LCA	ALC & LCA	ALC & LCA	ALC & LCA
els	14,968	3,154,804	876,929 a	14,904	3,461,387	716,624	15,165	3,767,977	804,822
emc	3,782	1,527,945	1,041,447	3,753	1,515,975	908,342	3,832	1,985,890	731,510
feb	4,329	1,250,466	627,536	NA	NA	NA	2,047	696,660	1,020,972
fmc	54,145 a	30,525,352 a	6,648,248 a	54,764 a	32,853,491 a	7,555,713 a	54,198	35,056,434	8,051,593
fum	51,691	9,437,724	2,328,137	51,248	9,551,765	2,449,731	50,601	10,334,180	2,597,215
ggb	74,159	14,967,312	1,547,038	75,028	15,816,060	1,473,070	NA	NA	NA
lca	2,176,991	371,981,816	87,439,137	2,173,558	404,300,509	82,862,299	2,176,265	435,564,519	83,217,264
lms	1,973,958	390,756,268	66,626,364	1,983,198	429,910,406	86,341,102	1,961,260	468,468,156	75,457,846
mch	99,511	28,846,931	16,437,738	99,651	31,304,278	17,448,024	101,501	33,583,338	17,981,274
mgc	36,644 a	6,796,330 a	5,976,652 a	36,609 a	7,857,792 a	7,203,240 a	37,007 a	8,438,680 a	7,705,419 a
mus	MCH & MGC	MCH & MGC	MCH & MGC	MCH & MGC	MCH & MGC	MCH & MGC	MCH & MGC	MCH & MGC	MCH & MGC
mca	24,863	5,178,444	860,399	24,500	5,675,495	831,177	24,669	6,049,857	812,015
nab	43,041	12,453,858	3,972,485	43,146	15,513,286	4,420,403	42,735	17,302,952	4,597,515
opc	11,553 a	5,235,294	1,235,849	11,884 a	5,939,983	1,382,451	11,956 a	6,512,125 a	1,430,061 a
pch	3,262,086	820,218,732	176,172,729	3,202,392	896,641,430	188,576,382	3,157,372	970,223,947	199,331,832
rca	210,762	70,733,297	17,313,239 b	210,312	77,044,709	18,193,793 b	211,168	82,656,050	19,418,165 b
sda	571,141	121,484,768	205,783,385	588,536	133,088,131	297,838,046	606,310	136,877,455	299,437,917
sbc	13,600,126	2,080,375,258	400,976,072	13,782,644	2,336,062,506	443,931,179	13,991,709	2,628,272,553	486,402,607
ucc	1,736,244	278,546,571	44,042,186	1,726,535	300,730,591	48,329,399	1,708,847	323,725,191	52,738,069
wel	308,620	60,624,862	16,037,844	311,351	68,056,396	18,261,099	312,195	71,891,457 a	18,677,343
Total	28,907,543	5,402,940,515	1,348,988,968	29,021,608	5,953,905,556	1,492,894,895	29,103,610	6,517,294,764	1,536,261,770

a Data obtained from denominational source.
b empty tomb review of RCA directory data.

Appendix B-1: Church Member Giving 1968-2000 (continued)

	Data Year 1983			Data Year 1984			Data Year 1985		
	Full/Confirmed Members	Congregational Finances	Benevolences	Full/Confirmed Members	Congregational Finances	Benevolences	Full/Confirmed Members	Congregational Finances	Benevolences
abc	965,117 a	254,716,036	43,683,021	953,945 a	267,556,088	46,232,040	894,732 a	267,694,684	47,201,119
alc	1,756,420	375,500,188	84,633,617	1,756,558	413,876,101	86,601,067	1,751,649	428,861,660	87,152,699
arp	31,738	10,640,050 a	2,180,230 a	31,355	11,221,526 a	3,019,456 a	32,051	12,092,868 a	3,106,994 a
bcc	14,782	7,638,413	1,858,632	15,128	8,160,359	2,586,843	15,535 a	8,504,354 a	2,979,046 a
ccd	761,629	241,934,972	35,809,331	755,233	263,694,210	38,402,791	743,486	274,072,301	40,992,053
cga	182,190	81,309,323	13,896,753	185,404	86,611,269	14,347,570	185,593	91,078,512	15,308,954
cgg	5,759	1,981,300	412,000	4,711	2,211,800	504,200	4,575	2,428,730	582,411
chb	164,680	39,726,743	14,488,192	161,824	37,743,527	15,136,600	159,184	40,658,904	16,509,718
chn	506,439	237,220,642	57,267,073 a	514,937	253,566,280	60,909,810 a	520,741	267,134,078	65,627,515 a
ccc	26,691 a	9,189,221 a	2,980,636	28,383	10,018,982	3,051,425	28,624	11,729,365	3,350,021
cpc	87,186 a	19,252,942 a	3,028,953 a	86,995 a	20,998,768 a	3,331,065 a	85,346 a	22,361,332 a	3,227,932 a
ecc	26,769 a	9,505,479 a	2,019,373 a	26,375 a	10,302,554 a	2,220,852 a	26,016	8,134,641 a	1,777,172
ecv	82,943	53,279,350 a	10,615,909	84,185	60,295,634 a	11,243,908	85,150	63,590,735 a	13,828,030
elc	ALC & LCA	ALC & LCA	ALC & LCA	ALC & LCA	ALC & LCA	ALC & LCA	ALC & LCA	ALC & LCA	ALC & LCA
els	15,576	3,842,625	838,788	15,396	4,647,714	931,677 a	15,012	4,725,783	791,586
emc	3,857	1,930,689	738,194	3,908	2,017,565	862,350	3,813	2,128,019	1,058,040
feb	2,094	622,467	1,466,399	NA	NA	NA	2,107 a	1,069,851 a	402,611 a
fmc	56,442 a	36,402,355 a	8,334,248 a	56,667 a	39,766,087 a	8,788,189 a	56,242	42,046,626 a	9,461,369 a
fum	49,441	11,723,240	2,886,931	48,713	11,549,163	2,875,370	48,812	12,601,820	3,012,658
ggb	75,133	17,283,259	1,733,755	75,028	17,599,169	1,729,228	73,040	18,516,252	1,683,130
lca	2,176,772	457,239,780	88,909,363	2,168,594	496,228,216	99,833,067	2,161,216	539,142,069	103,534,375
lms	1,984,199	499,220,552	76,991,991 a	1,986,392	539,346,935	81,742,006 a	1,982,753	566,507,516	83,117,011 a
mch	103,350 a	34,153,628	17,581,878	90,347	37,333,306	16,944,094	91,167	34,015,200	25,593,500
mgc	36,318 a	8,702,849 a	7,661,415 a	35,951 a	9,197,458 a	7,795,680 a	35,356 a	9,217,964 a	7,070,700 a
mus	MCH & MGC	MCH & MGC	MCH & MGC	MCH & MGC	MCH & MGC	MCH & MGC	MCH & MGC	MCH & MGC	MCH & MGC
mca	24,913	6,618,339	911,787	24,269	7,723,611	1,183,741	24,396	8,698,949	1,170,349
nab	43,286	18,010,853	5,132,672	43,215	19,322,720	5,724,552	42,863	20,246,236	5,766,686
opc	12,045	6,874,722	1,755,169	12,278 a	7,555,006	2,079,924	12,593 a	8,291,483	2,204,998
pch	3,122,213	1,047,756,995	197,981,080	3,092,151	1,132,098,779	218,412,639	3,057,226 a	1,252,885,684 a	232,487,569 a
rca	211,660	92,071,986	20,632,574	209,968 b	100,378,778	21,794,880	209,395	103,428,950	22,233,299
sda	623,563	143,636,140	323,461,439	638,929	155,257,063	319,664,449	651,594	155,077,180	346,251,406
sbc	14,178,051	2,838,573,815	528,781,000	14,341,822	3,094,913,877	567,467,188	14,477,364	3,272,276,486	609,868,694
ucc	1,701,513	332,613,396	55,716,557	1,696,107	385,786,198	58,679,094	1,683,777	409,543,989	62,169,679 a
wel	313,883	76,133,614 a	24,169,441	315,466	82,884,471 a	22,951,699	316,297 a	87,194,889 a	22,376,423 a
Total	29,346,652	6,975,305,963	1,638,558,401	29,460,234	7,589,863,214	1,727,047,454	29,477,705	8,045,957,110	1,841,897,747

a Data obtained from denominational source.
b empty tomb review of RCA directory data.

Appendix B-1: Church Member Giving 1968-2000 (continued)

	Data Year 1986			Data Year 1987			Data Year 1988		
	Full/Confirmed Members	Congregational Finances	Benevolences	Full/Confirmed Members	Congregational Finances	Benevolences	Full/Confirmed Members	Congregational Finances	Benevolences
abc	862,582 [a]	287,020,378 [a]	49,070,083 [a]	868,189 [a]	291,606,418 [a]	55,613,855	825,102 [a]	296,569,316 [a]	55,876,771
alc	1,740,439	434,641,736	96,147,129	See ELCA	See ELCA	See ELCA	See ELCA	See ELCA	See ELCA
arp	32,438 [a]	12,336,321 [a]	3,434,408 [a]	32,289	13,553,176 [a]	3,927,030 [a]	31,922	13,657,776 [a]	5,063,036 [a]
bcc	15,911	10,533,883	2,463,558	16,136	11,203,321	3,139,949	16,578 [a]	13,522,101 [a]	4,346,690 [a]
ccd	732,466	288,277,386	42,027,504	718,522	287,464,332	42,728,826	707,985	297,187,996	42,226,128
cga	188,662	91,768,855	16,136,647	198,552	124,376,413	20,261,687	198,842	132,384,232	19,781,941
cgg	NA	NA	NA	4,348	2,437,778	738,818	4,394 [a]	2,420,600 [a]	644,000 [a]
chb	155,967	43,531,293	17,859,101	154,067	45,201,732	19,342,402	151,169	48,008,657	19,701,942 [a]
chn	529,192	283,189,977	68,438,998 [a]	541,878	294,160,356	73,033,568 [a]	550,700	309,478,442	74,737,057 [a]
ccc	28,948	15,559,846 [a]	3,961,037	29,429	15,409,349 [a]	3,740,688	29,015	13,853,547	4,120,974
cpc	84,579 [a]	22,338,090 [a]	3,646,356 [a]	85,781	22,857,711	3,727,681	85,304	23,366,911 [e]	3,722,607
ecc	25,625	10,977,813 [a]	2,422,879 [a]	25,300	14,281,140 [a]	2,575,415 [a]	24,980	12,115,762	2,856,766 [a]
ecv	86,079	67,889,353 [a]	14,374,707	86,741	73,498,123 [a]	14,636,000	87,750	77,504,445 [a]	14,471,178
elc	ALC & LCA	ALC & LCA	ALC & LCA	3,952,663	1,083,293,684	169,685,942	3,931,878	1,150,483,034	169,580,472
els	15,083 [a]	4,996,111 [a]	1,050,715 [a]	15,892	5,298,882	1,082,198	15,518 [a]	5,713,773 [a]	1,043,612 [a]
emc	NA	NA	NA	3,841	2,332,216	1,326,711	3,879	2,522,533	1,438,459
feb	NA	NA	NA	NA	NA	NA	NA	NA	NA
fmc	56,243	46,150,881	9,446,120	57,262	47,743,298	9,938,096	57,432	48,788,041	9,952,103
fum	48,143	12,790,909	2,916,870	47,173	13,768,272	3,631,353	48,325	14,127,491	3,719,125
ggb	72,263	19,743,265	1,883,826	73,515	20,850,827	1,789,578	74,086	21,218,051	1,731,299
lca	2,157,701	569,250,519	111,871,174	See ELCA	See ELCA	See ELCA	See ELCA	See ELCA	See ELCA
lms	1,974,798	605,768,688	87,803,646 [a]	1,973,347	620,271,274	86,938,723 [a]	1,962,674	659,288,332	88,587,175 [a]
mch	91,467 [a]	40,097,500 [a]	24,404,200 [a]	92,673 [a]	43,295,100	25,033,600	92,682	47,771,200	27,043,900
mgc	35,170	10,101,306 [a]	7,717,998 [a]	34,889	11,560,998	8,478,414	34,693	11,399,995	9,638,417
mus	MCH & MGC	MCH & MGC	MCH & MGC	MCH & MGC	MCH & MGC	MCH & MGC	MCH & MGC	MCH & MGC	MCH & MGC
mca	24,260	8,133,127	1,155,350	24,440	9,590,658	1,174,593	23,526	9,221,646	1,210,476
nab	42,084	20,961,799	5,982,391	42,150 [a]	23,773,844 [a]	7,873,096 [a]	42,629	24,597,288	6,611,840
opc	12,919 [a]	9,333,328 [a]	2,347,928 [e]	13,013 [a]	9,884,288	2,425,480	13,108 [a]	10,797,786 [a]	2,648,375 [a]
pch	3,007,322	1,318,440,264	249,033,881	2,967,781	1,395,501,073	247,234,439	2,929,608	1,439,655,217	284,989,138
rca	207,993	114,231,429	22,954,596	203,581	114,652,192 [b]	24,043,270	200,631	127,409,263	25,496,802 [b]
sda	666,199	166,692,974	361,316,753	675,702	166,939,355	374,830,065	687,200	178,768,967	395,849,223
sbc	14,613,638	3,481,124,471	635,196,984	14,722,617	3,629,842,643	662,455,177	14,812,844	3,706,652,161	689,366,904
ucc	1,676,105	429,340,239 [a]	63,808,091	1,662,568	451,700,210	66,870,922	1,644,787	470,747,740	65,734,348
wel	316,416	92,662,969 [a]	22,448,920	317,294	97,567,101 [a]	22,207,123	316,987	101,975,092 [a]	22,406,238
Total	29,500,692	8,517,884,710	1,931,321,850	29,641,633	8,943,915,764	1,960,484,699	28,781,126	9,271,207,395	2,054,596,996

[a] Data obtained from denominational source.

[b] empty tomb review of RCA directory data.

[e] A *YACC* prepublication data table listed 23,366,911 for Congregational Finances which, added to Benevolences, equals the published Total of 27,089,518.

Appendix B-1: Church Member Giving 1968-2000 (continued)

	Data Year 1989			Data Year 1990			Data Year 1991		
	Full/Confirmed Members	Congregational Finances	Benevolences	Full/Confirmed Members	Congregational Finances	Benevolences	Full/Confirmed Members	Congregational Finances	Benevolences
abc	789,730 [a]	305,212,094 [a]	55,951,539	764,890 [a]	315,777,005 [a]	54,740,278	773,838 [a]	318,150,548 [a]	52,330,924
alc	See ELCA	See ELCA	See ELCA	See ELCA	See ELCA	See ELCA	See ELCA	See ELCA	See ELCA
arp	32,600	16,053,762 [a]	4,367,314 [a]	32,817 [a]	17,313,355 [a]	5,031,504 [a]	33,494 [a]	17,585,273 [a]	5,254,738 [a]
bcc	16,842	12,840,038	3,370,306	17,277	13,327,414	3,336,580	17,456 [a]	14,491,918 [a]	3,294,169 [a]
ccd	690,115	310,043,826	42,015,246	678,750	321,569,909	42,607,007	663,336	331,629,009	43,339,307
cga	199,786	134,918,052	20,215,075	205,884	141,375,027	21,087,504	214,743 [a]	146,249,447 [a]	21,801,570 [a]
cgg	4,415	3,367,000	686,000	4,399	3,106,729	690,000	4,375	2,756,651	662,500
chb	149,681	51,921,820	19,737,714 [a]	148,253	54,832,226	18,384,483 [a]	147,954	55,035,355	19,694,919 [a]
chn	558,664	322,924,598	76,625,913 [a]	563,756 [a]	333,397,255 [a]	77,991,665 [a]	572,153	352,654,251	82,276,097 [a]
ccc	28,413	18,199,823	4,064,111	28,355	16,964,128	4,174,133	28,035	17,760,290	4,304,052
cpc	84,994 [a]	25,867,112 [a]	4,086,994 [a]	85,025 [a]	27,027,650 [a]	4,139,967 [a]	84,706 [a]	28,069,681 [a]	5,740,846 [a]
ecc	24,606	13,274,756 [a]	2,703,095 [a]	24,437	12,947,150 [a]	2,858,077 [a]	24,124 [a]	13,100,036 [a]	3,074,660 [a]
ecv	89,014	80,621,293 [a]	15,206,265	89,735	84,263,236 [a]	15,601,475	89,648	87,321,563 [a]	16,598,656
elc	3,909,302	1,239,433,257	182,386,940	3,898,478	1,318,884,279	184,174,554	3,890,947	1,375,439,787	186,016,168
els	15,740	6,186,648	1,342,321	16,181	6,527,076	1,193,789	16,004	6,657,338	1,030,445
emc	3,888	2,712,843	1,567,728	4,026	2,991,485	1,800,593	3,958	3,394,563	1,790,115
feb	NA	NA	NA	NA	NA	NA	2,008 [a]	1,398,968 [a]	500,092 [a]
fmc	59,418 [a]	50,114,090 [a]	10,311,535 [a]	58,084	55,229,181	10,118,505	57,794	57,880,464	9,876,739
fum	47,228	16,288,644	4,055,624	45,691	10,036,083	2,511,063	50,803 [f]	NA	NA
ggb	73,738	23,127,835	1,768,804	74,156	23,127,835	1,737,011	71,119	22,362,874	1,408,262 [a]
lca	See ELCA	See ELCA	See ELCA	See ELCA	See ELCA	See ELCA	See ELCA	See ELCA	See ELCA
lms	1,961,114	701,701,168 [a]	90,974,340 [a]	1,954,350	712,235,204	96,308,765 [a]	1,952,845	741,823,412	94,094,637 [a]
mch	92,517	55,353,313	27,873,241	92,448 [a]	65,709,827	28,397,083	93,114 [a]	68,926,324	28,464,199
mgc	33,982	12,096,435	9,054,682	33,535	13,669,288	8,449,395	33,937	13,556,484	8,645,993
mus	MCH & MGC	MCH & MGC	MCH & MGC	MCH & MGC	MCH & MGC	MCH & MGC	MCH & MGC	MCH & MGC	MCH & MGC
mca	23,802	10,415,640	1,284,233	23,526	10,105,037	1,337,616	22,887	10,095,337	1,205,335
nab	42,629	28,076,077	3,890,017	44,493	31,103,672	7,700,119	43,187 [a]	27,335,239 [a]	7,792,876 [a]
opc	12,573 [a]	11,062,590 [a]	2,789,427 [a]	12,177 [a]	10,631,166 [a]	2,738,295 [a]	12,265	11,700,000	2,700,000
pch	2,886,482	1,528,450,805	295,365,032	2,847,437	1,530,341,707	294,990,441	2,805,548	1,636,407,042	311,905,934 [a]
rca	198,832	136,796,188 [b]	29,456,132 [b]	197,154	144,357,953 [b]	27,705,029 [b]	193,531 [b]	147,532,382 [b]	26,821,721 [b]
sda	701,781	196,204,538	415,752,350	717,446	195,054,218	433,035,080	733,026	201,411,183	456,242,995
sbc	14,907,826	3,873,300,782	712,738,838	15,038,409	4,146,285,561	718,174,874	15,232,347	4,283,283,059	731,812,766
ucc	1,625,969	496,825,160	72,300,698	1,599,212	527,378,397	71,984,897	1,583,830	543,803,752	73,149,887
wel	317,117	110,575,539 [a]	22,811,571	316,813	116,272,092 [a]	24,088,568	316,929 [a]	121,835,547 [a]	24,276,370 [a]
Total	29,582,798	9,793,965,726	2,134,753,085	29,617,194	10,261,841,145	2,167,088,350	29,719,138	10,659,647,777	2,226,106,972

[a] Data obtained from denominational source.

[b] empty tomb review of RCA directory data.

[f] Inclusive membership, obtained from the denomination and used only in Chapter 5 analysis.

Appendix B-1: Church Member Giving 1968-2000 (continued)

	Data Year 1992			Data Year 1993			Data Year 1994		
	Full/Confirmed Members	Congregational Finances	Benevolences	Full/Confirmed Members	Congregational Finances	Benevolences	Full/Confirmed Members	Congregational Finances	Benevolences
abc	730,009 [a]	310,307,040 [a]	52,764,005	764,657 [a]	346,658,047 [a]	53,562,811	697,379 [a]	337,185,885 [a]	51,553,256 [e]
alc	See ELCA	See ELCA	See ELCA	See ELCA	See ELCA	See ELCA	See ELCA	See ELCA	See ELCA
arp	33,550	18,175,957 [a]	5,684,008 [a]	33,662 [a]	20,212,390 [a]	5,822,845 [a]	33,636	22,618,802 [a]	6,727,857
bcc	17,646 [a]	15,981,118 [a]	3,159,717 [a]	17,986	13,786,394	4,515,730 [a]	18,152	14,844,672	5,622,006
ccd	655,652	333,629,412	46,440,333	619,028	328,219,027	44,790,415	605,996	342,352,080	43,165,285
cga	214,743	150,115,497	23,500,213	216,117	158,454,703	23,620,177	221,346 [a]	160,694,760 [a]	26,262,045 [a]
cgg	4,085	2,648,085	509,398	4,239	2,793,000	587,705	3,996	2,934,843	475,796
chb	147,912	57,954,895	21,748,320	146,713	56,818,998	23,278,848	144,282	57,210,682	24,155,595
chn	582,804 [a]	361,555,793 [a]	84,118,580 [a]	589,398	369,896,767	87,416,378 [a]	595,303	387,385,034	89,721,860 [a]
ccc	30,387	22,979,946	4,311,234	36,864	24,997,736 [a]	5,272,184	37,996 [a]	23,758,101 [a]	5,240,805 [a]
cpc	85,080 [a]	27,813,626 [a]	4,339,933 [a]	84,336 [a]	27,462,623 [a]	4,574,550 [a]	83,733 [a]	29,212,802 [a]	4,547,149 [a]
ecc	24,150	13,451,827 [a]	3,120,351 [a]	23,889	13,546,159 [a]	3,258,595 [a]	23,504	13,931,409	3,269,986
ecv	90,985 [a]	93,071,869 [a]	16,732,701 [a]	89,511	93,765,006 [a]	16,482,315	90,919 [a]	101,746,341 [a]	17,874,955 [a]
elc	3,878,055	1,399,419,800	189,605,837 [a]	3,861,418	1,452,000,815	188,393,158	3,849,692	1,502,746,601	187,145,886
els	15,929 [a]	6,944,522 [a]	1,271,058 [a]	15,780	6,759,222 [a]	1,100,660	15,960	7,288,521	1,195,698
emc	4,059	3,839,838 [a]	1,403,001 [a]	4,130 [a]	4,260,307 [a]	1,406,682 [a]	4,225 [a]	4,597,730 [a]	1,533,157 [a]
feb	1,872 [a]	1,343,225 [a]	397,553 [a]	1,866 [a]	1,294,646 [a]	429,023 [a]	1,898 [a]	1,537,041 [a]	395,719 [a]
fmc	58,220	60,584,079	10,591,064	59,156	62,478,294	10,513,187	59,354	65,359,325 [a]	10,708,854 [a]
fum	50,005 [f]	NA	NA	45,542 [f]	NA	NA	44,711 [f]	NA	NA
ggb	72,388 [a]	21,561,432 [a]	1,402,330 [a]	73,129 [a]	22,376,970 [a]	1,440,342 [a]	71,140 [a]	19,651,624 [a]	2,052,409 [a]
lca	See ELCA	See ELCA	See ELCA	See ELCA	See ELCA	See ELCA	See ELCA	See ELCA	See ELCA
lms	1,953,248	777,467,488	97,275,934 [a]	1,945,077	789,821,559	96,355,945 [a]	1,944,905	817,412,113	96,048,560 [a]
mch	94,222 [a]	68,118,222	28,835,719	95,634	71,385,271	27,973,380	87,911 [a]	64,651,639	24,830,192
mgc	34,040	14,721,813 [a]	8,265,700	33,629	14,412,556	7,951,676	32,782	16,093,551 [a]	8,557,126 [a]
mus	MCH & MGC	MCH & MGC	MCH & MGC	MCH & MGC	MCH & MGC	MCH & MGC	MCH & MGC	MCH & MGC	MCH & MGC
mca	22,533	10,150,953	1,208,372	22,223	9,675,502	1,191,131	21,448	9,753,010	1,182,778
nab	43,446	28,375,947	7,327,594	43,045	30,676,902	7,454,087	43,236	32,800,560	7,515,707
opc	12,580 [a]	12,466,266 [a]	3,025,824 [a]	12,924 [a]	13,158,089 [a]	3,039,676 [a]	13,970	14,393,880	3,120,454
pch	2,780,406	1,696,092,968	309,069,530	2,742,192	1,700,918,712	310,375,024	2,698,262	1,800,008,292	307,158,749
rca	190,322 [b]	147,181,320 [b]	28,457,900 [b]	188,551 [b]	159,715,941 [b]	26,009,853 [b]	185,242	153,107,408	27,906,830
sda	748,687	191,362,737	476,902,779	761,703	209,524,570	473,769,831	775,349	229,596,444	503,347,816
sbc	15,358,866	4,462,915,112	751,366,698	15,398,642	4,621,157,751	761,298,249	15,614,060	5,263,421,764	815,360,696
ucc	1,555,382	521,190,413	73,906,372	1,530,178	550,847,702	71,046,517	1,501,310	556,540,722	67,269,762
wel	316,183 [a]	127,858,970 [a]	26,426,128 [a]	315,871	137,187,582	24,587,988	315,302	142,851,919	23,998,935
Total	29,757,441	10,959,280,170	2,283,168,186	29,731,548	11,314,263,241	2,287,518,962	29,792,288	12,195,687,555	2,367,945,929

a Data obtained from denomination source.
b empty tomb review of RCA directory data.
f Inclusive membership, obtained from the denomination and used only in Chapter 5 analysis.

Appendix B-1: Church Member Giving 1968-2000 (continued)

	Data Year 1995			Data Year 1996			Data Year 1997		
	Full/Confirmed Members	Congregational Finances	Benevolences	Full/Confirmed Members	Congregational Finances	Benevolences	Full/Confirmed Members	Congregational Finances	Benevolences
abc	726,452 [a]	365,873,197 [a]	57,052,333 [a]	670,363 [a]	351,362,401 [a]	55,982,392 [a]	658,731 [a]	312,860,507 [a]	54,236,977 [a]
alc	See ELCA	See ELCA	See ELCA	See ELCA	See ELCA	See ELCA	See ELCA	See ELCA	See ELCA
arp	33,513	23,399,372 [a]	5,711,882 [a]	34,117	23,419,989 [a]	5,571,337 [a]	34,344	25,241,384	6,606,829
bcc	18,529	16,032,149	5,480,828	18,424	16,892,154	4,748,871	19,016 [a]	17,456,379 [a]	5,934,414 [a]
ccd	601,237	357,895,652	42,887,958	586,131	370,210,746	42,877,144	568,921	381,463,761	43,009,412
cga	224,061	160,897,147	26,192,559	229,240	180,581,111	26,983,385	229,302	194,438,623	29,054,047
cgg	3,877	2,722,766	486,661	3,920	2,926,516	491,348	3,877	2,987,337	515,247
chb	143,121	60,242,418	22,599,214	141,811	60,524,557 [a]	19,683,035 [a]	141,400	60,923,817 [a]	19,611,047 [a]
chn	598,946	396,698,137	93,440,095	608,008	419,450,850	95,358,352	615,632	433,821,462	99,075,440
ccc	38,853 [a]	24,250,819 [a]	5,483,659 [a]	38,469 [a]	25,834,363 [a]	4,989,062 [a]	38,956	28,204,355	5,167,644
cpc	81,094 [a]	31,072,697 [a]	4,711,934 [a]	80,122 [a]	31,875,061 [a]	5,035,451 [a]	79,576 [a]	32,152,971 [a]	5,152,129 [a]
ecc	23,422	14,830,454	3,301,060	23,091	14,692,608	3,273,685	22,957	15,658,454	3,460,999
ecv	91,458	109,776,363 [a]	17,565,085 [a]	91,823 [a]	115,693,329 [a]	18,726,756 [a]	93,414	127,642,950	20,462,435
elc	3,845,063	1,551,842,465	188,107,066	3,838,750	1,629,909,672	191,476,141	3,844,169	1,731,806,133	201,115,441
els	16,543	7,712,358 [a]	1,084,136	16,511	8,136,195	1,104,996	16,444	8,937,103	1,150,419
emc	4,284 [a]	5,321,079 [a]	1,603,548 [a]	4,201	5,361,912 [a]	1,793,267 [a]	4,348 [a]	7,017,588 [a]	2,039,740 [a]
feb	1,856 [a]	1,412,281 [a]	447,544 [a]	1,751 [a]	1,198,120 [a]	507,656 [a]	1,763	1,120,222 [a]	518,777 [a]
fmc	59,060	67,687,955	11,114,804	59,343 [a]	70,262,626	11,651,462	62,191	78,687,325	12,261,465
fum	43,440 [f]	NA	NA	42,918 [f]	NA	NA	41,040 [f]	NA	NA
ggb	70,886 [a]	24,385,956 [a]	1,722,662 [a]	70,562 [a]	27,763,966 [a]	1,832,909 [a]	72,326	28,093,944	1,780,851
lca	See ELCA	See ELCA	See ELCA	See ELCA	See ELCA	See ELCA	See ELCA	See ELCA	See ELCA
lms	1,943,281	832,701,255	98,139,835 [a]	1,951,730	855,461,015	104,076,876 [a]	1,951,391	887,928,255	110,520,917
mch	90,139 [a]	71,641,773	26,832,240	90,959	76,669,365	27,812,549	92,161	76,087,609 [a]	25,637,872 [a]
mgc	35,852	15,774,961 [a]	7,587,049 [a]	35,333	18,282,833	7,969,999	34,731	14,690,904	6,514,761
mus	MCH & MGC	MCH & MGC	MCH & MGC	MCH & MGC	MCH & MGC	MCH & MGC	MCH & MGC	MCH & MGC	MCH & MGC
mca	21,409	10,996,031	1,167,513	21,140	11,798,536	1,237,349	21,108	12,555,760	1,148,478
nab	43,928	37,078,473	7,480,331	43,744 [a]	37,172,560 [a]	7,957,860 [a]	43,850	37,401,175	7,986,099
opc	14,355	16,017,003	3,376,691	15,072 [a]	17,883,915 [a]	3,467,207 [a]	15,072	20,090,259	3,967,490
pch	2,665,276	1,855,684,719	309,978,224	2,631,466	1,930,179,808	322,336,258	2,609,191	2,064,789,378	344,757,186
rca	183,255	164,250,624	29,995,068	182,342	183,975,696 [a]	31,271,007	180,980 [a]	181,977,101 [a]	32,130,943 [a]
sda	790,731	240,565,576	503,334,129	809,159	242,316,834	524,977,061	825,654	249,591,109	552,633,569
sbc	15,663,296	5,209,748,503	858,635,435	15,691,249 [a]	5,987,033,115	891,149,403 [a]	15,891,514	6,098,933,137	930,176,909
ucc	1,472,213	578,042,965	67,806,448	1,452,565	615,727,028	69,013,791	1,438,181	651,176,773	70,180,193
wel	314,188 [a]	150,853,785 [a]	33,193,286 [a]	314,379 [a]	156,966,741 [a]	47,436,904	315,355	164,256,655	52,322,175
Total	29,820,178	12,405,408,933	2,436,519,277	29,755,775	13,489,563,622	2,530,793,513	29,926,555	13,947,992,430	2,649,129,905

[a] Data obtained from denominational source.

[f] Inclusive membership, obtained from the denomination and used only in Chapter 5 analysis.

Appendix B-1: Church Member Giving 1968-2000 (continued)

	Data Year 1998			Data Year 1999			Data Year 2000		
	Full/Confirmed Members	Congregational Finances	Benevolences	Full/Confirmed Members	Congregational Finances	Benevolences	Full/Confirmed Members	Congregational Finances	Benevolences
abc	621,232 a	326,046,153 a	53,866,448 a	603,014 a	331,513,521 a	58,675,160	593,113	359,484,902	63,042,002 a
alc	See ELCA	See ELCA	See ELCA	See ELCA	See ELCA	See ELCA	See ELCA	See ELCA	See ELCA
arp	34,642 a	28,831,982 a	7,378,121 a	35,643 a	33,862,219 a	7,973,285 a	35,022 a	33,004,995 a	25,148,657 a
bcc	19,577	24,116,889	5,274,612	20,010	22,654,566	5,913,551	20,587	25,148,637	5,703,506
ccd	547,875 a	395,699,954 a	45,576,436 a	535,893	410,583,119	47,795,574	527,363	433,965,354	48,726,350
cga	234,311 f	NA	NA	235,849 f	NA	NA	238,891 f	NA	NA
cgg	3,824	3,087,000	689,756	4,083	3,357,300	503,365	4,037	3,232,160	610,173
chb	140,011 a	57,605,960 a	22,283,498 a	138,304 a	63,774,756 a	21,852,687 a	135,978	67,285,361	25,251,272 a
chn	623,028	460,776,715	104,925,922	626,033 a	487,437,668 a	110,818,743 a	633,264	516,708,125	122,284,063
ccc	38,996	28,976,122	5,194,733	40,414	31,165,218	5,931,456	40,974 a	33,537,589 a	6,360,912 a
cpc	80,829 a	33,623,232 a	5,412,917 a	79,452 a	36,303,752 a	5,879,014 a	86,519	39,533,829	6,591,617
ecc	22,868	15,956,209	3,599,440	22,349	16,574,783	3,587,877	21,939	17,656,789	1,982,328
ecv	96,552	140,823,872	20,134,436	98,526 a	161,361,490 a	23,237,513 a	101,317 a	181,127,526 a	25,983,315 a
elc	3,840,136	1,822,915,831	208,853,359	3,825,228	1,972,950,623	220,647,251	3,810,785	2,067,208,285	231,219,316
els	16,897	9,363,126	1,120,386	16,734	10,062,900	1,129,969	16,569	10,910,109	949,421
emc	4,646 a	6,472,868 a	1,854,222 a	4,511 a	7,528,256 a	1,982,985 a	4,929	8,289,743 a	2,085,475 a
feb	1,828 a	1,433,305 a	502,839 a	1,936 a	1,496,949 a	534,203 a	1,764 a	1,360,133 a	373,067 a
fmc	62,176	82,254,922	12,850,607	62,368 a	86,906,899	12,646,064	62,453	98,853,770	13,430,274
fum	33,908 f	NA	NA	34,863 f	NA	NA	41,297 f	NA	NA
ggb	67,314 a	28,533,439 a	2,594,098 a	55,549 a	22,857,097 a	2,331,087 a	66,296 a	30,470,298 a	2,950,915 a
lca	See ELCA	See ELCA	See ELCA	See ELCA	See ELCA	See ELCA	See ELCA	See ELCA	See ELCA
lms	1,952,020	975,113,229	121,536,226	1,945,846	986,295,136	123,632,549	1,934,057	1,101,690,594	127,554,235
mch	92,002 a	75,796,469 a	26,452,444 a	See MUS	See MUS	See MUS	See MUS	See MUS	See MUS
mgc	36,600	14,786,936 a	5,853,292 a	See MUS	See MUS	See MUS	See MUS	See MUS	See MUS
mus	MCH & MGC	MCH & MGC	MCH & MGC	120,381 a	95,843,112 a	34,821,702 a	NA	NA	NA
mca	20,764	13,082,671	1,131,742	20,400	11,527,684	849,837	20,281	13,391,991	945,165
nab	43,844 a	41,939,978 a	7,731,550 a	45,738	47,207,867	9,055,128	47,097	54,866,431	9,845,352
opc	15,936	22,362,292	4,438,333	17,279 a	24,878,935	4,920,310	17,914	28,120,325	5,978,474
pch	2,587,674	2,173,483,227	355,628,625	2,560,201	2,326,583,688	384,445,608	2,525,330	2,517,278,130	398,602,204
rca	179,085	189,390,759	33,890,048	178,260 a	216,305,458 a	36,158,625 a	177,281	226,555,821	37,221,041
sda	839,915	269,679,595	588,227,010	861,860	301,221,572	629,944,965	880,921	316,562,375	675,000,508
sbc	15,729,356	6,498,607,390	953,491,003	14,001,690 g	6,001,443,051 g	795,207,316 g	15,221,959 g	7,037,051,273 g	936,520,383 g
ucc	1,421,088	678,251,694	74,861,463	1,401,682	700,645,114	76,550,398	1,377,320	744,991,925	78,525,195
wel	315,581 a	178,509,021 a	44,674,782 a	315,637 a	182,185,390 a	49,215,524 a	316,386	194,799,255 a	52,998,892 a
Total	29,456,296	14,597,520,840	2,720,028,348	27,639,021	14,594,528,123	2,676,241,746	28,681,455	16,163,550,725	2,888,784,036

a Data obtained from denominational source.

f Inclusive membership, obtained from the denomination and used only in Chapter 5 analysis.

g The 1999 and 2000 data for the Southern Baptist Convention used in the 1968-2000 analysis includes data only for those State Conventions that provided a breakdown of Total Contributions between Congregational Finances and Benevolences for that year. For the Eleven Denominations 1921-2000 analysis, 1999 and 2000 Southern Baptist Convention Total Contributions are $7,772,452,961 and $8,437,177,940, respectively. For the Eleven Denominations 1921-2000 analysis, and the Membership Trends analysis, 1999 and 2000 Southern Baptist Convention Membership is 15,581,756 and 15,960,308, respectively.

Appendix B-2: Church Member Giving for 44 Denominations, 1999-2000

	Data Year 1999			Data Year 2000		
	Full/Confirmed Members	Congregational Finances	Benevolences	Full/Confirmed Members	Congregational Finances	Benevolences
African Methodist Episcopal Zion Church	1,060,256	82,340,065	3,221,303	1,080,256	95,966,232	3,271,303
Allegany Wesleyan Methodist Connection (Original Allegheny Conference)	1,768 [a]	4,258,815	1,067,924	1,734	4,178,221	1,097,005
Apostolic Faith Mission Church of God	8,301	420,000	574,000	8,291	390,000	579,000
Baptist General Conference	142,871 [a]	160,485,560 [a]	23,322,007 [a]	141,781 [a]	136,546,920 [a]	22,572,695
Bible Fellowship Church	7,142 [a]	8,779,515 [a]	2,360,503 [a]	7,258	10,342,940	2,620,065
Church of Christ (Holiness) U.S.A.	10,509 [a]	8,084,857 [a]	405,638 [a]	10,475	9,106,063	443,937
Church of Lutheran Brethren of America	8,229	10,363,380	1,921,186	8,207 [a]	11,159,060 [a]	2,064,723 [a]
Church of the Lutheran Confession	6,475	4,252,615	705,728	6,527	4,625,633	768,464
Churches of God General Conference	32,045	19,597,034	4,390,455	32,380	21,078,740	4,495,037
The Episcopal Church	1,814,380 [a]	1,884,535,013 [a]	262,300,705 [a]	1,806,185 [a]	1,978,394,026 [a]	251,111,600 [a]
The Evangelical Church	12,879 [a]	12,104,167 [a]	2,783,478 [a]	12,475	12,784,502	2,848,483
International Church of the Foursquare Gospel	233,412	495,911,270 [a]	12,500,000	242,616	540,000,000	36,162,641
International Pentecostal Church of Christ	2,420	3,059,829	3,185,239	2,184 [a]	2,867,887 [a]	3,888,865 [a]
Presbyterian Church in America	235,661 [a]	340,377,605 [a]	96,219,775 [a]	247,010	384,909,043	98,600,797
The Romano Byzantine Synod of the Orthodox Catholic Church	23,000 [a]	58,000 [a]	27,000 [a]	25,000	61,000	30,000
The United Methodist Church	8,377,662	3,639,161,294	884,123,557	8,340,954	3,854,328,165	906,820,115
The Wesleyan Church	112,615	179,035,829 [a]	27,805,260	114,084	204,711,754	28,136,843

[a] Data obtained from denominational source.

127

Appendix B-3.1: Church Member Giving for Eleven Denominations, 1921-1952, in Current Dollars

Year	Total Contributions	Members	Per Capita Giving
1921	$281,173,263	17,459,611	$16.10
1922	345,995,802	18,257,426	18.95
1923	415,556,876	18,866,775	22.03
1924	443,187,826	19,245,220	23.03
1925	412,658,363	19,474,863	21.19
1926	368,529,223	17,054,404	21.61
1927	459,527,624	20,266,709	22.67
1928	429,947,883	20,910,584	20.56
1929	445,327,233	20,612,910	21.60
1930	419,697,819	20,796,745	20.18
1931	367,158,877	21,508,745	17.07
1932	309,409,873	21,757,411	14.22
1933	260,366,681	21,792,663	11.95
1934	260,681,472	22,105,624	11.79
1935	267,596,925	22,204,355	12.05
1936	279,835,526	21,746,023	12.87
1937	297,134,313	21,906,456	13.56
1938	307,217,666	22,330,090	13.76
1939	302,300,476	23,084,048	13.10
1940	311,362,429	23,671,660	13.15
1941	336,732,622	23,120,929	14.56
1942	358,419,893	23,556,204	15.22
1943	400,742,492	24,679,784	16.24
1944	461,500,390	25,217,019	10.30
1945	551,404,448	25,898,642	21.29
1946	608,165,179	26,158,559	23.25
1947	684,393,895	27,082,905	25.27
1948	775,360,993	27,036,992	28.68
1949	875,069,944	27,611,824	31.69
1950	934,723,015	28,176,095	33.17
1951	1,033,391,527	28,974,314	35.67
1952	1,121,802,639	29,304,909	38.28

Appendix B-3.2: Church Member Giving for Eleven Denominations, 1953-1967

	Data Year 1953		Data Year 1954		Data Year 1955	
	Total Contributions	Per Capita Total Contributions	Total Contributions	Per Capita Total Contributions	Total Contributions	Per Capita Total Contributions
American Baptist (Northern)	$66,557,447 a	$44.50 b	$65,354,184	$43.17	$67,538,753 d	$44.19 d
Christian Church (Disciples of Christ)	60,065,545 c	32.50 b	65,925,164	34.77	68,611,162 d	35.96 d
Church of the Brethren	7,458,584	43.78	7,812,806	45.88	9,130,616	53.00
The Episcopal Church	84,209,027	49.02	92,079,668	51.84	97,541,567 b	50.94 b
Evangelical Lutheran Church in America						
The American Lutheran Church						
American Lutheran Church	30,881,256	55.24	34,202,987	58.83	40,411,856	67.03
The Evangelical Lutheran Church	30,313,907	48.70	33,312,926	51.64	37,070,341	55.29
United Evangelical Lutheran Ch.	1,953,163	55.85	2,268,200	50.25	2,635,469	69.84
Lutheran Free Church	Not Reported: YACC 1955, p. 264		2,101,026	44.51	2,708,747	55.76
Evan. Lutheran Churches, Assn. of	Not Reported: YACC 1955, p. 264		Not Reported: YACC 1956, p. 276		Not Reported: YACC 1957, p. 284	
Lutheran Church in America						
United Lutheran Church	67,721,548	45.68	76,304,344	50.25	83,170,787	53.46
General Council Evang. Luth. Ch.						
General Synod of Evan. Luth. Ch.						
United Syn. Evang. Luth. South	Not Reported: YACC 1955, p. 264		Not Reported: YACC 1956, p. 276		Not Reported: YACC 1957, p. 284	
American Evangelical Luth. Ch.						
Augustana Lutheran Church	18,733,019	53.98	22,203,098	62.14	22,090,350	60.12
Finnish Lutheran Ch. (Suomi Synod)	744,971	32.12	674,554	29.47	1,059,682	43.75
Moravian Church in Am. No. Prov.	1,235,534	53.26	1,461,658	59.51	1,241,008	49.15
Presbyterian Church (U.S.A.)						
United Presbyterian Ch. in U.S.A.						
Presbyterian Church in the U.S.A.	141,057,179	56.49	158,110,613	61.47	180,472,698	68.09
United Presbyterian Ch. in N.A.	13,204,897	57.73	14,797,353	62.37	16,019,616	65.39
Presbyterian Church in the U.S.	56,001,996	73.99	59,222,983	75.54	66,033,260	81.43
Reformed Church in America	13,671,897	68.57	14,740,275	71.87	17,459,572	84.05
Southern Baptist Convention	278,851,129	39.84	305,573,654	42.17	334,836,283	44.54
United Church of Christ						
Congregational Christian	64,061,866	49.91	71,786,834	54.76	80,519,810	60.00
Congregational						
Evangelical and Reformed	31,025,133	41.24	36,261,267	46.83	41,363,406	52.74
Evangelical Synod of N.A./German						
Reformed Church in the U.S.						
The United Methodist Church						
The Evangelical United Brethren	36,331,994	50.21	36,609,598	50.43	41,199,631	56.01
The Methodist Church	314,521,214	34.37	345,416,448	37.53	389,490,613	41.82
Methodist Episcopal Church						
Methodist Episcopal Church South						
Methodist Protestant Church						
Total	$1,318,601,306		$1,446,219,640		$1,600,655,226	

a In data year 1953, $805,135 has been subtracted from the 1955 *Yearbook of American Churches* (Edition for 1956) entry. See 1956 *Yearbook of American Churches* (Edition for 1957), p. 276, n.1.

b This Per Capita Total Contributions figure was calculated by dividing (1) revised Total Contributions as listed in this Appendix, by (2) Membership that, for purposes of this report, had been calculated by dividing the unrevised Total Contributions by the Per Capita Total Contributions figures that were published in the *YACC* series.

c In data year 1953, $5,508,883 has been added to the 1955 *Yearbook of American Churches* (Edition for 1956) entry. See 1956 *Yearbook of American Churches* (Edition for 1957), p. 276, n. 4.

d Total Contributions and Per Capita Total Contributions, respectively, prorated based on available data as follows: American Baptist Churches, 1954 and 1957 data; Christian Church (Disciples of Christ), 1954 and 1956 data; and The Episcopal Church, 1954 and 1956 data.

Appendix B-3.2: Church Member Giving for Eleven Denominations, 1953-1967 (continued)

	Data Year 1956		Data Year 1957		Data Year 1958	
	Total Contributions	Per Capita Total Contributions	Total Contributions	Per Capita Total Contributions	Total Contributions	Per Capita Total Contributions
American Baptist (Northern)	$69,723,321 e	$45.21 e	$71,907,890	$46.23	$70,405,404	$45.03 e
Christian Church (Disciples of Christ)	71,397,159	37.14	73,737,955	37.94	79,127,458	41.17
Church of the Brethren	10,936,285	63.15	11,293,388	64.43	12,288,049	70.03
The Episcopal Church	103,003,465	52.79	111,660,728	53.48	120,687,177	58.33
Evangelical Lutheran Church in America						
The American Lutheran Church						
American Lutheran Church	45,316,809	72.35	44,518,194	68.80	47,216,896	70.89
The Evangelical Lutheran Church	39,096,038	56.47	44,212,046	61.95	45,366,512	61.74
United Evangelical Lutheran Ch.	2,843,527	73.57	2,641,201	65.46	3,256,050	77.38
Lutheran Free Church	2,652,307	53.14	3,379,882	64.70	3,519,017	66.31
Evan. Lutheran Churches, Assn. of	Not Reported: YACC 1958, p. 292		Not Reported: YACC 1959, p. 277		Not Reported: YACC 1960, p. 276	
Lutheran Church in America						
United Lutheran Church	93,321,223	58.46	100,943,860	61.89	110,179,054	66.45
General Council Evang. Luth. Ch.						
General Synod of Evan. Luth. Ch.						
United Syn. Evang. Luth. South						
American Evangelical Luth. Ch.	Not Comparable YACC 1958, p. 292		935,319	59.45	1,167,503	72.98
Augustana Lutheran Church	24,893,792	66.15	28,180,152	72.09	29,163,771	73.17
Finnish Lutheran Ch. (Suomi Synod)	1,308,026	51.56	1,524,299	58.11	1,533,058	61.94
Moravian Church in Am. No. Prov.	1,740,961	67.53	1,776,703	67.77	1,816,281	68.14
Presbyterian Church (U.S.A.)						
United Presbyterian Ch. in U.S.A.					243,000,572	78.29
Presbyterian Church in the U.S.A.	204,208,085	75.02	214,253,598	77.06		
United Presbyterian Ch. in N.A.	18,424,935	73.30	19,117,837	74.24		
Presbyterian Church in the U.S.	73,477,555	88.56	78,426,424	92.03	82,760,291	95.18
Reformed Church in America	18,718,003	88.56	19,658,604	91.10	21,550,017	98.24
Southern Baptist Convention	372,136,675	48.17	397,540,347	49.99	419,619,438	51.04
United Church of Christ						
Congregational Christian	89,914,505	65.18	90,333,453	64.87	97,480,446	69.55
Congregational						
Evangelical and Reformed	51,519,531	64.88	55,718,141	69.56	63,419,468	78.56
Evangelical Synod of N.A./German						
Reformed Church in the U.S.						
The United Methodist Church						
The Evangelical United Brethren	44,727,060	60.57	45,738,332 e	61.75 e	46,749,605 e	62.93 e
The Methodist Church	413,893,955	43.82	462,826,269 e	48.31 e	511,758,582	52.80
Methodist Episcopal Church						
Methodist Episcopal Church South						
Methodist Protestant Church						
Total	$1,753,253,223		$1,880,324,622		$2,012,064,649	

e Total Contributions and Per Capita Total Contributions, respectively, prorated based on available data as follows: American Baptist Churches 1954 and 1957 data; The Evangelical United Brethren, 1956 and 1960 data; and The Methodist Church, 1956 and 1958 data.

Appendix B-3.2: Church Member Giving for Eleven Denominations, 1953-1967 (continued)

	Data Year 1959		Data Year 1960		Data Year 1961	
	Total Contributions	Per Capita Total Contributions	Total Contributions	Per Capita Total Contributions	Total Contributions	Per Capita Total Contributions
American Baptist (Northern)	$74,877,669	$48.52	$73,106,232	$48.06	$104,887,025	$68.96
Christian Church (Disciples of Christ)	84,375,152 f	51.22	86,834,944	63.26	89,730,589	65.31
Church of the Brethren	12,143,983	65.27	12,644,194	68.33	13,653,155	73.33
The Episcopal Church	130,279,752	61.36	140,625,284	64.51	154,458,809	68.30
Evangelical Lutheran Church in America						
The American Lutheran Church	50,163,078	73.52	51,898,875	74.49	113,645,260	73.28
The Evangelical Lutheran Church	49,488,063	65.56	51,297,348	66.85		
United Evangelical Lutheran Ch.	Not Reported: YACC 1961, p. 273		Not Reported: YACC 1963, p. 273			
Lutheran Free Church	3,354,270	61.20	3,618,418	63.98	4,316,925	73.46
Evan. Lutheran Churches, Assn. of	Not Reported: YACC 1961, p. 273		Not Reported: YACC 1963, p. 273			
Lutheran Church in America						
United Lutheran Church	114,458,260	68.29	119,447,895	70.86	128,850,845	76.18
General Council Evang. Luth. Ch.						
General Synod of Evan. Luth. Ch.						
United Syn. Evang. Luth. South						
American Evangelical Luth. Ch.	1,033,907	63.83	1,371,600	83.63	1,209,752	74.89
Augustana Lutheran Church	31,279,335	76.97	33,478,865	80.88	37,863,105	89.37
Finnish Lutheran Ch. (Suomi Synod)	1,685,342	68.61	1,860,481	76.32	1,744,550	70.60
Moravian Church in Am. No. Prov.	2,398,565	89.28	2,252,536	82.95	2,489,930	90.84
Presbyterian Church (U.S.A.)						
United Presbyterian Ch. in U.S.A.	259,679,057	82.30	270,233,943	84.31	285,380,476	87.90
Presbyterian Church in the U.S.A.						
United Presbyterian Ch. in N.A.						
Presbyterian Church in the U.S.	88,404,631	99.42	91,582,428	101.44	96,637,354	105.33
Reformed Church in America	22,970,935	103.23	23,615,749	104.53	25,045,773	108.80
Southern Baptist Convention	453,338,720	53.88	480,608,972	55.68	501,301,714	50.24
United Church of Christ						
Congregational Christian	100,938,267	71.12	104,862,037	73.20	105,871,158	73.72
Congregational						
Evangelical and Reformed	65,541,874	80.92	62,346,084	76.58	65,704,662	80.33
Evangelical Synod of N.A./German						
Reformed Church in the U.S.						
The United Methodist Church						
The Evangelical United Brethren	47,760,877 g	64.10 g	48,772,149	65.28	50,818,912	68.12
The Methodist Church	532,854,842 g	53.97 g	553,951,102	55.14	581,504,618	57.27
Methodist Episcopal Church						
Methodist Episcopal Church South						
Methodist Protestant Church						
Total	$2,127,026,579		$2,214,409,136		$2,365,114,612	

f The 1961 YACC, p. 273 indicates that data for this year is not comparable with data for the previous year.

g Total Contributions and Per Capita Total Contributions, respectively, prorated based on available data as follows: The Evangelical United Brethren, 1956 and 1960 data; and The Methodist Church, 1958 and 1960 data.

Appendix B-3.2: Church Member Giving for Eleven Denominations, 1953-1967 (continued)

	Data Year 1962		Data Year 1963		Data Year 1964	
	Total Contributions	Per Capita Total Contributions	Total Contributions	Per Capita Total Contributions	Total Contributions	Per Capita Total Contributions
American Baptist (Northern)	$105,667,332	$68.42	$99,001,651	$68.34	$104,699,557	$69.99
Christian Church (Disciples of Christ)	91,889,457	67.20	96,607,038	75.81	102,102,840	86.44
Church of the Brethren	14,594,572	77.88	14,574,688	72.06	15,221,162	76.08
The Episcopal Church	155,971,264	69.80	171,125,464	76.20	175,374,777	76.66
Evangelical Lutheran Church in America						
The American Lutheran Church	114,912,112	72.47	136,202,292	81.11	143,687,165	83.83
American Lutheran Church						
The Evangelical Lutheran Church						
United Evangelical Lutheran Ch.						
Lutheran Free Church	4,765,138	78.68				
Evan. Lutheran Churches, Assn. of						
Lutheran Church in America	185,166,857	84.98	157,423,391	71.45	170,012,096	76.35
United Lutheran Church						
General Council Evang. Luth. Ch.						
General Synod of Evan. Luth. Ch.						
United Syn. Evang. Luth. South						
American Evangelical Luth. Ch.						
Augustana Lutheran Church						
Finnish Lutheran Ch. (Suomi Synod)						
Moravian Church in Am. No. Prov.	2,512,133	91.92	2,472,273	89.29	2,868,694	103.54
Presbyterian Church (U.S.A.)						
United Presbyterian Ch. in U.S.A.	288,496,652	88.08	297,582,313	90.46	304,833,435	92.29
Presbyterian Church in the U.S.A.						
United Presbyterian Ch. in N.A.						
Presbyterian Church in the U.S.	99,262,431	106.96	102,625,764	109.46	108,269,579	114.61
Reformed Church in America	25,579,443	110.16	26,918,484	117.58	29,174,103	126.44
Southern Baptist Convention	540,811,457	53.06	556,042,694	53.49	591,587,981	55.80
United Church of Christ	164,858,968	72.83	162,379,019	73.12	169,208,042	75.94
Congregational Christian						
Congregational						
Evangelical and Reformed						
Evangelical Synod of N.A./German						
Reformed Church in the U.S.						
The United Methodist Church						
The Evangelical United Brethren	54,567,962	72.91	49,921,568	67.37	56,552,783	76.34
The Methodist Church	599,081,561	58.53	613,547,721	59.60	508,841,881	59.09
Methodist Episcopal Church						
Methodist Episcopal Church South						
Methodist Protestant Church						
Total	$2,448,137,339		$2,486,424,360		$2,582,434,095	

Note: Data for the years 1965 through 1967 was not available in a form that could be readily analyzed for the present purposes, and therefore data for 1965-1967 was estimated as described in the introductory comments to Appendix B. See Appendix B-1 for 1968-1991 data except for The Episcopal Church and The United Methodist Church, available data for which is presented in the continuation of Appendix B-3 in the table immediately following.

Appendix B-3.3: Church Member Giving for Eleven Denominations,

The Episcopal Church and The United Methodist Church, 1968-2000

The Episcopal Church			The United Methodist Church		
Data Year	Total Contributions	Full/Confirmed Membership	Data Year	Total Contributions	Full/Confirmed Membership
1968	$202,658,092 [c]	2,322,911 [c]	1968	$763,000,434 [a]	10,849,375 [b]
1969	209,989,189 [c]	2,238,538	1969	800,425,000	10,671,774
1970	248,702,969	2,208,773	1970	819,945,000	10,509,198
1971	257,523,469	2,143,557	1971	843,103,000	10,334,521
1972	270,245,645	2,099,896	1972	885,708,000	10,192,265
1973	296,735,919 [c]	2,079,873 [c]	1973	935,723,000	10,063,046
1974	305,628,925	2,069,793	1974	1,009,760,804	9,957,710
1975	352,243,222	2,051,914 [c]	1975	1,081,080,372	9,861,028
1976	375,942,065	2,021,057	1976	1,162,828,991	9,785,534
1977	401,814,395	2,114,638	1977	1,264,191,548	9,731,779
1978	430,116,564	1,975,234	1978	1,364,460,266	9,653,711
1979	484,211,412	1,962,062	1979	1,483,481,986	9,584,771
1980	507,315,457	1,933,080 [c]	1980	1,632,204,336	9,519,407
1981	697,816,298	1,930,690	1981	1,794,706,741	9,457,012
1982	778,184,068	1,922,923 [c]	1982	1,931,796,533	9,405,164
1983	876,844,252	1,906,618	1983	2,049,437,917	9,291,936
1984	939,796,743	1,896,056	1984	2,211,306,198	9,266,853
1985	1,043,117,983	1,881,250	1985	2,333,928,274	9,192,172
1986	1,134,455,479	1,772,271 [c]	1986	2,460,079,431	9,124,575
1987	1,181,378,441	1,741,036	1987	2,573,748,234	9,055,145
1988	1,209,378,098	1,725,581	1988	2,697,918,285	8,979,139
1989	1,309,243,747	1,714,122	1989	2,845,998,177	8,904,824
1990	1,377,794,610	1,698,240	1990	2,967,535,538	8,853,455
1991	1,541,141,356 [c]	1,613,825 [c]	1991	3,099,522,282	8,789,101
1992	1,582,055,527 [c]	1,615,930 [c]	1992	3,202,700,721 [c]	8,726,951 [c]
1993	1,617,623,255 [c]	1,580,339 [c]	1993	3,303,255,279	8,646,595
1994	1,679,250,095 [c]	1,578,282 [c]	1994	3,430,351,778	8,584,125
1995	1,840,431,636 [c]	1,584,225 [c]	1995	3,568,359,334 [c]	8,538,808 [c]
1996	1,731,727,725 [c]	1,593,756 [c]	1996	3,744,692,223	8,496,047 [c]
1997	1,832,000,448 [c]	1,717,069 [c]	1997	3,990,329,491 [c]	8,452,042 [c]
1998	1,977,012,320 [c]	1,765,562 [c]	1998	4,219,596,499 [c]	8,411,503 [c]
1999	2,146,835,718 [c]	1,814,380 [c]	1999	4,523,284,851	8,377,662
2000	2,229,505,626 [c]	1,806,185 [c]	2000	4,761,148,280	8,340,954

a The Evangelical United Brethren Data Not Reported: YACC 1970, p. 198-200. This figure is the sum of The Methodist Church in 1968, and the Evangelical United Brethren data for 1967.

b This membership figure is an average of the sum of 1967 membership for The Methodist Church and the Evangelical United Brethren and 1969 data for The United Methodist Church.

c Data obtained directly from denominational source.

APPENDIX B-4: *Trends in Giving and Membership*

Appendix B-4.1: Membership for Seven Denominations, 1968-2000

Year	American Baptist Churches (Total Mem.)	Assemblies Of God	Baptist General Conference	Christian and Missionary Alliance	Church of God (Cleveland, TN)	Roman Catholic Church	Salvation Army
1968	1,583,560	610,946	100,000	71,656	243,532	47,468,333	329,515
1969	1,528,019	626,660	101,226	70,573	257,995	47,872,089	331,711
1970	1,472,478	625,027	103,955	71,708	272,276	48,214,729	326,934
1971	1,562,636	645,891	108,474	73,547	287,099	48,390,990	335,684
1972	1,484,393	679,813	111,364	77,991	297,103	48,460,427	358,626
1973	1,502,759	700,071	109,033	77,606	313,332	48,465,438	361,571
1974	1,579,029	751,818	111,093	80,412	328,892	48,701,835	366,471
1975	1,603,033	785,348	115,340	83,628	343,249	48,881,872	384,817
1976	1,593,574	898,711	117,973	83,978	365,124	49,325,752	380,618
1977	1,584,517	939,312	120,222	88,763	377,765	49,836,176	396,238
1978	1,589,610	932,365	131,000	88,903	392,551	49,602,035	414,035
1979	1,600,521	958,418	126,800	96,324	441,385	49,812,178	414,659
1980	1,607,541	1,064,490	133,385	106,050	435,012	50,449,842	417,359
1981	1,621,795	1,103,134	127,662	109,558	456,797	51,207,579	414,999
1982	1,637,099	1,119,686	129,928	112,745	463,992	52,088,774 [a]	419,475
1983	1,620,153	1,153,935	131,594 [a]	117,501	493,904	52,392,934	428,046
1984	1,559,683	1,189,143	131,162 [a]	120,250	505,775	52,286,043	420,971
1985	1,576,483	1,235,403	130,193 [a]	123,602	521,061 [b]	52,654,908	427,825
1986	1,568,778 [a]	1,258,724	132,546 [a]	130,116	536,346 [b]	52,893,217	432,893
1987	1,561,656 [a]	1,275,146	136,688 [a]	131,354	551,632 [b]	53,496,862	434,002
1988	1,548,573 [a]	1,275,148	134,396 [a]	133,575	556,917 [b]	54,918,949 [a]	433,448
1989	1,535,971 [a]	1,266,982	135,125 [a]	134,336	582,203	57,019,948	445,566
1990	1,527,840 [a]	1,298,121	133,742 [a]	138,071	620,393	58,568,015	445,991
1991	1,534,078 [a]	1,324,800	134,717 [a]	141,077	646,201 [b]	58,267,424	446,403
1992	1,538,710 [a]	1,337,321	134,658 [a]	142,346	672,008	59,220,723	450,028 [a]
1993	1,516,505	1,340,400	134,814 [a]	147,367	700,517	59,858,042	450,312 [a]
1994	1,507,934 [a]	1,354,337	135,128	147,560 [a]	722,541	60,190,605	443,246
1995	1,517,400	1,377,320	135,008	147,955	753,230	60,280,454	453,150
1996	1,503,267 [a]	1,407,941	136,120	143,157	773,483 [a]	61,207,914	462,744 [a]
1997	1,478,534 [a]	1,419,717	134,795	146,153	815,042 [a]	61,563,769 [a]	468,262 [a]
1998	1,507,824 [a]	1,453,907	141,445	163,994	839,857 [a]	62,018,436	471,416
1999	1,454,388	1,492,196	142,871 [a]	164,196	870,039	62,391,484	472,871
2000	1,436,909	1,506,834	141,781 [a]	185,133	895,536	63,683,030 [a]	476,887 [a]

a Data obtained from a denominational source.
b Extrapolated fron YACC series.
Note regarding American Baptist Churches in the U.S.A. Total Membership data: Total Membership is used for the American Baptist Churches in the U.S.A. for anlyses that consider membership as a percentage of U.S. population. The ABC denominational office is the source for this data in the years 1968 and 1970. The year 1978 Total Membership data figure is an adjustment of YACC data based on 1981 YACC information.

APPENDIX C: *Income, Deflators, and U.S. Population*

Income, 1929-2000

Per Capita Disposable Personal Income in Current Dollars: U.S. Department of Commerce, Bureau of Economic Analysis; "Table 8.7. Selected Per Capita Product and Income Series in Current and Chained Dollars;" Line 4: "Disposable personal income;" National Income and Product Accounts Tables; <http://www.bea.doc.gov/bea/dn/nipaweb/TableViewFixed.asp#Mid> via <http://www.bea.doc.gov/bea/dn/nipaweb/SelectTable.asp?Selected=Y>: Selections: First Year = 1929-A, Last Year = 2001-A & Q, Annual, Get all years; Last Revised on August 29, 2002; (Generated by empty tomb, inc.: 29 August 2002).

Deflator, 1996 Dollars, 1929-2000

Gross National Product: Implicit Price Deflators for Gross National Product [1996=100]: U.S. Bureau of Economic Analysis; "Table 7.3. Quantity and Price Indexes for Gross National Product and Command-Basis Gross National Product;" Line 4: "Implicit price deflator;" National Income and Product Accounts Tables; < http://www.bea.doc.gov/bea/dn/nipaweb/TableViewFixed.asp#Mid> via <http://www.bea.doc.gov/bea/dn/nipaweb/SelectTable.asp?Selected=Y>: Selections: First Year = 1929-A, Last Year = 2001-A & Q, Annual, Get all years; Last Revised on August 29, 2002; (Generated by empty tomb, inc.: 30 August 2002).

Consumer Price Index (CPI-U) [1982-84 = 100], 1968-2001

U.S. Bureau of Labor Statistics; "Consumer Price Index-All Urban Consumers, Series ID: CUUR0000SA0, Not Seasonally Adjusted, Area: U.S. city average, All items, 1982-84=100;" <http://data.bls.gov/cgi-bin/surveymost?cu> via <http://www.bls.gov/cpi/#data>: Selection: "Consumer Price Index-All Urban Consumers: U.S. All items, 1982-84=100 - CUUR0000SA0"; Change Output Options: From = 1968, To = 2002; (Data extracted by empty tomb, inc.: 3 September 2002).

Population, 1929-2000

U.S Bureau of Economic Analysis; "Table 8.7. Selected Per Capita Product and Income Series in Current and Chained Dollars;" Line 16: "Population (mid-period, thousands)"; National Income and Product Accounts Tables; <http://www.bea.doc.gov/bea/dn/nipaweb/TableViewFixed.asp#Mid> via <http://www.bea.doc.gov/bea/dn/nipaweb/SelectTable.asp?Selected=Y>: Selections: First Year = 1929-A, Last Year = 2001-A & Q, Annual, Get all years; Last Revised on August 29, 2002; (Generated by empty tomb, inc.: 29 August 2002).

Appendix C.1: Per Capita Disposable Personal Income and Deflators, 1921-2000

Year	Current $s Per Capita Disposable Personal Income	Implicit Price Deflator GNP [1958=100]	Implicit Price Deflator GNP [1996=100]	Year	Current $s Per Capita Disposable Personal Income	Implicit Price Deflator GNP [1996=100]	Consumer Price Index (CPI-U) [1982-1984=100]
1921	$555	54.5		1961	$2,081	22.43	
1922	$548	50.1		1962	$2,174	22.74	
1923	$623	51.3		1963	$2,249	22.99	
1924	$626	51.2		1964	$2,412	23.34	
1925	$630	51.9		1965	$2,567	23.77	
1926	$659	51.1		1966	$2,742	24.45	
1927	$650	50.0		1967	$2,899	25.21	
1928	$643	50.8		1968	$3,119	26.29	34.8
1929	$683		12.60	1969	$3,329	27.59	36.7
1930	$605		12.14	1970	$3,591	29.05	38.8
1931	$517		10.87	1971	$3,860	30.52	40.5
1932	$393		9.60	1972	$4,138	31.82	41.8
1933	$365		9.35	1973	$4,619	33.60	44.4
1934	$417		9.87	1974	$5,013	36.62	49.3
1935	$465		10.06	1975	$5,470	40.03	53.8
1936	$525		10.18	1976	$5,960	42.31	56.9
1937	$560		10.61	1977	$6,519	45.03	60.6
1938	$512		10.29	1978	$7,253	48.24	65.2
1939	$545		10.18	1979	$8,033	52.26	72.6
1940	$581		10.33	1980	$8,869	57.05	82.4
1941	$703		11.02	1981	$9,773	62.38	90.9
1942	$880		11.89	1982	$10,364	66.26	96.5
1943	$990		12.52	1983	$11,036	68.89	99.6
1944	$1,072		12.81	1984	$12,215	71.45	103.9
1945	$1,087		13.10	1985	$12,941	73.70	107.6
1946	$1,145		14.76	1986	$13,555	75.32	109.6
1947	$1,194		16.34	1987	$14,246	77.58	113.6
1948	$1,307		17.28	1988	$15,312	80.22	118.3
1949	$1,281		17.25	1989	$16,235	83.28	124.0
1950	$1,388		17.45	1990	$17,176	86.53	130.7
1951	$1,499		18.70	1991	$17,664	89.67	136.2
1952	$1,552		18.99	1992	$18,524	91.84	140.3
1953	$1,622		19.24	1993	$18,979	94.06	144.5
1954	$1,629		19.43	1994	$19,624	96.02	148.2
1955	$1,715		19.77	1995	$20,358	98.11	152.4
1956	$1,800		20.45	1996	$21,069	100.00	156.9
1957	$1,867		21.12	1997	$21,881	101.93	160.5
1958	$1,899		21.63	1998	$23,031	103.17	163.0
1959	$1,983		21.88	1999	$23,742	104.65	166.6
1960	$2,026		22.18	2000	$25,205	106.86	172.2
				2001			177.1

Appendix C.2: U.S. Population, 1921-2000

Year	U.S. Population	Year	U.S. Population
1921	108,538,000	1961	183,742,000
1922	110,049,000	1962	186,590,000
1923	111,947,000	1963	189,300,000
1924	114,109,000	1964	191,927,000
1925	115,829,000	1965	194,347,000
1926	117,397,000	1966	196,599,000
1927	119,035,000	1967	198,752,000
1928	120,509,000	1968	200,745,000
1929	121,878,000	1969	202,736,000
1930	123,188,000	1970	205,089,000
1931	124,149,000	1971	207,692,000
1932	124,949,000	1972	209,924,000
1933	125,690,000	1973	211,939,000
1934	126,485,000	1974	213,898,000
1935	127,362,000	1975	215,981,000
1936	128,181,000	1976	218,086,000
1937	128,961,000	1977	220,289,000
1938	129,969,000	1978	222,629,000
1939	131,028,000	1979	225,106,000
1940	132,122,000	1980	227,726,000
1941	133,402,000	1981	230,008,000
1942	134,860,000	1982	232,218,000
1943	136,739,000	1983	234,332,000
1944	138,397,000	1984	236,394,000
1945	139,928,000	1985	238,506,000
1946	141,389,000	1986	240,682,000
1947	144,126,000	1987	242,842,000
1948	146,631,000	1988	245,061,000
1949	149,188,000	1989	247,387,000
1950	151,684,000	1990	249,981,000
1951	154,287,000	1991	252,677,000
1952	156,954,000	1992	255,403,000
1953	159,565,000	1993	258,107,000
1954	162,391,000	1994	260,616,000
1955	165,275,000	1995	263,073,000
1956	168,221,000	1996	265,504,000
1957	171,274,000	1997	268,087,000
1958	174,141,000	1998	270,560,000
1959	177,073,000	1999	272,996,000
1960	180,760,000	2000	282,489,000